Technological Competition, Employment and Innovation Policies in OECD Countries

Springer
Berlin
Heidelberg
New York
Barcelona
Budapest
Hong Kong
London
Milan
Paris
Santa Clara
Singapore
Tokyo

Paul J.J. Welfens · David Audretsch
John T. Addison · Hariolf Grupp

Technological Competition, Employment and Innovation Policies in OECD Countries

With 16 Figures
and 20 Tables

 Springer

Professor Dr. Paul J.J. Welfens, University of Potsdam,
European Institute for International Economic Relations,
August-Bebel-Str. 89, 14482 Potsdam, Germany

Professor Dr. David B. Audretsch, Georgia State University,
School of Policy Studies, University Plaza,
Atlanta, Georgia 30303-3083, USA

Professor Dr. John T. Addison, John M. Olin Visiting Professor of Labor
Economics and Public Policy, Center for the Study of American Business,
Washington University in St. Louis, One Brookings Drive,
St. Louis, MO 63130-4899, USA
and
University of South Carolina, Department of Economics,
College of Business Administration, The H. William Close Building,
Columbia, SC 29208, USA

Dr. habil. Hariolf Grupp, Fraunhofer-Institute for Systems
and Innovation Research (ISI), Breslauer Str. 48,
76139 Karlsruhe, Germany

ISBN 3-540-63439-8 Springer-Verlag Berlin Heidelberg New York

Cataloging-in-Publication Data applied for
Die Deutsche Bibliothek - CIP-Einheitsaufnahme

Technological competition, employment and innovation policies in
OECD countries : with 20 tables / Paul J.J. Welfens ... - Berlin ;
Heidelberg ; New York ; Barcelona ; Budapest ; Hong Kong ;
London ; Milan ; Paris ; Santa Clara ; Singapore ; Tokyo : Springer,
1998
  ISBN 3-540-63439-8

© Springer-Verlag Berlin · Heidelberg 1998
Printed in Germany

The use of general descriptive names, registered names, trademarks, etc. in this publica-
tion does not imply, even in the absence of a specific statement, that such names are
exempt from the relevant protective laws and regulations and therefore free for general
use.

Product liability: The publishers cannot guarantee the accuracy of any information about
the application of operative techniques and medications contained in this book. In every
individual case the user must check such information by consulting the relevant literature.

Hardcover-Design: Erich Kirchner, Heidelberg

SPIN 10642969   43/2202-5 4 3 2 1 0 – Printed on acid-free paper

JK

Table of Contents

Introduction

The international innovation race has intensified in the 1980s and 1990s, with EU firms facing new competitors from Asia and postsocialist countries of eastern Europe, but also - after 1990 - a reorientation of US technology policy towards a dominant commercial orientation after decades of a dual focus on commercial and military projects, where the latter had only indirect effects on the US international competitiveness. With the exception of France which followed the US reorientation in innovation policy, EU countries on the continent need to adjust to high technology competition on the one hand and to a broader technological catching up process on the other hand. This requires structural adjustment in the economy and appropriate policy changes. The worldwide increase in unskilled labor supply during the 1980s and 1990s poses an additional challenge, since it requires a corresponding adjustment in relative wage rates (skilled versus unskilled workers) if employment is to grow. In fact, among OECD countries only the US, the UK, Australia, Canada and New Zealand achieved timely adjustment in this respect. A third challenge concerns the apparent weakness of major EU countries in lagging behind the US in terms of capital productivity. If capital productitivity could be increased, more investment would be profitable and hence more employment feasible. This question raises the issue of problems in capital markets and national systems of financing innovations.

While the US achieved an unemployment rate of 5% in 1996 and hence full employment, the EU rate of 11 % pointed to serious labor market problem including reduced regional labor market mobility. Moreover, in the US the employment rate increased from 67 to 79 % in the period 1970-95, while that of the EU stagnated at 66.5% (in Germany a slight increase was recorded).

The intensified international technology race has led to a rise in the demand for skilled labor. Thus, high technology manufacturing was indeed the sector which recorded employment growth in OECD countries, while employment growth was also achieved in the service sector in some EU countries. The higher demand for skilled labor, coupled with the expansion in the supply of unskilled labor following the economc opening up of China and postsocialist countries in eastern Europe, implies a relative fall in wages of unskilled workers. Given relative wage rigidity in many continental EU countries increased unemployment of unskilled workers is to be expected. To the extent that this in turn reduces effective demand this could translate also into unemployment of skilled workers. Moreover, if the intensified technology race requires faster structural change and higher regional mobility, impediments to mobility as well as skill mismatches will raise the unemployment rate. Indeed, unemployment in continental EU countries strongly increased in the 1980s and early 1990s. By contrast, employment growth in the US was remarkable. The question arises which role global technology competition play in the different employment growth record of the US and continental EU countries and which remedies are adequate for employment problems in Germany and most other EU countries.

The 1990s are characterized by true globalization of industry in the sense that foreign investors face locational opportunities worldwide and therefore enjoy new advantages from mobility. Exporters from eastern Europe and the Asian NICs capture an increasing share of EU markets in certain fields. Thus, since the 1980s Asian NICs are increasingly specializing in medium and high technology products. At the same time Asian markets, where EU firms are underrepresented, are enjoying high economic growth. Transforming economies also have weak trade relations with Asian NICs although this is changing gradually.

Trade between the EU and eastern Europe grew very dynamically in the 1990s both on the import and export side. From a theoretical perspective rapidly growing trade between the EU and eastern Europe clearly could be anticipated on the basis of the gravity equation. Globalization defined as a combination of rising export-GDP ratios and rising foreign direct investment relative to domestic investment is affecting EU countries in several ways.

Between 1950 and 1990 three main indicators of cognitive skills - substantive complexity, general educational development and average years of schooling measured in 1970 - showed positive growth; the same holds for interactive skills. With rising world market orientation of firms competition is intensifying and better skills are required. However, there is no general shortage of skilled employees since an increasing number of vocational training schemes, high school and universities turn out more and more skilled people in OECD countries.

Economic integration in the EU increased between 1968 (formation of a customs union) and the 1990s. The single market project was implemented at the end of 1992 - with some latecomer sectors following only in 1994/95. It is clear that the creation of a single market for goods and services facilitates the exploitation of static and dynamic economies of scale so that considerable productivity increases and specific growth impacts can be expected for certain industries. However, with respect to employment impacts one should not overlook the development of the overall aggregate investment output ratio which was not favorable in the EU. Within two decades, output growth fell from 4% to 2.5% p.a., while the investment-output ratio dropped by five percentage points as emphasized by the EUROPEAN COMMISSION in 1993. The single market program stimulated growth only moderately.

The EU has recently assumed the position of a high unemployment region, having overtaken the US in this regard in the early 1980s. For its part, the US has continued to generate private sector jobs at a rapid pace. These jobs are moreover not predominantly of the hamburger-flipper variety. The European problem is one of sluggish employment growth, high and rising unemployment and, relatedly, persistent long-term unemployment.

Yet it is difficult to quantify the causes of the unfavorable EU labor market record, while that of the US has to be qualified by a pronounced growth in earnings inequality and sluggish earnings growth. Adverse movements in the terms of trade and counter inflationary demand policies though they have undoubtedly contributed to higher EU unemployment do not really get to grips with the persistence of high unemployment in the region. Here the candidates include insider-outsider considerations and outsider characteristics. The balance of the evidence suggests that the latter may have been most responsible for mismatch, taken in conjunction with wage rigidities.

Restrictions on the freedom of employers to shed labor may also assist in explaining the upward drift in unemployment. Thus, there are signs that more generous severance pay is associated with reduced employment and heightened joblessness and that more generally the stringency of a nation's labor market regulatory apparatus may be associated with a number of adverse labor market outcomes. But the evidence is not overwhelming. The safest conclusion pending further and improved empirical analysis is that much (though not all) employment regulation has contributed to the employment/unemployment problem by raising employment adjustment costs even if the precise magnitudes are unclear at this time. (The contribution of fixed employment costs is more opaque.) The mixed evidence on the effects of employment regulation may also in part reflect the outcome of a market escape route favoring so-called "atypical employment," which is currently the source of much debate but little hard evidence.

With major privatizations organized in several EU countries in the early 1990s one would expect overmanning to fall immediately after privatization. Major layoffs occurred in the context of privatization of telecoms network operators in almost all EU countries; this was also the case in the electricity sector in the UK which was privatized in the 1980s.

With the economic opening up of eastern Europe and the advances of NICs in the world market global competition has intensified - especially in the field of labor intensive products and medium intensive technologies. For EU countries facing intensified import competition and the relocation of production in the context of foreign direct investment outflows it is therefore important to increasingly position themselves in advanced technology fields, which typically is one of the few areas in which continental EU countries recorded job growth in the 1980s. Hence R&D is increasingly important for growth, international competitiveness, employment and ecological progress.

R&D is needed for process innovations which allow costs to be cut and hence markets to be widened - this could facilitate the exploitation of static and dynamic economies of scale. R&D is also a requirement for product innovations which allow firms to charge higher prices. Firms that are eager to recover R&D investment costs and to earn a Schumpeterian rent from innovation will try to ensure intellectual property rights, typically via patents. They will also massively invest into marketing in order to create preferences in favor of the novel products. R&D as well as marketing expenditures create market entry barriers because they largely represent sunk costs; newcomers will find it therefore difficult to successfully enter the market. Innovative firms thus can enjoy extra profits which partly will have to be shared with workers since trade unions in highly profitable industries will strongly lobby for wage rises. With continued product innovations the value-added by the firm will indeed rise continuously such that the wage bargaining process will result in rising real wage rates and higher real incomes in some sectors. This in turn will result in multiplier effects in the overall economy.

Launching product innovations will stimulate the growth of demand directly as was emphasized by SCHUMPETER, who also stressed that entrepreneurship is the basis for long-term growth and economic cycles. Both for R&D devoted to product innovations and to process innovations it holds that unit R&D costs can be reduced if large output volumes are realized during a given innovation cycle. From this perspective the gradual increase of R&D expenditure-GNP ratios in OECD countries is bound to stimulate exports and trade.

In a large integrated market facing global competition one should expect EU firms to develop a special innovation profile which reflects its comparative advantages and policy priorities for R&D. The US achieved a much stronger change in patent specialization than the EU-12-Community (or Germany). The degree of specialization measured by an appropriate Herfindahl index was much higher in the US and Japan than in the Community. Indeed the EU-12 group suffered from an overall decline in specialization in the period 1982/92. This points to unexploited EU potentials for economies of scale in R&D in the sense that a stronger concentration on profitable innovation fields lets one expect that R&D unit costs could be reduced under such a strategy. Lack of innovation specialization in the EU is probably due to parallel R&D programs of various EU countries. While a simple switching to fully integrated supranational R&D programs certainly would reduce useful variety of competing R&D approaches in the Community it seems that the present situation offers considerable room for improved policy coordination. Since figures for Germany showed a better adaptation of small and medium sized firms to international technology trends (i.e. activities in the most dynamic patenting fields - with high growth rates) one may doubt that creating bigger EU firms via merger and acquisitions will automatically improve the innovativeness and technological adaptability of firms in the Community. This does not rule out that there are industries with further opportunities for mergers and acquisitions which then in turn would generate an endogenous clearance mechanism across firms. At the bottom line the global division of R&D is characterized by insufficient specialization in the EU and poor flexibility of big firms.

The EU's research base is probably less market oriented than that of the US, and in addition fewer human resources are devoted to R&D: Scientific research personnel represents only 0.47% of the labor force, compared to 0.74% in the US and 0.80 % in Japan. Moreover, between 1984 and 1993 the EU lost share in patents in all sectors except aerospace and transport equipment. Since the Community Innovation Survey indicated that EU companies which engaged in technical cooperation agreements usually have a much larger proportion of new or improved products in their total sales EU programs which support cooperation among innovative firms should be strengthened.

Whither science and technology in the decades ahead? All leading industrial nations have been looking for plausible answers to this question. There is a constant temptation for technical observation to restrict itself to describing the potential supply of scientific and technical solutions. However, it must do far more than depict the supply factors. The importance of technology in the future depends just as much on the pressure of social, ecological and economic problems which are expected to arise, and which will make important demands on science and technology in the future. For this reason, any discussion of problems must focus increasingly on factors relating to demand. If the real challenges for a particular policy in the area of high technology originate from increasing social, economic, and environmental problems, the aim of the respective policy is to make the innovation system adaptive enough to meet those challenges.

The ability to develop and exploit new business opportunities, i. e., the *economic competence*, is generally difficult to determine quantitatively. One is tempted to 'measure' economic competence by its outcomes - successful innovation. A patent is often applied long before the invention ever sees the market. In this respect, such inventions are the result of innovative processes. Europe (EU-15 by artificially adding up the then non-members and East Germany) was unreservedly one of the world's two leading economic regions in terms of the number of patent applications filed annually at the beginning of the 1980s. During the 1980s, patent productivity and technological competition both increased. However, the number of European patents with world market relevance has been on the decline since the early 1990s, largely due to diminishing patent activity on the part of major EU nations. This trend parallels the drop in R&D activity in some European countries. On the other hand, among Europe's smaller nations, Belgium, Finland and Spain have increased their patent activity to such an extent that the approximate overall EU level could be maintained, or, after 1992, even improved a bit.

High R&D expenditures of innovative sectors is only one key to high productivity growth, the other is rapid diffusion - i.e. application - of new technologies. While most new technologies are developed in high technology manufacturing industries (information technology, pharmaceuticals, aerospace) the most important user is the service sector whose role in international technology trade increased in the 1980s.

Germany and many other continental EU countries suffer from high unemployment rates which largely reflect an underdeveloped service sector, insufficient R&D expenditures and lack of training and education as well as inadequate diffusion policies. Labor market rigidities and insufficient wage dispersion also impair regaining full employment. Part of the existing productivity gap in continental EU countries vis-à-vis the US is apparently related to underdeveloped stock markets and rather poor capital productivity compared to the US. Germany and France as well as other continental EU countries should launch new initiatives to reinforce the role of stock markets and venture capital markets. It is obvious that insufficient growth of the service sector in many EU countries is related to difficulties for new firms from the service sector to finance business expansion. The low capital intensity of the service sector - relative to manufacturing industry - render financing of newcomers rather difficult in the banking-dominated continental Europe since they can offer less collateral than a typical firm from the manufacturing sector.

The role of the stock market could also increase because the age of high technology competition at the turn of the century will reduce the relative importance of banks in financing innovative firms. Asymmetric information problems between the innovator and the bank are typical of innovation projects so that insufficient access to (cheap) capital could limit the innovativeness of firms in the EU. The role of equity capital should be strengthened in the late 1990 in Europe. With workers facing a weaker bargaining position in the new environment of economic globalization one may consider tax incentives for workers encouraging them to allocate savings to investment funds (of a certain minimum rating). The role of capital markets could also be reinforced by reforming the social security systems, namely by partly replacing the current pay-as-you-go systems with capital funded security programs.

Since labor market rigidities and insufficient wage dispersion have characterized Germany and other EU countries for about two decades and since R&D-GDP ratios declined in the period 1990-96 there are no fast remedies for higher employment. If, however, adequate wage policy reforms (including a new incentive compatible reform of the unemployment insurance system) are combined with a new innovation policy initiative and the expansion of the service sector promoted there are prospects for gradually increasing employment on the continent. If Germany, France, Spain and Italy were to reform labor markets and social security systems while stimulating innovation and diffusion one may hope to achieve higher growth not only in continental EU countries but in the whole EU. Since the EU-15 countries are rather interdependent economies it is obvious that higher growth in some EU countries reinforces overall EU growth. Higher economic growth certainly would be favorable also for the sustainability of the European Monetary Union, which would face the risk of instability if high unemployment rates and slow growth were to lead to major conflicts about macroeconomic policies.

In the following study which grew out of project No. IV/96/10 for the European Parliament the authors summarize the main strands of the existing literature and analyze the link between innovation and employment, providing new insights into the adjustment problems and policy options faced by Europe. Parts of our study are reproduced here with the permission of the European Parliament. We emphasize that this report can be only a first step towards a broader understanding of the problems of R&D and employment in the age of high technology.

In conclusion, I would like to thank Jörg Höfling, Juliane Kinsele, Alison Sinclair and Frank Wilk for research assistance and Rainer Hillebrand for excellent editorial support.

Potsdam, July 1997

Paul J.J. Welfens
(Coordinator)

Executive Summary[1]

The EU labor market participation rate fell slightly between 1960 and 1995, while that of the US strongly increased. Although new jobs were created in the EU in the 1980s, this was insufficient given the strong growth of labor supply. Continental EU countries suffer from a high rate of long-term unemployment. Furthermore, in almost all EU countries the share of those with a low educational level among the unemployed is close to or above 50%. This is of particular importance since NICs and countries form eastern Europe are moving upwards on the technology ladder so that EU countries need to specialize more in high technology. Unskilled workers will, therefore, face reduced employment prospects. High long term unemployment implies problems for social security financing, potential instability and even resistance against technological progress. High regional unemployment disparities have become a structural phenomenon in the EU in the 1980s, so that measures to encourage regional labor mobility are required.

Employment growth is unevenly spread across households in the EU, with new jobs predominantly going to families in which there already is one bread-winner while other households face continued unemployment and the threat of poverty.

Narrowing wage dispersion in continental Europe stands in marked contrast to rising wage dispersion in the US and the UK in the 1980s and early 1990s. In a period of global economic opening up from China to eastern Europe, and hence an increase in unskilled labor worldwide a widening wage gap is required. A wider wage gap does not necessarily imply social conflicts as long as appropriate income tax reforms and savings incentives for low income households help to maintain the overall net income position of unskilled workers. Sufficient wage differentials between skilled and unskilled labor are required not only to minimize the incentive for firms to substitute capital for labor but also to encourage further education and on the job training. This is an important aspect for the EU if it wants to specialize in high technology products in the future.

R&D expenditure relative to GDP is lower in the EU than in the US and Japan. Moreover, the EU's patenting pattern is different from that in the US and

---

[1] This is a joint project of Prof. Dr. Paul J.J. Welfens (Coordinator), University of Potsdam and European Institute for International Economic Relations, Prof. Dr. John Addison, John M. Olin Visiting Professor of Labor Economics and Public Policy, Washington University and University of South Carolina, Prof. Dr. David Audretsch, Georgia State University, and Dr. Hariolf Grupp, Fraunhofer Institute: Systems and Innovation Research, Karlsruhe.

Japan. While these countries recorded a rising technology specialization in the 1980s, the EU's specialization index reduced.

According to the modern theory of economic integration product and process innovations are easier to achieve in large integrated markets than in small national ones. This points to benefits from EU integration. The service sector is increasingly important for R&D and international technology trade, and hence the single market program, which in particular liberalized services, should yield additional benefits in the future. Higher EU exports in the future can only be expected if EU firms record a rising share in global patents.

The EU has recently assumed the position of a high unemployment region, having overtaken the US in this regard in the early 1980s. For its part, the US has continued to generate private sector jobs at a rapid pace. These jobs are moreover not predominantly of the hamburger-flipper variety. The European problem is one of sluggish employment growth, high and rising unemployment and, relatedly, persistent long-term unemployment.

Yet it is difficult to quantify the causes of the unfavorable EU labor market record, while that of the US has to be qualified by a pronounced growth in earnings inequality and sluggish earnings growth. Adverse movements in the terms of trade and counter inflationary demand policies though they have undoubtedly contributed to higher EU unemployment do not really get to grips with the persistence of high unemployment in the region. Here the candidates include insider-outsider considerations and outsider characteristics. The balance of the evidence suggests that the latter may have been most responsible for mismatch, taken in conjunction with wage rigidities.

Restrictions on the freedom of employers to shed labor may also assist in explaining the upward drift in unemployment. Thus, there are signs that more generous severance pay is associated with reduced employment and heightened joblessness and that more generally the stringency of a nation's labor market regulatory apparatus may be associated with a number of adverse labor market outcomes. But the evidence is not overwhelming. The safest conclusion pending further and improved empirical analysis is that much (though not all) employment regulation has contributed to the employment/unemployment problem by raising employment adjustment costs even if the precise magnitudes are unclear at this time. (The contribution of fixed employment costs that would also include the probabilistic costs of employment protection rules is opaque.) The mixed evidence on the effects of employment regulation may also in part reflect the outcome of a market escape route favoring so-called "atypical employment," which is currently the source of much debate but little hard evidence.

The subsidization of unemployment though the unemployment insurance system has also been allied to rising EU unemployment but there is doubt as to whether the more generous rates of income maintenance observed in the EU vis-à-vis the US have contributed substantially to differential unemployment development in the two blocs, even if certain hysteresis effects have been identified by the OECD for high-benefit countries. Interestingly, the disemployment effects of minimum wages found de facto or de jure in most EU member states appear muted in practice, though this perhaps surprising result emphatically does not favor policy activism in this area.

Finally, drawing on the US evidence, there is the suggestion that biased technical change may well provide a common theme underpinning a number of the apparently very different labor market developments observed in the US and the EU, once account is taken of differences in institutions. This is one aspect of the increased need for flexibility, which (elusive) concept may in turn explain why it has been so difficult to explain differential labor market outcomes at a time when regulations may have been broadly unchanged.

Continued downsizing by the existing large manufacturing firms has caused unemployment to ratchet higher throughout the 1990s. But unemployment is not an isolated economic problem. Two additional problems are a lack of innovative activity and a deterioration of international competitiveness. These three problems are interrelated and exacerbated by the increasing degree of globalization.

Among the most cited sources of evidence for the existence of a European innovation crisis is the declining share of patent and R&D activity vis-à-vis Japan and the United States. But a more careful inspection reveals that the relative technological advantage of European companies in the industries in which Europe has traditionally held the comparative advantage, such as chemicals, specialized machine tools, and automobiles, has not greatly deteriorated over the past decade.

The innovation challenge in Europe does not seem to exist in the industries in which Europe has traditionally held the comparative advantage. Rather, the innovation challenge confronting Europe seems to lie in newly emerging industries such as computers, software, semiconductors and biotechnology. It is the inability of European firms to innovate and participate in these new industries that is underlying the real innovation crisis in Europe.

The problem in the more traditional industries may have less to do with a lack of innovativeness and more to do with remaining competitive in markets that are increasingly globally linked. High wages and other costs of production dictate that production be shifted out of high-cost locations and into lower-cost locations. Because production processes in traditional industries tend to become relatively standardized, they can be duplicated at much lower costs in non-European countries. The continued transfer of production facilities out of Europe and into lower-cost countries through outward foreign direct investment, along with corporate restructuring, has left large numbers of displaced workers unlikely to be re-employed, even once economic recovery has taken hold.

Substituting technology and organizational innovations for labor has resulted in substantial productivity gains in traditional European industries. This has had a positive impact on firm efficiency. But at the same time it places downward pressure on the number of jobs available in these traditional industries, how and under what conditions can these displaced workers, as well as new entrants to the labor force, be absorbed into productive activity? The answer suggested in this study is through shifting economic activity out of traditional industries and into newly emerging industries. As industries mature, it becomes less costly to duplicate their production processes and apply them in a less costly location, even so-called high-technology industries can become increasingly based upon information (which can be communicated almost costlessly across geographic space) and less based on tacit knowledge (which dictates proximity for transmission) as they mature. In contrast, newer industries have a higher component of tacit knowledge and thus are less vulnerable to competition form lower production cost locations.

There are, however, a number of barriers in Europe to shifting economic activity out of traditional industries and into new industries. These barriers are generally linked to a broad set of institutions ranging from finance to labor market policies. The institutional structure of Europe, which encompasses national systems of innovation have been designed for industrial stability and the application of new technological knowledge only within the existing technological trajectories. And yet, as the comparative advantage of Europe become increasingly based on earlier stages of industry life cycle, the underlying knowledge conditions associated with tacit knowledge, such as greater uncertainty, knowledge asymmetries, and costs of transaction, dictate not stability but rather mobility.

Europe had the comparative advantage in moderate-technology and traditional industries throughout most of the post-war period. This meant that diffusing technology along existing technological trajectories was sufficient to preserve the international competitiveness of firms and ensure a rising standard of living for the domestic population. But a shift in the comparative advantage of Europe away form such traditional industries has left a void. The economic challenge confronting Europe at the turn of the century will be to generate a new renaissance of employment creation by shifting its industry structure away from mature industries and products and towards newly emerging technologies and industries.

The US has high R&D spending which has remained at around 2.5 percent of GDP over the last four decades. The US spends more on R&D than any other country, with the exception of Japan, but today a number of countries have higher ratios of nondefense R&D. The Federal share of R&D spending has however declined through time, currently standing at 36 percent of all R&D outlays. (If the goal of balancing the budget by 2002 is achieved, this decline may be expected to continue.) Employment in R&D represents less than 1 percent of civilian employment.

Changes in US R&D policy have mirrored concerns over the erosion that country's technological leadership as expressed in a number of indicators. The current administration seeks to achieve a balance between Federal and civilian defense expenditures by 1998; the defense share currently being around 56 percent. Aspects of the attempt to realign Federal spending include the use of "dual use" R&D programs that exploit goods with both military and commercial uses under the Technology Reinvestment Program; enhanced commercial justification for certain Department of Defense administered programs; a new role for the Department of Commerce (viz. its Advanced Technology Program) as a funding mechanism for technology projects performed by industry, and other private-public partnerships in specific areas held to be critical to the nation's competitiveness (e.g. advanced manufacturing technology development and high performance computing and communications); and technology transfer. A further (perhaps more fundamental) aspect of US R&D policy is the ongoing process of regulatory reform.

Despite these changes, however, the notion of a national R&D policy outside the classic public good of defense (and basic research) apparently favored by the present administration lacks widespread acceptance - and this is underscored by the globalization debate - while resource constraints ensure that policy initiatives will remain marginal.

Whither science and technology in the decades ahead? All leading industrial nations have been looking for plausible answers to this question. There is a constant temptation for technical observation to restrict itself to describing the potential supply of scientific and technical solutions. However, it must do far more than depict the supply factors. The importance of technology in the future depends just as much on the pressure of social, ecological and economic problems which are expected to arise, and which will make important demands on science and technology in the future. For this reason, any discussion of problems must focus increasingly on factors relying to demand. If the real challenges for a particular policy in the area of high technology originate from increasing social, economic, and environmental problems, the aim of the respective policy is to make the innovation system adaptive enough to meet those challenges.

The ability to develop and exploit new business opportunities, i. e., the *economic competence*, is generally difficult to determine quantitatively. One is tempted to 'measure' economic competence by its outcomes - successful innovation. A patent is often applied for long before the invention ever sees the market. In this respect, such inventions are the result of innovative processes. Europe (EU-15 by artificially adding up the then non-members and East Germany) was unreservedly one of the world's two leading economic regions in terms of the number of patent applications filed annually at the beginning of the 1980s. During the 1980s, patent productivity and technological competition both increased. However, the number of European patents with world market relevance has been on the decline since the early 1990s, largely due to diminishing patent activity on the part of major EU nations. This trend parallels the drop in R&D activity in some European countries. On the other hand, among Europe's smaller nations, Belgium, Finland and Spain have increased their patent activity to such an extent that the approximate overall EU level could be maintained, or, after 1992, even improved a bit.

The relative strengths in Europe's technology activity are clearly to be found in the automotive engineering, mechanical engineering and chemical sectors. These strengths reflect the international division of labor in R&D and foreign trade - how could it be otherwise? The microelectronics and instrument engineering industries report below-average 'R&D output'. The almost complementary structure of specialization patterns found in Japan and Europe is striking; Japan has weaknesses in those areas in which Europe shows its strength - and vice versa.

Overall, the R&D level of the United States and Europe is still above Japan. Areas in which Europe is assessed as having a high level of R&D are mineral and water resources, urbanization and construction, agriculture and food, environment, energy, and transportation. In these six areas, Europe's R&D level is assumed to be among the most advanced in the world. In contrast, areas in which Europe's R&D level is assessed as low are information and electronics, as the lowest, followed by communications.

The USA has massive comparative advantages throughout the entire range of leading-edge technologies in the narrower sense. As is also the case in France and Great Britain, the USA's stable position in leading-edge technologies is strongly dependent upon substantial R&D activity in military-related areas which are not likely to enjoy the same preferential treatment in future government R&D budgets as they have in the past. Japan has unusually strong advantages arising from its specialization in advanced technologies *and* leading-edge technologies. Imports of research-intensive products have a much lower share in the domestic market in Japan than in countries of comparable size, while there is a dependence on leading-edge technology imports.

Although less specialized than Japan in R&D-intensive products, Germany has approximately the same level of specialization as Switzerland and an even greater level than the USA. Other industrialized nations such as Belgium and Great Britain follow at some distance. The research-intensive sector in France, Sweden and Spain represents approximately an average share in the world market. No other EU country has comparative advantages in these markets. In this context, 'specialization' and 'comparative advantages' mean that the ratio of exports to imports is better than the average for the respective industry. Great Britain - and the USA in particular - would rank considerably higher if export performance were the only factor taken into consideration, as is done when calculating specialization values. These countries are relatively open to technological imports. On the other hand, Germany, and Japan in particular, have strong import-substitution sectors as well.

Contemporary R&D policy has moved away from the idea that the State could direct basic research over technological developments right down to individual national innovations. Equally outmoded is the idea that the State could be satisfied with the role of a subsidiary supporter of basic research and leave the control of technology in the future to anonymous market processes. R&D policy for the start of the twenty-first century requires a middle way, an active role for the State as an intermediary between social players (companies, associations, interest groups, science communities, consumers, media, employers' and employees' representatives etc.).

This intermediary role must also take account of the fact that European R&D policy is restricted in its scope from below. The activities of the European Communities must always be seen in context with the efforts of national policies and, in addition in some member countries, with below-national policies as in federal states to promote research on a regional basis.

It follows from these general trends in R&D policy, that European support for oriented basic research, in so far as it is concerned with technology at the start of the twenty-first century, cannot be replaced by other, for example indirect, instruments of R&D policy. In the field of preventive research in particular, selective project support continues to be of the greatest importance. One new task will be that R&D policy in basic research should in future not only examine technological options but also indicate creative perspectives. This relates to research-related evaluation of the consequences of basic research.

Through demand from the public sector, the government bodies on European, national and below-national levels offer a high demand potential, which in Europe has until now been only inadequately used for R&D policy. Lead projects in R&D policy which represent outline solutions to large, global, economic, social, societal and ecological problems, and above all the visionary view of technological development and the challenges now facing us throw up other, more radical questions of R&D policy than those set out above in respect of the short-term view. It was not the aim of this study to give those concrete form. It was however possible to indicate that the trends described in technology policy up to the start of the twenty-first century can themselves provide the key to further-reaching changes in future policy and the technology of the next decade can point the way to the lead projects of the twenty-first century. R&D policy for the day after tomorrow must be in place by tomorrow.

One interpretation of the evidence reviewed in section 1.3 is that the unfavorable effects of labor market regulation may be more muted than basic economic theory might suggest. If this is because national social systems have ultimately to stand a market test, then one inference is that supranational social legislation both introduced and envisaged by the Community is contraindicated once one begins to stray far beyond national practice while at the same time ossifying employment protection. At a practical level, the evaluative apparatus of DGV - its so-called "fiches d'impact" - should now be subject to the most careful scrutiny. The basic goal must be to sustain flexibility which apparently still exists in surprising measure in the economies of the EU.

The analysis of job flow data, and, in particular, the high rates of job destruction, underscores the need for a flexible workforce. Here there is clear consensus on the crucial role of improved schooling (primary, secondary, and tertiary) as a long-term solution to the problems of low skill, arguably the most fundamental source of inflexibility. Altogether more problematic, however, is the issue of post-school training and the short term. Although market failure stemming from imperfect capital markets is an issue in the area of post-school training, there would seem to be no general presumption in favor of massive retraining programs. The position of the currently unskilled/disadvantaged is however a legitimate cause for concern by virtue of their exclusion from private sector training. Some have interpreted this phenomenon as indicating that such workers are in fact not worth training. Quite apart from the fact that such workers may not be able to pay for their training through lower wages (e.g. because of wage floors), there may be a good case for programs carefully targeted toward disadvantaged workers. The Community focus on exchange of national experience may be particularly valuable in this connection. Disadvantage is perhaps more easily measured in a US context but the problem of long-term unemployment in Europe as manifested in human capital depreciation and stigmatization make the issue no less relevant in situations where there is no underclass per se. In neither case, however, is the quick fix a realistic option. Progress will necessarily be incremental rather than once for all.

Some piecemeal labor market reform measures that may commend themselves to Europeans might include the introduction of experience rating in unemployment insurance (UI) schemes and further action to minimize their disincentive effects. In broad terms, the general thrust of UI should shift away from income maintenance toward active reemployment assistance, involving profiling of claimants and job search assistance. (That said, greater income support may be required for some under targeted programs for those with pronounced skill deficits). Another UI initiative worth examining is reemployment bonuses.

On the thorny question of European wage rigidity, practical considerations perhaps rule out any simple policy conclusions. But policy makers might reasonably consider limiting the scope of erga omnes agreements, further facilitate product market deregulation, and (re)examine the efficacy of recent social chapter measures and procedures that may have the effect of promoting European-wide collective bargaining.

Comparing the EU as a group of 15 countries with the US and Japan is somewhat misleading, since R&D policies at the EU-level is largely insignificant in terms of expenditure. Thus, R&D and innovation policies are determined at the national level and varies substantially between different EU member states. International competitiveness of EU firms often can be strengthened by increasing product variety and a broader research portfolio. Nevertheless, some concentration of R&D efforts of EU industry could be useful in the future, namely to the extent that this reflects economies of scale, specialisation gains and the impulses of integrated EU capital markets.

To the extent that monetary integration creates bigger and efficient EU capital markets, one may expect rising intra-EU merger activities, which already were reinforced by the single market dynamics. Efficient capital markets could indirectly encourage firms to specialize in certain research fields. It should not be overlooked that coordinating and harmonizing national R&D policies of EU member countries can only be achieved at considerable political and economic transaction costs.

National R&D financing in the presence of high capital mobility and multinational companies, respectively, means that major benefits of public R&D support might occur abroad. This problem points to the need for a reorganization of European R&D policies. Following new growth theory R&D expenditures and investment in human capital are quite important for economic growth and employment. In a world of rising foreign direct investment flows, which are the basis of international technology transfers, continental EU countries - except the Netherlands, Belgium, Spain and Portugal - suffer from insufficient investment inflows. High EU unemployment could be reduced by a higher rate of capital formation which requires an accompanying environmental strategy in order to avoid that high output growth results in a degradation of the environment.

A specific problem of EU R&D policy is the emphasis on direct subsidies which is in marked contrast to the US focus on tax credits. The latter are quite adequate to stimulate both small and large companies. Under the present system of national R&D funding politically well-tied big companies are likely to absorb a dominant share of direct subsidies. As regards employment growth this is a problem because new and small/medium companies are crucial for innovation and employment growth.

The Community suffers from an uneven distribution of external foreign direct investment inflows. With respect to inflows from the US Germany and Italy ranked poorly in the early 1990s.

Liberalization of the telecommunications industry and the move towards an information society is likely to create new jobs. This holds less for network operation were overstaffing of dominant state operators will have to be reversed in the new competitive post-1998 framework. However, innovative telecoms services will result in new jobs and cheaper telecoms prices will stimulate the expansion of industries which use telecoms services as an input. Falling costs of international telephony will stimulate international data transmission and facilitate the multinationalization process. However, R&D results will also become more mobile internationally such that first mover advantages could become less relevant. Reinforcing patent rights and defining adequate rules for the data highway could therefore become quite important.

European R&D policy should be strengthened both at the national and the supranational level. Higher R&D related government expenditures (including tax credits) and incentives for retraining could stimulate economic growth and job creation. Measures should not only encourage EU-wide cooperation between technology-intensive firms but also stimulate the creation of new innovative firms. This will require a dynamic capital market, including adequate tax incentives for private households. Improved reporting on R&D at both the national and the supranational level could contribute to more efficient R&D policies. More emphasis on high technology and promotion of innovations will not be sufficient to achieve full employment. Thus, the unemployment insurance system needs to be reformed in line with basic principles of the private insurance sector. Achieving sufficient wage dispersion could also be quite important for avoiding strong incentives for rationalization investment.

Facing an eastern EU enlargement the Community will have to increasingly foster high technology industry and innovative services in order to create new employment opportunities. In the future EU regional policies should be designed in such a way as to encourage new and innovative firms. Switching to a high technology and service society will require accelerated structural adjustment in the EU - measures, that slow down this process are inadequate for the creation of sustainable full employment.

1. EU Labor Markets Facing Globalization and Intensified Technology Competition

The past decades saw intensified international competition as well as a rising R&D-GDP ratio in OECD countries. While labor productivity growth in the U.S. was low it was relatively high in EU countries which, however, suffered from high sustained unemployment rates after 1974. The US enjoyed high economic growth and was able to attract massive FDI inflows in the 1980s. At the same time US multinational companies (MNCs) were also increasingly active in western Europe and Asia, including Japan where EU firms faced problems in setting up subsidiaries. Foreign subsidiaries allow parent companies to observe new technologies in leading OECD countries and to tap the global innovation pool. Hence EU firms' weak presence with foreign direct investment (FDI) in Japan and elsewhere in Asia could undermine EU competitiveness in the long term. This holds the more the presence of MNCs facilitates exports from the parent company.

Since 1960 the EU created in net terms some 10 million new jobs which is less than 1/5 created in the US, where the employment rate increased from 66.2% in 1960 to 79.2% in 1995 (as a percentage of population employed at age of 15 to 64 years) - see Table 1. During the period 1960-95 the number of new entrants in the labor market was 1.5 times higher in the US than in Europe, allowing the US to reach the high Japanese employment rate. By contrast, the employment rate in the EU slightly fell during this period, and during 1980-95 the unemployment rate was about twice as high as in the US This comparison with the US needs certain qualifications as some observers argue that the US suffers from job insecurity, growth of mainly unskilled jobs, pay stagnation and underemployment (ECONOMIC POLICY INSTITUTE, 1996). However, in the EU there are also employees who would like to work longer working hours than is currently the case, US pay stagnation has been only transitory and is not inconsistent with economic theory given the high rate of female entrants into the labor market. Furthermore the presumed dominance of unskilled jobs in US employment growth is simply a prejudice as the following chapters of this report will show.

In a recent study the Commission identified insufficient public investment, high public deficits and growing taxation - in particular of labor - as well as high capital costs and insufficient R&D expenditures as major reasons for the poor employment

Table 1: Employment Rates in the Triade (In percent)

	1960	1970	1980	1995
EU	68.5	66.5	66.5	66.5
US	66.2	66.9	72.0	79.2
Japan	75.6	71.8	71.8	76.3

Source: Eurostat/European Commission.

record in the EU (EUROPEAN COMMISSION, 1996). However, this explains only in part the high unemployment rates. Traditional analyses have focused on labor market problems from either a pure macroeconomic or industrial economics perspective, while innovation and growth theory has been used to analyze the role of R&D for economic development not taking into account the labor market. The following analysis adopts a more integrated approach to discuss the links between capital formation, R&D, market dynamics and employment.

The share of long-term unemployment is rather high in EU countries except for Austria, Finland, Luxembourg and Sweden. In 1994 the share of people with a low educational level among the unemployed was particularly high in all EU countries, usually lying above 50%, with the exception of Germany (and possibly Austria, Finland and Sweden for which no data were available) - see Table 2. Higher levels of education (university degree) in OECD countries have implied lower unemployment rates than the average OECD. Thus, on the one hand educational efforts have to be improved, and on the other hand „wage structure policies" which raise the wages of skilled labor relative to unskilled are required.

Table 2: Main Features of Unemployment in the EU, 1994

	Unemployment rate of total labor force	Share of long-term unemployed[b] among all unemployed	Share of those with low educational level[c] among unemployed	Unemployment rate for 'youth' (15-24 yrs)
EUR 12	11,4	48,1	49,9	22,0
France	12,7	37,5	46,4	28,8
Germany	8,7	44,3	21,9	9,0
Italy	11,3	61,5	58,7	31,6
Spain	24,3	52,7	67,9	45,1
United Kingdom	9,7	45,4	58,0	16,3
Austria	3,9[a]	15,6	..	3,5
Belgium	9,6	58,3	51,8	21,8
Denmark	8,0	32,1	30,6	10,2
Finland	18,5	21,4	..	32,5
Greece	8,9	50,5	40,0	27,7
Ireland	14,7	59,1	63,5[a]	23,0
Luxembourg	3,5	29,6	62,8	7,9
Netherlands	7,2	49,4	31,7	11,3
Portugal	6,7	43,4	78,7	14,5
Sweden	8,1[a]	9,7	..	18,2[d]

a) 1993.
b) unemployed for more than 12 months.
c) educational level lower than upper secondary; share calculated for persons aged 15 to 59 years.
d) Sweden uses age group 16-24 years.

Source: EUROSTAT Labour Force Survey 1994 and National Statistical Institutes for Austria, Finland and Sweden.

While national unemployment rates have differed between OECD countries in the 1980s, a clear upward trend was observable in EU countries. Possible explanations for this trend can be found in hysteresis theories (e.g. JACKMANN et al., 1990; survey: BEAN, 1994; FRANZ, 1997) and insider-outsider theories (LINDBACK and SNOWER, 1990). The latter emphasize the wage pressure coming (through collective bargaining) from skilled workers which have been with the firm for many years and thus perceive the personal wage-unemployment risk as rather weak. This could create persisting excess wage pressure relative to the level compatible with full employment.

The move towards a knowledge-based society and higher R&D intensities could reinforce the insider-outsider problem in Europe in the long run. The problem is less severe in the US and Japan because wage bargaining occurs at the firm level, while EU countries typically have national or regional bargaining systems, so that there is a built-in tendency for insufficient wage dispersion with respect to regions, skills and firms in western Europe.

Long-term unemployment is particularly high among young people and among workers aged over 50. Lack of experience impairs the job opportunities for young people. The more serious problem is, however, "old unemployment" because this indeed might be a hysteresis phenomenon. This new variant of explaining hysteresis unemployment says the following: experienced employees around 50 will tend to enjoy an insider wage bonus which is linked to the firm specific skills acquired over many years, and if such employees are laid off it will be practically impossible for them to find a job at the former high gross wage in a different firm. Facing rather generous unemployment compensation and severance payments, there are only weak incentives to actively seek a new job (especially in a different sector) that would offer a lower income than previously. A solution for this problem would be to offer reentrants in the labor markets a temporary tax credit, thereby reducing the divergence between net income at the old and the new job and avoiding unemployment ratchet effects. Overall unemployment rates will increase gradually if negative external shocks gradually affect various sectors of the economy, and negative Keynesian multiplier and accelerator effects could indeed accentuate the problem.

Persistence of Regional Unemployment Differentials
One important feature of high unemployment rates in EU countries in the 1980s as compared to 1970 is the high standard deviation of regional unemployment rates (PETIT, 1995). In 1970 OECD countries except for Italy and Spain, recorded standard deviations below 1.5 - Germany, the Netherlands, Japan and Australia together recorded the smallest figures, respectively 0.26, 0.29, 0.38 and 0.38. But in 1987 only Norway, Sweden, Austria, Japan and Australia were lying below the 1.5 threshold, and even the US experienced an one-third increase to 1.73 (the OECD average being 2.18). This points to malfunctioning labor markets in the EU as unemployed workers from high unemployment areas are not moving into low-unemployment regions where the probability to find a new job is higher. Rules for unemployment benefits at present do not encourage such mobility - certainly a point for potential reform options. The rising female labor market participation rate has also contributed to low family mobility across regions. Furthermore, subsidized local

housing raises the cost of mobility in the EU, since tenants might be unable to find subsidized housing in a region with better employment prospects.

EU Unemployment Problems, Income Developments and Economic Integration
Economic integration has deepened in western Europe in the 1980s and early 1990s. The single market project was implemented at the end of 1992, although some sectors were effectively fully opened up to competition only in 1994/95 (the insurance sector was the last to be opened in 1995). Competition has intensified in the single market which also is an enlarged market of 270 million consumers.

After 1975 the European Union suffered from growing unemployment rates, with an acceleration occurring in the first half of the 1990s. While millions of jobs were lost in the manufacturing industry some 18 million jobs were created during the last 15 years in the expanding service sector. Standardized unemployment rates in western Europe reached almost 10% in 1994/95, in southern Europe (Italy, Portugal and Spain) about 15%; Finland which was strongly hit by the disintegration of the former socialist CMEA recorded a steep increase: from 3.4 % in 1990 to a peak-rate of 18.2 in 1994. For various reasons Sweden's unemployment rate also strongly increased, namely from 1.8% in 1990 to 9.2% in 1995. This is in marked contrast to the US and Japan which recorded 5.5% and 3.1% in 1995, respectively (see Table 3).

Table 3:   Standardized Unemployment Rates in 18 OECD Countries
(As percent of total labor force)

	1983	1990	1991	1992	1993	1994	1995
North America	9,7	5,8	7,2	7,9	7,3	6,5	5,9
Canada	11,9	8,1	10,3	11,3	11,2	10,3	9,5
United States	9,5	5,6	6,8	7,5	6,9	6,0	5,5
Japan	2,6	2,1	2,1	2,2	2,5	2,9	3,1
Central and Western Europe	9,8	6,9	7,4	8,1	9,5	9,7	9,2
Belgium	12,1	7,2	7,2	7,7	8,6	9,6	9,4
France	8,3	8,9	9,4	10,3	11,7	12.3	11,6
Germany[a]	7,7	4,8	4,2	4,6	7,9	8,4	8,2
Ireland	14,0	13,3	14,7	15,5	15,6	14,3	12,9
Netherlands	12,0	7,5	7,0	5,6	6,2	6,8	6,5
Switzerland	..	..	1,8	2,8	3,7	3,8	3,3
United Kingdom	12,4	6,9	8,8	10,1	10,4	9,6	8,7
Southern Europe	11,4	11,6	11,4	12,5	14,1	15,3	15,4
Italy	8,8	10,3	9,9	10,5	10,2	11,1	12,2
Portugal	7,8	4,6	4,1	4,1	5,5	6,8	7,1
Spain	17,0	15,9	16,0	18,1	22,4	23,8	22,7
Nordic Countries	4,2	3,0	5,0	7,8	10,9	11,1	10,3
Finland	5,4	3,4	7,5	13,0	17,7	18,2	17,1
Norway	3,4	5,2	5,5	5,9	6,0	5,4	4,9
Sweden	3,9	1,8	3,3	5,8	9,5	9,8	9,2
Oceania	..	7,0	9,6	10,6	10,6	9,4	8,1
Australia	9,9	6,9	9,5	10,7	10,8	9,7	8,5
New Zealand	..	7,7	10,3	10,2	9,4	8,1	6,3
Total of above countries	8,6	6,1	6,8	7,5	8,0	7,9	7,6

a) Up to and including 1992, western Germany; subsequent data concern the whole of Germany

Note: In so far as possible, the data have been adjusted to ensure comparability over time and to conform to the guidelines of the International Labour Office. All series are benchmarked to labor-force-survey-based estimates. In countries with annual surveys, monthly estimates are obtained by interpolation/extrapolation and by incorporating trends in administrative data, where available. The annual figures are then calculated by averaging the monthly estimates (for both unemployed and the labor force). For countries with monthly or quarterly surveys, the annual estimates are obtained by averaging the monthly or quarterly estimates, respectively. For several countries, the adjustment procedure used is similar to that of the Bureau of Labor Statistics, US Department of Labor. For EU countries, the procedures are similar to those used in deriving the Comparable Unemployment Rates (CURs) of the Statistical Office of the European Communities. Minor differences may appear mainly because of various methods of calculating and applying adjustment factors, and because EU estimates are based on the civilian labor force.

Table 4: Incidence of Long-term Unemployment from Survey-based Data in Selected OECD Countries [a,b,c,d,e] (As percent of total unemployment)

	1983		1991		1995	
	6 months and over	12 months and over	6 months and over	12 months and over	6 months and over	12 months and over
Austria	..	..	..	..	30,0	17,4
Belgium	81,9	64,2	76,7	62,0	77,7	62,4
Czech Republic	..	..	..	..	52,5	30,6
Denmark	65,8	43,4	53,4	31,4	46,6	27,9
Finland	30,0	19,2	32,6	9,2	47,4	32,3
France	66,9	42,4	58,0	37,2	68,9	45,6
Germany	65,8	41,6	54,1	31,5	65,4	48,3
Greece	58,2	33,1	71,5	47,6	71,9	50,9
Ireland	62,8	36,0	76,3	60,5	..	..
Italy	80,9	57,1	84,2	68,0	79,4	62,9
Luxembourg[f]	(55,1)	(34,7)	(37,5)	(20,8)	(47,5)	(22,4)
Netherlands	69,2	47,8	59,6	45,5	74,4	43,2
Portugal	..	..	58,4	38,6	62,3	48,7
Spain	72,8	52,4	68,4	51,1	72,2	56,5
Sweden	24,9	10,3	16,8	4,0	35,2	15,7
Switzerland	..	..	26,5	16,2	49,6	32,3
United Kingdom	65,7	45,2	46,6	28,5	60,7	43,5
Japan	32,8	13,3	37,5	19,1	38,2	18,1
United States	23,9	13,3	12,9	6,3	17,3	9,7

a) While data from labor force surveys make international surveys easier, compared to a mixture of surveys and registration data, they are not perfect. Questionnaire wording and design, survey timing, differences across countries in the age groups covered, and other reasons mean that care is required in interpreting cross-country differences in levels.

b) The duration of unemployment database maintained by the Secretariat is composed of detailed duration categories disaggregated by age and sex. All totals are derived by adding each component. Thus, the total for men is derived by adding the number of unemployed men by each duration and age group category. Since published data are usually rounded to the nearest thousand, this method sometimes result in slight differences between the percentages shown here and those that would be obtained using the available published figures.

c) Data are averages of monthly figures for Sweden and the United States, averages of quarterly figures for Czech Republic and Spain. The reference period for the remaining countries is as follows (among EU countries it occasionally varies from year to year): Austria, April; Belgium, April; Denmark, April-May; Finland, autumn; France, March; Germany, April; Greece, March-July; Ireland, May; Italy, April; Japan, February; Luxembourg, April; Netherlands, March-May; Portugal, February-April; Switzerland, second quarter; and the United Kingdom, March-May.

d) Data refer to persons aged 15 and over in Austria, Belgium, Czech Republic, Denmark, France, Germany, Greece, Ireland, Italy, Japan, Luxembourg, Netherlands, Portugal and Switzerland; and aged 16 and over in Spain, the United Kingdom and the United States. Data for Finland refer to persons aged 15-64 (excluding unemployment pensioners). Data for Sweden refer to persons aged 16-64.

e) Persons for whom no duration of unemployment was specified are excluded.

f) Data in brakets are based on small sample sizes and, therefore, must be treated with care.

Source: OECD (1996a), Employment Outlook, July 1996, p. 202.

A major difference between the early 1990s and the early 1980s is that the incidence of long-term unemployment strongly increased in EU countries, except for the United Kingdom. When considering high Swedish unemployment rates in 1995 one has to take into account that the share of long-term unemployed - e.g. 12 months and over - (as percent of total unemployed) was rather modest at a level of 15.7% in 1995. By contrast, the respective figure for France, Germany and Italy was 45.6%, 48.3% and 62.9% (see Table 4).

Labor force participation rates in almost all OECD countries strongly increased between 1973 and 1995 (see appendix 1, Table A1). The rising labor supply was bound to require wage moderation if full employment was to be restored. With the economic opening up of China in the 1980s and the rapid expansion of Asian NICs global competition intensified, most notably in product markets which required unskilled labor. In such a situation some EU countries were characterized by collective bargaining arrangements which reduced earnings dispersion; by contrast, Australia, Canada, the Czech Republic, Japan, New Zealand and the US recorded growing earnings dispersion in the 1980s and the early 1990s (OECD, 1996a, p. 61/62). Among EU countries only the UK recorded rising wage dispersion.

Unemployment in OECD countries is unevenly distributed across households so that relative household income positions differ internationally. A particular economic and social problem are households in which nobody has a job ("workless households", see Table 5). In this respect employment gains were more evenly distributed in Spain than in the UK: while Spain had a much higher unemployment rate than the UK in the mid 1990s the share of workless households was similar in both countries, namely around 20%. In the UK the benefit of job creation was mostly in favor of households in which one family member already had a job ("mixed households").

Table 5: The Changing Distribution of Work in Households
(Employment polarisation in OECD countries)

	Workless		Mixed		All work		Unemployment rate
%	1994	*1983*	1994	*1983*	1994	*1983*	1994
Germany	**15,5**	*15,0[a]*	**25,6**	*32,5*	**58,9**	*52,5*	**6,9**
France	**16,5**	*12,5*	**27,9**	*30,6*	**55,7**	*56,9*	**12,5**
Italy	**17,2**	*13,2*	**42,8**	*47,4*	**40,0**	*39,4*	**11,1**
UK	**18,9**	*16,0*	**18,6**	*30,1*	**62,1**	*53,9*	**9,5**
Spain	**20,1**	*19,4[b]*	**48,1**	*54,5*	**31,8**	*26,2*	**23,8**
Canada	**15,1**	*15,2*	**35,9**	*35,7*	**49,0**	*49,1*	**10,3**
US	**11,5[c]**	*13,1*	**24,9**	*32,3*	**63,6**	*54,6*	**6,0**

a) 1984 data
b) 1986 data
c) 1993 data

Source: GREGG, P. and WADSWORTH, J., It takes two - Employment Polarisation in the
OECD, here: table taken from Financial Times, 08.01.1997, p. 10.

Given intensified competition through trade, EU countries were facing strong structural adjustment pressures. Expanding production and exports of capital goods (human-capital intensive) and expanding the service sector were two potential reactions of EU countries. However, not all leading EU countries successfully organized structural change consistent with changing international labor scarcity and shifts in international comparative advantage.

European R&D Policy and Economic Integration
Comparing the US and the EU in the 1980s and the 1990s it is clear that R&D expenditures relative to GDP are too low in the Community; a fact already noted by the Commission's Green Paper on Innovation (EUROPEAN COMMISSION, 1995a). The US lead in manufacturing industry is partly due to the fact that public support is more generous in the US than in the EU. An additional aspect is that R&D policies - and economic policy in general - in the EU are hesitant in supporting innovative services which have become increasingly important in the 1980s and 1990s.

R&D expenditures in the EU are insufficient compared to the US and Japan. Thus, in 1995 industry's R&D expenditure-GDP ratio was less than 1/2 of that in Japan and the overall R&D-GDP ratio of the US was about 1/3 higher than that of the EU (see Table 6). Since US subsidiaries are strongly represented in the EU where they undertake R&D and EU firms are less active in the US it is obvious that US firms' global R&D efforts are much stronger than those of EU firms, and much stronger than the figures in Table 6 suggest.

Table 6: R&D Expenditures in the Triade

	Total R&D Spending (% of GDP) in 1995	R&D Spending by Industry (% of GDP) in 1995
EU	1.9	1.0
US	2.5	1.6
Japan	3.0	2.2

Source: EUROPEAN COMMISSION, (1996), Benchmarking the Competitiveness of European Industry, Brussels, COM(96) 463 final, p.8.

GRUPP, MÜNT and SCHMOCH (1994) have shown for the case of Germany, that lagged shares in world patents in a sector i are strongly correlated with the respective sector's relative export performance. For the Community this would mean - mutatis mutandis - that the Community's external trade balance will worsen if EU patenting is weakening in fields of crucial technological and commercial importance.

EU technological competition has intensified for various reasons. First, the single market's strong competition induces firms to step up product and process innovations since such innovations are an active way to defend market shares (WELFENS, 1992a). Second, in principle the large EU market allows firms to spread R&D costs over larger sales volumes which could stimulate R&D. However, temporarily falling market shares of firms as well as declining profit margins due to intensified competition could reduce firms' ability to finance high R&D expenditures. Third, there is the challenge of the newly industrializing countries which increasingly have captured market shares in medium technology (and high technology) so that firms from EU countries are forced to move up the technology ladder. After 1990 in addition to the Asian NIC's strong export drive there is the new and rapidly rising

EU import penetration from postsocialist eastern European countries. Fourth, a broad shift from military R&D towards higher shares of civilian R&D is occurring since the end of the Cold War. Military R&D traditionally accounted for about 50% of overall R&D expenditures in the UK, France and the US, with the share lying at a similar level in the USSR. Germany and Japan, which after 1945 had modest defense outlays and insignificant military R&D expenditures, thus, no longer stand to benefit from an exceptional situation in which their competitors' R&D budgets were largely absorbed by military R&D projects as in the 1970s.

1.1 New Competitors from NICs and Transforming Economies in Eastern Europe

While the 1970s brought two oil price shocks for western Europe leading to rising unemployment, the 1980s brought a new challenge: a rapid increase in foreign direct investment flows of OECD countries where Asian countries - including China - became important destinations. In these countries an unorthodox mixture of outward oriented policies and government R&D promotion stimulated technological catching up and economic growth which in turn facilitated exploitation of dynamic scale economies. East Asian countries moved up the technological ladder and improved their market shares in EU countries; moreover, Asian Newly Industrializing Countries (NICs) became important source countries of foreign direct investment themselves, directing part of their MNCs' investment budgets towards the EU whose single market program reinforced its attractiveness for outside investors. At the end of the 1980s the demise of the socialist CMEA and the disintegration of the Soviet Union became major impulses for the EU which enjoyed new market access in the rapidly opening up Visegrad countries.

By offering well-skilled personnel but wage costs that are 1/10 of the EU average, these countries are creating new investment opportunities for EU firms, especially those from high wage countries in proximity to eastern Europe (i.e. in particular Germany, Italy, Austria, Finland, Sweden).

The post-socialist countries in central and eastern Europe are facing specific problems of systemic transformation which include institutional innovations, macroeconomic stabilization and supply-side adjustments in combination with economic opening up. The economic opening-up process, reinforced by EBRD and

OECD support as well as EU activities (e.g. Phare, ACE), will lead to a new European division of labor, a new international economic order and a dynamic structural change in Europe. Economic and technological catching up of CEECs will be crucial for sustained transformation and - from a long-term perspective - will reduce the need of an enlarged EU to provide structural funds to new member states from central and eastern Europe. The second action under the 4th Framework Programme already envisages supporting the participation of Phare countries in Community programs.

Studies on German unification as well as studies on the impact of EU accession in Austria and Sweden (plus Finland) show a strong impact of the single market with respect to structural changes and innovation dynamics. However, as the example of the recent EU member country Austria shows, it is not easy even for an economically leading country's industry to quickly and efficiently integrate itself into Community programs. For prospective new EU member countries in eastern Europe the structural adjustment pressure from the single market will add to that of systemic transformation which brought major changes in the sectoral structure, the size of firms and the regional allocation of economic activities. A major feature of the transformation and economic opening up process in CEECs is that transportation intensity is rising in the sense that the average haul length of transportation is increasing, while the former east-east orientation of trade has been replaced by a new east-west-orientation. Traffic bottlenecks and rising transportation intensity in the whole of Europe will reinforce environmental problems and finding a solution - already a priority in the 4th Framework Program - will therefore become even more important in the future.

A future eastern enlargement of the EU, which silently began with German unification, will raise various problems that can be assessed on the basis of modern theory, including the gravity equation (BALDWIN, 1994; WELFENS, 1996b; WELFENS, 1997e). While the creation of a larger customs union will reinforce the exploitation of economies of scale and trade in differentiated products it is unclear whether there will be economic convergence within central Europe and among the newcomers (e.g. Visegrad countries). The longer the economic catching up process takes the higher will be the EU budgetary transfers necessary for the newcomers, and this will be a major political issue in the Community as long as high unemployment rates persist. Europe's history of interwar disintegration shows that protectionism can rapidly emerge from a situation of political instability and high unemployment rates (TILLY and WELFENS, 1996). A comprehensive theory of integration will have to take into account unemployment differentials among countries - affecting labor mobility even under factor equalization - and the impact of multinational companies (WELFENS, 1997b). The most recent strand of research integrates the effects of foreign direct investment on regional integration and takes into account the reduction of global political transactions cost. This literature strongly supports the case of regional integration provided that it is embedded into the overarching framework of the World Trade Organization.

Asian NICs

Asian NICs were particularly successful in technological and economic catching-up, where the process was organized in several stages by government which combined a policy of promoting education and R&D with an outward oriented policy that encouraged firms to increase their exports to contested OECD markets. It took the Republic of Korea some 15 years to reduce the export share of food and live animals from 30.4% in 1960 to 11.9 % in 1975 and to raise the share of machinery and transport equipment from 0.3 to 13.8%. The dynamic adjustment in production and exports can be summarized as follows (SONG, 1990, p.105): "The predominant export manufactures shifted over time from (1) labor-intensive goods to (2) other capital-intensive goods, (3) capital-intensive goods and skill-intensive goods, (4) capital- and-technology-intensive and high-wage goods, and (5) research-, capital-, and high skill-intensive goods." For the process of economic catching-up Korea relied strongly (and over time increasingly) on the import of machinery and transport equipment which accounted for about 1/3 of its imports in the late 1980s; the import share of professional and scientific instruments doubled between 1960 and 1987. Taiwan, Singapore and Hongkong followed a similar path of economic and technological catching-up which resulted in a combined export share equal to that of Japan in 1995.

The four "Asian Tiger countries" partly relied on foreign direct investment - very strongly as in the case of Singapore, sometimes in the weak form of subcontracting as in Korea. The ingredients for economic catching-up are fairly obvious, although it is clear that the prerequisite of political stability is not easy to achieve (AIZENMAN, 1997). Eastern Europe's postsocialist economies could follow a similar catching-up path which would imply for EU countries new opportunities to export R&D- and skill-intensive machinery and transport equipment, but this requires appropriate policy impulses, especially in the field of education and high technology R&D support. The EU would import low technology machinery and equipment as well as manufactured goods and chemicals from postsocialist eastern Europe (including Russia).

Globalization

The 1990s are characterized by true globalization of industry in the sense that foreign investors face locational opportunities worldwide and therefore enjoy new advantages from mobility. Exporters from eastern Europe and the Asian NICs capture an increasing share of EU markets in certain fields. In the 1980s Asian NICs increasingly specialized in medium and high technology products. Asian markets where EU firms are underrepresented enjoy high economic growth. Transforming economies also have weak trade relations with Asian NICs although this is changing gradually.

Trade between the EU and eastern Europe grew very dynamically in the 1990s both on the import and export side. From a theoretical perspective rapidly growing trade between the EU and eastern Europe clearly could be anticipated on the basis of the gravity equation (e.g. BALDWIN, 1994). Globalization defined as a combination of rising export-GDP ratios and rising foreign direct investment relative to domestic investment is affecting EU countries in several ways.

Between 1950 and 1990 three main indicators of cognitive skills - substantive complexity, general educational development and average years of schooling measured in 1970 - showed positive growth; the same holds for interactive skills. With rising world market orientation of firms competition is intensifying and better skills are required. However, there is no general shortage of skilled employees since an increasing number of vocational training schemes, high school and universities turn out more and more skilled people in OECD countries (WOLFF, 1996). It seems that the demand for skills is mainly increasing as a consequence of new vintages of capital so that the pace of new investment, the rate of computerization and R&D intensity are stimulating the demand for more educated workers (BARTELS and LICHTENBERG, 1987).

From a theoretical perspective there are various links between employment and innovation where the latter depends crucially on economic integration and science and technology policy. Innovation will cause regional and structural change and require job reallocation across sectors and firms so that labor mobility is important. With an increasing role of innovative services for the overall innovation process (DEUTSCHE BUNDESBANK, 1996) analysis will have to focus on expansion of services, in particular telecommunications. In liberalized telecoms markets there will be increasing mobility of service providers and users as well as improved prospects for the growth of mobile skilled services. Expanding services mainly are input for manufacturing industry so that industrial development (as well as regional and structural change) is important for job reallocation and employment. Economic integration facilitates regional specialization in industry, exploitation of scale economies and trade in differentiated products. National science and technology policy is often rather inefficient in such an international setting because R&D will have international spillover effects; indeed R&D policies which reinforce ownership specific advantages as the required basis for multinationalization could stimulate FDI outflows causing net employment losses. A wider two-way FDI network in turn could raise regional (international) trade which contributes to growth and employment.

Figure 1: Building Blocs of Innovation in Europe

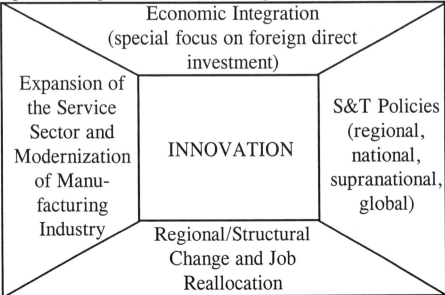

1.2 Integration, R&D Dynamics and Technological Specialization

Economic integration in the EU increased between 1968 (formation of a customs union) and the 1990s. The single market project was implemented at the end of 1992 - with some latecomer sectors following only in 1994/95. It is clear that the creation of a single market for goods and services will facilitate the exploitation of static and dynamic economies of scale so that considerable productivity increases and specific growth impacts can be expected for certain industries. However, with respect to employment impacts one should not overlook the development of the overall aggregate investment output ratio which was not favorable in the EU. Within two decades, output growth fell from 4% to 2.5% p.a., while the investment-output ratio dropped by five percentage points as emphasized by the EUROPEAN COMMISSION (1993, p. 9). The single market program stimulated growth only moderately.

With major privatizations organized in several EU countries in the early 1990s one would expect overmanning to fall immediately after privatization. Major layoffs occurred in the context of privatization of telecoms network operators in almost all EU countries; this was also the case in the electricity sector in the UK which was privatized in the 1980s.

R&D Dynamics
With the economic opening up of eastern Europe and the advances of NICs in the world market global competition has intensified - especially in the field of labor intensive products and medium intensive technologies. For EU countries facing intensified import competition and the relocation of production in the context of foreign direct investment outflows it is therefore important to increasingly position themselves in advanced technology fields, which typically is one of the few areas in which continental EU countries recorded job growth in the 1980s. Hence R&D are increasingly important for growth, international competitiveness, employment and ecological progress.

R&D is needed for process innovations which allow costs to be cut and hence markets to be widened - this could facilitate the exploitation of static and dynamic economies of scale. R&D is also a requirement for product innovations which allow firms to charge higher prices. Firms that are eager to recover R&D

investment costs and to earn a Schumpeterian rent from innovation will try to ensure intellectual property rights, typically via patents. They will also massively invest into marketing in order to create preferences in favor of the novel products. R&D as well as marketing expenditures create market entry barriers because they largely represent sunk costs; newcomers will find it therefore difficult to successfully enter the market. Innovative firms thus can enjoy extra profits which partly will have to be shared with workers since trade unions in highly profitable industries will strongly lobby for wage rises. With continued product innovations the value-added by the firm will indeed rise continuously such that the wage bargaining process will result in rising real wage rates and higher real incomes in some sectors. This in turn will result in multiplier effects in the overall economy.

Launching product innovations will stimulate the growth of demand directly as was emphasized by SCHUMPETER, who also stressed that entrepreneurship is the basis for long-term growth and economic cycles. Both for R&D devoted to product innovations and to process innovations it holds that unit R&D costs can be reduced if large output volumes are realized during a given innovation cycle. From this perspective the gradual increase of R&D expenditure-GNP ratios in OECD countries is bound to stimulate exports and trade.

Firms which develop process innovations will benefit from rising sales and employment. Technometric analysis can identify the most dynamic technology fields across countries. Firms that apply process innovations could, however, substitute capital for labor so that the overall impact of R&D on labor markets is unclear. To the extent that technological progress is capital embodied the countries with a strong investment goods industry will particularly benefit. Empirical analysis has to show which net effect will prevail.

Technological Specialization
In a large integrated market facing global competition one should expect EU firms to develop a special innovation profile which reflects its comparative advantages and policy priorities for R&D. The US achieved a much stronger change in patent specialization than the EU-12-Community (or Germany) as is shown in Table 7 and 8. The degree of specialization measured by an appropriate Herfindahl index was much higher in the US and Japan than in the Community. Indeed the EU-12 group suffered from an overall decline in specialization in the period 1982/92. This points

to unexploited EU potentials for economies of scale in R&D in the sense that a stronger concentration on profitable innovation fields lets one expect that R&D unit costs could be reduced under such a strategy. Lack of innovation specialization in the EU is probably due to parallel R&D programs of various EU countries. While a simple switching to fully integrated supranational R&D programs certainly would reduce useful variety of competing R&D approaches in the Community it seems that the present situation offers considerable room for improved policy coordination. Since figures for Germany showed a better adaptation of small and medium sized firms to international technology trends (i.e. activities in the most dynamic patenting fields - with high growth rates) one may doubt that creating bigger EU firms via merger and acquisitions will automatically improve the innovativeness and technological adaptability of firms in the Community. This does not rule out that there are industries with further opportunities for mergers and acquisitions which then in turn would generate an endogenous clearance mechanism across firms. At the bottom line the global division of R&D is characterized by insufficient specialization in the EU and poor flexibility of big firms.

Table 7: Adjustment of the Technology Portfolio of Branches
(Sum of absolute differences of shares 1982-1992[a])

Country of origin	Period 1982/92	Period 1987/92	Average p.a. 1982-1992
Germany	6,5	4,0	2,8
EU(12)	10,0	5,5	2,1
USA	16,4	10,9	3,1
Japan	11,8	4,5	3,6
World Total	12,4	5,7	2,1

a) Sum A of absolute differences of the shares of inventions with international patent applications that are alloted to each branch between the years 1982 respectively 1987 and 1992:

$$A = \sum_i \left| \frac{p_{it}}{p_t} - \frac{p_{iT}}{p_T} \right|$$; p_{it} = patents in sector i in period t; T = reference year

Source: *FAUST, K. (1996), Internationale Patentstatistik: Technologische Positionen und strukturelle Probleme der deutschen Industrieforschung, Ifo-Schnelldienst 12/96, p. 12.*

Table 8:   Degree of Technological Specialization According to Industrial Sectors

(Herfindahl index[b] according to international patenting)

Country of origin	Year of announcement 1992	Changes 1992/82
Germany	13,8	0,09
EU(12)	12,9	-0,15
USA	16,0	1,25
Japan	23,2	2,40
World Total	14,9	0,83

b) Sum of the squared shares of the individual branches of industry in the total number of inventions of the country of origin concerned, multiplied by 100. The Herfindahl-Index is a measure for concentration that is 100% in case of full concentration while approaching 0 in case of very diversified patent patterns.

Source: FAUST, K. (1996), Internationale Patentstatistik: Technologische Positionen und strukturelle Probleme der deutschen Industrieforschung, Ifo-Schnelldienst 12/96, p. 12.

Privatization, Competition and Productivity Problems

The McKINSEY (1996) report showed that Germany and other EU countries strongly lag behind the US in capital productivity in many fields, often because of dominance of state firms and lack of competition. An important example is telecommunications where US capital productivity exceeds that of Germany by about 1/3. The EU's costs disadvantage vis-à-vis the US in telecommunications, energy and transportation partly can be attributed to lack of competition in infrastructure industries. Due to liberalization initiatives of the European Commission this deficiency will be gradually remedied from the late 1990s onwards. Competition will improve the allocation process and facilitate to cope with capital shortage problems in the EU: Higher capital productivity allows to provide capital for more workers than at present.

The EU's research base probably is less market-oriented than that of the US, and in addition fewer human resources are devoted to R&D: Scientific research personnel represents only 0.47% of the labor force, compared to 0.74% in the US and 0.80 % in Japan. Moreover, between 1984 and 1993 the EU lost share in patents in all sectors except aerospace and transport equipment (EUROPEAN COMMISSION 1996, p.14). Since the Community Innovation Survey indicated that

EU companies which engaged in technical cooperation agreements usually have a much larger proportion of new or improved products in their total sales EU programs which support cooperation among innovative firms should be strengthened.

Lack of functional infrastructure in the single market is a crucial problem since infrastructure bottlenecks reduce private investment. Moreover, distortions in infrastructure pricing which result from external economic/environmental costs of alternatives modes of transportation lead to important misallocation problems in the Community. E.g. as long as interconnection among transportation modes remains poor the capital productivity of the overall transport infrastructure remains low in Europe; moreover, only with vertical disintegration of railway services and network operation plus privatization can capacity utilization of Europe's enormous railway system be improved.

1.3 Structural Aspects of European and US Labor Markets

Structural problems in Europe are manifested in sluggish employment growth coupled with high and persistent unemployment. There are fewer overt indications of structural problems in the US but a common structural theme is the difficulty confronting low skill workers, with widening skill (and unemployment) differentials in the US and deteriorating relative employment and unemployment for the low skilled in the Community.

Beginning with employment, the slow growth of employment in the European Union has long been a matter of concern. Figure A1 in appendix I reproduces a graph from the well-known OECD Jobs Study charting employment growth in OECD regions between 1960 and 1995. It reveals the lamentable Community record in generating jobs. Over the interval in question, employment growth averaged 1.8% a year in North America, 1.7% in Oceania, 1.2% in Japan, 0.6% in the EFTA group of countries, and just 0.3% in the twelve-nation EC group. The values given in the figure for 1993-95 are projections. The actual out-turn of events has been little different, with only modest net job creation in the European Union. But, after zero job growth between 1990 and 1992, the US added 7.05 million jobs to the civilian employment count (or 6%) between January 1993 and January 1996, and the pace seems to have accelerated markedly since then. Note also that job growth in the US and Japan has primarily occurred in the private sector whereas in the Community it has predominantly been in the public sector, albeit less so since the late 1980s. Another interesting difference between the Community and the US is the much lower share of the working age population in employment in the former: 60% as compared with 73%. Moreover, this employment population ratio in the Community is actually lower today than it was 25 years ago.

It is now clear that the allegation that US employment growth has largely occurred in low skill jobs can be firmly dispelled. Thus for example of the 22.2 million jobs created between 1983 and 1994 no less than 10 million, or 46%, were in the relatively high-paying managerial and professional occupations (60% of individuals holding these jobs have 4 or more years of college, more than twice the average for all occupations). Moreover, Bureau of Labor Statistics projections through 2005 point to a continued generation of good jobs. In fact, there are close similarities between the Community and the US in the changing structure of the workforce by occupation, which reflects the fact that there have been not dissimilar changes in the industrial structure of employment.

Sectoral shifts in employment can be measured using indices of structural change. Interestingly, for both the Union and the US, though there are signs of considerable churning or turbulence in the labor market, there is little indication that the pace of structural change has accelerated in recent years (OECD, 1994a, Part 1, Table 1.7; ALLEN and FREEMAN, 1995). In other words, at the very broadest level, the major shift into services over the last two decades has been no greater than the shift out of agriculture in earlier decades - and the same holds true for the industrial reallocation of labor at lower levels of aggregation. Increased turbulence could of course imply major problems for unemployment development. (We will comment on the reallocation of labor between establishments in section 5.8.)

Turning therefore to unemployment, Figure A2 in appendix I charts the course of joblessness in the Union between 1970 and 1995. Figure A3 in appendix I extends the time frame, again using data from the OECD Jobs Study, from which it is immediately apparent that the marked improvement in unemployment development in the Community between 1986 and 1990 was not to prove long lasting. (For a variety of unemployment performance indicators other than the conventional unemployment rate considered here, see SORRENTINO, 1995.) One interesting result is that the Community overtook the US as a high-unemployment region around 1983. The US record is particularly interesting because of the major improvement in its relative position, but even here there is every indication of some ratcheting up of US unemployment in the 1970s as compared with the 1950s and 1960s (ECONOMIC REPORT OF THE PRESIDENT, 1994, p. 103). Also, as we shall see, there is stronger evidence to suggest a rise in that country's long-term unemployment rate. The anomaly therefore is more Japan than the US Unemployment rates are typically higher for younger workers, blue-collar workers, and for women (and minorities) in both the Community and the US There are no signs that blue-collar employment has increased relatively to white-collar unemployment while the relative position of younger workers and women has actually improved. Interesting differences are recorded for unskilled workers, however. If we compare the unemployment rates for the bottom and top quartiles of the labor force ranked by education (from the lowest to the highest), higher ratios are observed over the 1980s for France, Germany, Italy, and the UK though not for the US (in the case of males). It is tempting to link these differences to a marked widening of earnings differentials in the US, but as we shall see this broad inter-quartile distinction is somewhat superficial since it does not truly get to grips with the issue of low skill.

Yet more powerful differences between the US and the Community are evident when we come to examine unemployment duration. In 1993 for example 20.4 (11.2)% of the US unemployed had been without work for 6 (12) months or more. Corresponding values for France, Germany, Italy, the Netherlands, Spain, and the UK were 58.2 (34.2)%, 60.1 (40.3)%, 76.5 (57.7)%, 79.1 (52.3)%, 69.6 (47.4)%, and 62.9 (42.5)%, respectively. It should also be noted, however, that long-term unemployment in the US is currently at a record high level for the present stage of the cycle - 18% of workers have been unemployed for more than 26 weeks at a time when the overall unemployment rate is just 5.3%. As was indicated earlier the troughs in the ratio of long-term to total unemployment have been at successively higher levels since 1970 (ECONOMIC REPORT OF THE PRESIDENT, 1994, Chart 3-4).

Let us now turn to the structure of earnings. The favorable US labor market performance relative to the Community evident in the preceding paragraphs has in part to be qualified by the trends in American earnings development. Consider first earnings differentials. Over the course of the 1980s the relative wage of low productivity workers (bottom decile) declined by 17%. In marked contrast, the relative wage of the low-skilled in most Community countries - the notable exception is the UK - were somewhat higher at the end of the 1980s than at the beginning of the decade. (Much the same is true of earnings differentials by education levels.) Moreover, not only did the relative earnings of low skill American workers fall in the 1980s but their real wages too: by more than 10%. No such fall in real wages of the low skilled is observed for in the Community - even in the UK, where the decline in relative wages was 25%, the real wages of the bottom decile of the earnings distribution increased by more than 10%.

Criticism of US labor market performance has thus switched from the ill-advised and frankly disingenuous charge that the job growth was of the hamburger flipper variety to the more substantive notion that its better performance than the Community on the employment front was achieved at the expense of wage growth and a growing number of working poor. But some important qualifications do need to be made in measuring trends in pay and inequality in the US First, the method of adjusting for inflation makes a big difference to outcomes: the CPI has overstated the rate of inflation in the US by as much as 1.5% recently, so that the decline in, say, real average hourly earnings observed over 1989-1995 using the official CPI becomes a modest gain of a little under 6% using an adjusted CPI. Second, wages differ from total compensation, such that given the continuing growth in fringes the latter series records a significantly larger growth rate than the former. Third, median and average wages differ, the larger increase in wages at the upper end of the distribution ensuring that the latter exceeds the former. Fourth, a variety of earnings series are available that again complicate the picture. (For the differences all these considerations make to the measurement of post-1988 earnings and compensation, see EMPLOYMENT POLICY FOUNDATION, 1996). Nevertheless, the fact remains that over the period since 1973 earnings in the US have slowed for most workers and stagnated for many. Figure A4 in appendix I charts the growth in various official measures of real pay for the US for the period 1963-91 and it can be seen that the break in the series after 1973 is acute. The figure implies that the middle of the distribution was hurt more by the slowdown than the top. This reflects a dramatic decline in the rewards offered those without a college degree. If one focuses on (unadjusted CPI) real hourly earnings then these actually fell for all but the highest paid - the exception to this statement is females whose real hourly wages increased and at all levels of the distribution.

We will return to the sources of sharply rising earnings inequality in the US below. In the interim we pause to document the very different path of real wages in the European Community. Figure A5 in appendix I is taken from the OECD Jobs Study and in addition to providing comparative information on real wages it also charts employment development. Real wage growth in the Community has outstripped productivity with obvious consequences for employment. If the US record in terms of earnings development is poor, the rise in earnings in the Community has clearly been excessive.

We now turn to the sources of unfavorable labor market developments in both the US and the Community. There are no simple explanations of the European predicament. Conventional arguments that have been put forward to explain the rise in Community unemployment, for example, are external developments in the form of adverse movements in the terms of trade and counter-inflationary demand policies. Such shocks, taken in association with real wage rigidity, appear to have had a major impact on unemployment levels. But there remains the issue of persistence since the above combination of factors would seem to have a temporary influence. It is precisely at this point that the water is muddied: there is no shortage of suggested mechanisms that have the effect of propagating persistent effects of temporary shocks. Some of the more popular of these are insider-outsider considerations and the characteristics of the unemployed. The burgeoning literature is reviewed by BEAN (1994). He concludes that insider-outsider models fail to explain the outward shift in the unemployment-vacancy (UV) relation observed for Europe (though not for the US). His evaluation comes down in favor of models that alternatively stress outsider characteristics. One such model is associated with the notion that a rise in unemployment serves to depreciate skills and weaken work habits. Taken in conjunction with wage rigidities, this could explain a rightward shift in the UV relation (and heightened wage pressure): a given level of vacancies will be now be associated with higher unemployment because of fewer successful job matches. At issue is whether jobless duration is long enough to explain persistence. A second argument of this genre is that firms will respond to deteriorating skill levels associated with lengthy unemployment by creating fewer jobs in the future, and a third, supply-side argument is that workers will give up searching and rely on UI benefits. In both such cases, the effective labor force declines and equilibrium wages rise. There is of course the empirical suggestion that rising long-term unemployment is associated with a outward shift of the UV curve and also evidence that a rising share of long-term unemployed in the unemployment count reduces downward wage pressure associated with a given (higher) aggregate unemployment rate.

Restrictions on the freedom of employers to lay off workers may also assist in the explanation of the upward drift of unemployment in Europe and by the same token the more favorable record of the US in this regard. This is a highly contentious issue in both Europe and the US We will again examine the flexibility argument in section 5.8, but would make the following necessarily summary remarks here. First, changes in regulations are necessary to produce persistence unless the need for flexibility has grown through time. Second, (rising) severance pay is associated with lower equilibrium levels of employment - both directly through increasing labor costs and indirectly by increasing insider power (LAZEAR, 1990). That said, the effect on unemployment is less clear empirically (ADDISON and GROSSO, 1996). Third, increases in unemployment are not confined to those European countries that increased severance pay so that the explanation is partial at best. Fourth, proceeding beyond severance pay, other employment protection regulations may have different effects; for example, advance notice of impending layoff may have beneficial effects on unemployment (ADDISON and GROSSO, 1996). Fifth, and relatedly, employment protection legislation is multifaceted, so that researchers have been drawn to constructing indices of the overall strictness of legislation. Research based on ranked indices has suggested, inter al., that employment-population ratios and part-time working (though not temporary work) are lower, the stricter is legislation (GRUBB and WELLS, 1993). Other research using cardinal measures has suggested that tighter regulation is associated with long-term unemployment, higher youth unemployment, and reduced outflows from the unemployment pool, inter al. (MOSLEY and KRUPPE, 1993). Such relationships are typically drawn from simple correlation analysis which is at best suggestive - and correlations based on rankings provide particularly blunt measures at that - and at all times the subjectivity of the coerciveness of legislation has to be borne in mind. More generally, the robustness of the estimated effects of employment regulation in ceteris paribus treatments is a real issue given the parsimonious nature of the estimating equations. Omitted variables bias could mean that the results are little more than noise.

In its own review of the employment protection issue, the OECD Jobs Study appears to conclude that although not the cause of high unemployment in Europe - other than perhaps in southern European nations (but see ADDISON and TEIXEIRA, 1996) - such regulations may add to adjustment difficulties once high levels of unemployment are reached. Nevertheless, the OECD (1994a, Part II, p. 80) comes down gingerly in favor of greater flexibility, noting among other things that "The duality among the employed that arises when temporary contracts are used seems preferable to `the graver social duality separating the employed from the unemployed'." Our own interpretation of the evidence is a little different: employment protection legislation is not the principal determinant of rising European unemployment but it contributes to that outcome by increasing employment adjustment costs and also by inhibiting the reallocation of labor between sectors, thereby leading to lower output and lower productivity (see BURGESS, 1994). (This interpretation is quite consistent with the argument that speed of employment adjustment within sectors may not be lower in Europe than in the US because of subsidized short time working.) The precise magnitudes are however opaque at this time. We shall subsequently argue that there is a clear danger of harmonizing employment protection rules across the Community.

As to the effects of other labor market regulations such as minimum wages and unemployment insurance (UI), the US evidence suggests that neither has had much material effect in lowering employment and elevating joblessness in the US Although minimum wage effects on unemployment also appear perhaps surprisingly to be muted in the case of Europe - though this absence of substantive overall effect provides the weakest of cases for minimum wage legislation, not least because young workers in Europe do appear to have been more adversely affected - the impact of UI benefits is rather more controversial. The conventional view is expressed by BURTLESS (1987), who argues that the potential unemployment effects of more generous benefit systems in some European countries relative to the US could have contributed only little to the observed differences in unemployment - just 2.5 to 4 weeks in the case of Germany in the early 1980s for example. In short, the elasticity of jobless duration with respect to benefits is too low to have had much effect (see also BEAN, 1994; ATKINSON and MICKLEWRIGHT, 1991). But the OECD Jobs Study is altogether less sanguine, noting in particular a form of unemployment hysteresis in high benefit countries following a deep recession, caused by higher unemployment reducing the monthly rate of job offers that an individual receives from the public employment service. For this and other disincentive-effect reasons the OECD proceeds to offer a specific and rigorous set of proposals to limit entitlements to benefits and refuse it to those who are not available for work.

Arguably the most interesting work on understanding the labor market problems of the 1980s and 1990s has been undertaken in the US The goal of this research has been to analyze the causes of rising wage and income inequality and the deteriorating position of low skilled workers. It is likely that the same processes are at work in Europe, where, because of greater wage rigidity, the inequality takes the form of widening unemployment differentials by skill rather than widening wage differentials. The US evidence suggests that a rising relative demand for skill has been in place for many decades, certainly dating back to the 1940s, and that the pace has not quickened in the most recent years. Rather what has occurred is a change in the composition of the change in the relative demand for skill. There has been a shift in demand within industries, while the contribution of sectoral (that is, industry) shifts may have actually declined through time. These results point to biased technical change (see JUHN and MURPHY, 1994; MURPHY and WELCH, 1993).

There is of course no shortage of explanations for rising inequality in the US, though each has to confront this within-industry shift in labor demand phenomenon. It seems that we can for the US discount the role of unemployment, demographics, and hours worked (see BURTLESS, 1990). More controversial is the contribution of international trade, immigration, and union decline. Although a number of studies have linked rising inequality with the growth of net imports, considerable doubt remains as to whether the number of trade-impacted workers are sufficient for the trade tail to wag the inequality dog (BURTLESS, 1995). Similarly, immigration which has had the effect of increasing the relative supply of unskilled workers and which rose in the latter half of the 1980s is unlikely to explain much of the rise in inequality (for undoubtedly upper-bound estimates, see BORJAS, FREEMAN and KATZ, 1992). But it has been calculated that the decline in unionization may have contributed up to one-fifth of the inequality in earnings over the 1980s (FREEMAN, 1993). The fact remains that earnings dispersion has increased as much among union as comparable nonunion workers, so that the primary cause of rising inequality must be found elsewhere.

In an interesting analysis of the fall in earnings of low skill (male) workers between 1973 and 1979, BLACKBURN, BLOOM, and FREEMAN (1990) confirm that roughly 80% of the decline is attributable to within-industry shifts in demand and 20% to inter-industry shifts in demand. They then attempt to ascertain the contribution of supply-side factors and institutional factors (minimum wages and declining unionization) in within-industry shifts. The supply-side analysis focuses shifts in the relative supply of workers with different educational qualifications. Assuming there were no shifts in relative demand, the authors first examine the increase in the differential between college-trained and high school graduates/dropouts between 1979 and 1987. Despite the growth in the proportion of college graduates in the workforce, the percentage that are college educated among those aged between 25 and 34 actually declined after 1979. The suggestion is that part of the increase in the observed differential(s) after 1979 could be due to this falling supply of young college graduates. It is reported that this decline could explain up to 30% of the rising differential observed among younger workers. In other words, this amount of the changes within industry may be attributed to a supply shift. Next, assuming that the rate of increase in relative demand was the same in the 1980s as in the 1970s (when the differential was fairly stable despite a sizable growth in the college-educated population), the authors estimate how the slowed growth in the relative supply of college educated workers in the 1980s contributed to the change in differentials between the periods 1979-87 and 1973-79. It is reported that the deceleration in the growth of college educated manpower can explain much but by no means all of the increase in the growth of the wage gap. In other words, the suggestion is that shifts in relative demand in favor of college educated manpower accelerated in the 1980s. Finally, it is found that although the effect of (declining) minimum wages had minimal effect on differentials, the decline in unionization may have contributed up to a fifth of the drop in relative wages received by low skill workers during the decade of the 1980s.

The basic issues raised by increasing returns to college-trained manpower are two-fold. First, is a Mincerian correction in sight, and second will labor force developments and in particular a likely slowdown in labor force growth provide a sufficiently tighter labor market to improve the employment and earnings of the less skilled. On the former question, there are signs that the gap between college and high school graduates has reached a plateau. Thus, in 1994 the college premium measured only 73%, down from 79% in 1990. Mincer himself has predicted that the premium will fall by 25% in the next six to seven years, other things being equal. On the second question, the projected slower labor force growth over the next few years should also improve the absolute earnings situation of the low skilled, assuming reasonable demand growth. The self correcting mechanisms of the US labor market coupled with demographics should therefore point to some real improvement but it is unlikely that there will be a massive improvement. Accordingly, in the US as elsewhere much attention has shifted to possible schooling and training initiatives, the effect of which will be discussed in section 5.8. The burden of our argument will be that the consensus as to the need to improve primary and secondary education, which is a long-run solution, evaporates when attention focuses on current actions to benefit low skill workers. Conventional training and other manpower programs have not been conspicuously successful in improving the lot of disadvantaged workers.

Finally, we should note that nearly all of the secular increase in unemployment (and nonparticipation) recorded in the US over, say, 1967-89 has fallen on less-skilled individuals despite the marked flexibility in their wages (TOPEL, 1993). In other words, the very considerable downward wage flexibility in the US has been accompanied by a material increase in the unemployment (and nonparticipation) of those in the lowest decile of the wage distribution. And markets are clearing! Unemployment rates for those above the median of the wage distribution have been largely unchanged over time.

1.4 Theoretical Aspects of Integration, Innovation and Innovation Policy in Open Economies

Integration Theories and R&D
In a two country model traditional economic theory shows that switching from autarky to free trade improves welfare in the sense that global consumption can be increased through trade. More generally, the elimination of tariff barriers is welfare improving for the world economy since the producers with the lowest costs can increase their market share. Dynamic models which take into account growth, R&D and multinational companies (TIRONI, 1982; ROMER, 1986; ETHIER, 1986; KLODT, 1992) will often lead to a different picture than short-term static analysis based on a partial equilibrium model.

If inter-industry trade is dominant, there could be serious transitory adjustment costs since the expansion of foreign firms in a certain sector will be accompanied by the contraction of this sector in the home country. Thus workers will have to shift from declining sectors to expanding industries. If intra-industry trade is dominant - a typical finding for EU countries - adjustment problems are relatively small; e.g. automotive firms in country II will specialize in the production and export of big cars, while the firms in country I will specialize in the production of small cars. Transitory adjustment problems, which are rarely considered in economic models, could become permanent problems if there is long-term unemployment eroding the human capital of workers. These workers facing a depreciation of human capital will find it impossible to find a new job at the old wage rate. Hence in a setting with sticky wages and time-consuming adjustment rising trade (or economic opening up of countries) could cause major economic problems unless exchange rate adjustments are possible; or other measures for regaining equilibrium in labor market exist.

It is not always clear that in a multi-country world the regional elimination of trade barriers makes the world economy better off (elimination of quantitative restrictions is always welfare-improving). The classical customs union theory of VINER analyzes within a partial equilibrium approach the main effects of countries which remove trade barriers among each other, while adopting a common external tariff vis-à-vis third countries (JOVANOVIC, 1992). While traditional trade theory of the VINER-type has no clear-cut results for regional economic integration schemes, modern theory which additionally includes product differentiation and innovation effects presents a stronger case for regional integration.

The European Community achieved within a decade the stage of a customs union (1968) and then proceeded towards further integration. Such integration has meant the abolishment of restrictions for trade in services and the creation of a common market with common competition policy rules. This was fully achieved in the 1992 single market project which also abolished physical trade barriers (border controls) and introduced the principle of mutual recognition of standards. The EU single market program brought major economic benefits, including an improvement in the terms of trade (see e.g. McKENZIE/VENABLES, 1991; AGEGAZ et al., 1994). But it is unclear whether benefits will be spread evenly among member countries and yield benefits for all main outsider trading partners (STRAUBHAAR, 1988; HUFBAUER, 1990; NEVEN, 1990; TICHY, 1992). Moreover there could be full liberalization of capital flows and even a currency union which establishes absolutely fixed exchange rates and a common currency (DE GRAUWE, 1992; WELFENS, 1996a). The highest form of economic integration is an economic and monetary union which the EU is envisaging for 1999 when the single market would be combined with a monetary union.

Integration Theory with a Spatial Dimension
Trade takes place in space so that distances and transportation costs are important. The gravity equation suggests that exports X from country i to j depend positively on per capita incomes y, GNP (as a proxy for market size) and negatively on distance, or more strictly, transportation costs T; in empirical analysis the latter is approximated by distance.

$$X_{i,j} = a_0 + a_1 y_i + a_2 y_j + a_3 GNP_i + a_4 GNP_j + a_5 T + u \quad (u = \text{error term})$$

The gravity equation implies that trade between neighboring countries should be relatively high, especially if the respective per capita incomes and GDP growth rates are high - the former offering opportunities for trade in differentiated products which require product innovations; in turn they often require new investment and thereby create additional employment.

Real capital mobility has increased worldwide after 1985, and the EU was able to attract rising foreign direct inflows, especially due to increasing intra-EU inflows. With ongoing privatization and deregulation of public utilities and other sectors there are new opportunities for the formation of EU multinationals.

A gravity equation for foreign direct investment flows might also be stated (WELFENS, 1997b):

$$I^*_{i,j} = b_0 + b_1 RCAP_i + b_2 y_i + b_3 y_j + b_4 GNPi + b_5 GNPj + b_6 T + b_7 q + b_8 D + u$$

The higher the revealed comparative advantage in patents RCAP (i.e. the higher its relative share in world patents), the greater the incentive for firms to produce abroad as a means of exploiting their know-how advantage while at the same time protecting it. From the perspective of an innovative firm licenses are very poor substitutes for foreign direct investment since the licensee is likely to reinforce cheaply its future competitive position, especially since information markets are rather imperfect and intellectual property rights rather weak. The terms of trade, denoted by q, play an important role in a world of imperfect capital markets. Following the theoretical and empirical analysis of FROOT and STEIN (1991), a real appreciation of the source country's currency will reinforce firms' ability to acquire firms abroad since foreign firms have become relatively cheaper in terms of the appreciated currency i.e. the raider firms have more capital - expressed in terms of the target country's currency. D is a dummy variable for similarity of language in the source and home country of foreign direct investment. If the host country has the same language as the source country one will expect higher FDI outflows since the absence of language barriers facilitates foreign investment abroad.

1.5 National R&D Financing and the Leakage Problem in the Presence of MNCs

Multinational companies (MNCs) are the most important route for international technology transfers which rely on trade in patents and licensing, including cross licensing. MNCs will be reluctant to transfer the latest technology if they do not enjoy clear intellectual property rights and full control of the foreign subsidiary; or at least a majority stake in the foreign firm. Therefore host country restrictions to foreign ownership - including hostile takeovers - are inappropriate if the international dissemination of R&D results is to be fostered. Stimulating international joint ventures can be a starting point for the creation of new multinational companies. Specific conditional public R&D support can help to reinforce ownership specific technological advantages of firms. Such advantages are considered to be the basis of successful foreign direct investment abroad (successful examples are the Asian NICs or Germany in the late 19th century). Foreign investment abroad in technologically leading countries can help the parent company to tap a larger global pool of technological advances which then can be exploited through the whole network of the MNC.

Countries with a liberal foreign investment regime have recorded high inward foreign direct investment (e.g. Belgium, Ireland, Spain) which has contributed to economic catching-up. The leading source countries of foreign investment (US, UK, Germany, Netherlands, Switzerland; exception being Japan which is only a major source country) are also leading host countries. To the extent that foreign subsidiaries have a natural preference for using the same machinery and equipment as the parent company the investment goods industry in the home country will benefit from FDI outflows: more equipment goods which typically represent a high R&D intensity will be exported.

MNCs produce similar products in different countries, where foreign direct investment can be - in net terms - a substitute for trade. From an environmental point of view this trade-refraining effect of MNCs is quite welcome since a large part of pollution damages is related to international traffic. For ecological reasons it might be useful to rely more on regional production networks that allow overall transportation volumes to be reduced. This could be a strong and new argument for economic policy to promote the multinationalization of firms.

Taxpayers' money is financing R&D programs which increasingly are those of multinational companies. A multinational EU company with large international production networks might use national research funds to develop new products where first generation production is immediately located outside the parent company country ("leakage problem"). If such patterns, in contrast with traditional product cycle trade models (which assume that first production occurs exclusively in the parent company country and is relocated abroad only later in the standardization stage production), would become dominant one may wonder whether national R&D programs still make sense from a political point of view. Cooperation among national R&D programs or a greater role for EU R&D programs could be an answer to the problem.

The leakage problem has been reinforced by the many privatizations of the 1980s and early 1990s leaving governments with less scope for more influencing industry directly. While reduced government interference could be beneficial for many reasons, governments have a legitimate interest to ensure that the incidence of R&D subsidies is in fact in favor of people employed within the country. As ongoing multinationalization undermines this rationale one might consider a greater role for EU R&D programs in the future. This, however, raises the problem of subsidiarity and, more importantly, of achieving efficient EU R&D programs which could be extremely difficult in the enlarged Community. The political principal-agent problem in a large community is severe so that one might expect considerable bureaucratic inefficiencies to follow from more comprehensive supranational R&D policy. A solution to this problem could be the creation of competing new private R&D administration firms - quoted at the stock market - which would act as agents for the Commission. The Community R&D budget would be allocated in an indirect way leading to superior results.

2. R&D Policy and Employment from a Theoretical Perspective

The new growth theory has emphasized the role of R&D, capital formation, learning by doing and technological spillovers for economic growth and prosperity (ROMER, 1986). Unfortunately, to date there is no comprehensive general equilibrium model which explicitly models the link between capital formation, R&D accumulation and employment effects. Such a model certainly should include a multi-sector approach integrating input output analysis. The basic idea of the new growth theory is that there exist economies of scale external to the firm which imply larger multiplier effects of investment in equipment, education and R&D than traditionally expected. There is still need to empirically estimate these multiplier effects and to derive consistent policy concepts.

The new growth theory suggests that the social benefits (and productivity growth) which can be achieved by investment, retraining and R&D is higher than perceived by the individual investor. Government should therefore subsidize investment in high-technology industries, retraining and education. A crucial problem emerging is that smoke-stack industries will also call for subsidization. This already points to a need for a two-pronged subsidy policy in the future, namely a strict distinction between productivity-enhancing subsidies in expanding industries and subsidies for declining sectors; the latter type is, of course, economically undesirable while vested interests will be rather strong in these very sectors.

2.1 R&D, New Growth Theory and Employment

New Growth Theory, Trade and Direct Investment
The new theory of integration focuses on internal economies of scale (average costs in a large firm are lower than in small firms) or external scale economies (firms which are proximate enjoy certain spillover effects, e.g. the research and development of an innovator can be observed by the neighboring firms). With regional integration economies of scale can be more easily exploited within the group of integrating countries. However, firms from outsider countries might suffer from rising costs as their exports to the customs union countries could fall. External economies of scale in a customs union can also be exploited by outsiders to the extent that there are no restrictions on foreign direct investment inflows.

Product differentiation also plays a role in recent models which assume that the larger variety of goods produced in a large customs union - compared to isolated countries - will benefit consumers. ETHIER (1982), ROMER (1986) and HELPMAN and KRUGMAN (1985) analyze scale economies and show that free trade will ensure that both the country producing under economies of scale and the importing country has benefits from trade. Indeed, trade is shown to be a full substitute to factor mobility and, following ROMER (1986), it can be shown that dynamic scale economies achieved via the single market program could yield a permanent increase in the EU growth rate (BALDWIN, 1989). Benefits from regional free trade in the presence of economies of scale will accrue differently to the countries involved in a customs union depending on the type of specialization pursued by individual countries. For example, country A specializing in aerospace production will enjoy a larger benefit from trade if economic rents in the aerospace industry are higher than in the locomotive industry. One may note, however, that benefits across countries could be shared more equally if foreign direct investment flows from country B to A, i.e. if part of A's aerospace industry is owned by citizens of country B. This problem still has to be explored analytically.

Trade with differentiated products leads to oligopolistic interdependence which can stimulate different forms of strategic pricing and investment behavior. Recent approaches emphasize the role of research and development in combination with dynamic economies of scale. Dynamic scale economies imply unit cost reduction as a function of cumulated output which explicitly can be modeled in the industry's learning curve for a given generation of products; e.g., the first 1000 units of a new chip generation will have a high percentage of technical misprints on the chip surface - say, only 50% are error free and can be sold - but after 100,000 units the failure rate falls to 10%. Following BRANDER and SPENCER (1981, 1985), this implies that regional integration can reinforce the customs union's international competitiveness because a larger domestic market in combination with government procurement in favor of domestic firms or government R&D subsidies will facilitate the innovative firms' attempt to quickly move down the learning curve. This in turn means that foreign markets can be attacked with relatively low prices.

Trade diversion might indeed be welcomed by members of the customs union because this implies difficulties for foreign competitors in high technology industries to quickly move down the learning curve. In the absence of innovation and economies of scale trade diversion for outsiders still could be welcomed by the customs union to the extent that it can improve its terms of trade. This would be the case if as a consequence of trade diversion excess capacities of outsiders depress world market prices for those goods as well as intermediate inputs which then can be imported at relatively reduced prices by the customs union members. GROSSMAN and HELPMAN (1991) introduce R&D in a model with trade in differentiated products where the number of products is increasing at an equilibrium rate in the steady state. This assumes, of course, that there is a constant share of real R&D expenditures relative to national output. In a customs union consumers will enjoy a greater variety of products as firms can spread fixed R&D costs over a greater number of consumers. Since large countries have relatively favorable starting conditions already under autarky for engaging in high technology products whose R&D costs have to be spread over a large number of consumers, the formation of a customs union might reinforce such first mover advantages in the international technology race. Thus, people living in large countries could benefit more from a customs union than those in small countries. The EU-15 group enjoys good opportunities to benefit from a large integrated "home market" which facilitates spreading of R&D costs and gaining first-mover-advantages.

An important issue of integration concerns foreign direct investment. WELFENS (1996c) has emphasized the reduction of political risk as a consequence of a common market so that new member countries of a customs union will benefit from additional foreign direct investment flows from source countries in the union. Indeed the overall investment output ratio in the union will increase so that there should be positive growth effects. This will hold in particular if the increased presence of foreign investors brings positive technology spillover effects for the host country so that the marginal product of capital is increasing in both the tradables and the non-tradables sector (WELFENS, 1992b). Indeed, Spain and Portugal recorded high per capita FDI inflows after joining the Community - even in the run up to 1986 which certainly has contributed to economic growth on the Iberian peninsula. In the 1980s Greece was a counterexample because poor domestic macroeconomic policies and lack of privatization rendered the country rather unattractive for foreign investors.

One may emphasize that economic integration increasingly relies on multinational companies which account for about 1/3 of OECD trade and for most of international technology trade. Intra-company trade in goods and technologies play an important role in technology intensive industries whose role is likely to increase in the future in the EU. This follows from the economic opening up of eastern Europe whose producers easily can invade markets with standard products so that EU firms will have an incentive to move up the technology ladder. Since firm specific advantages - typically tied to innovations - are the basis for multinational investment abroad it is clear that EU firms will increasingly be multinational companies. This tendency is reinforced both by Community R&D programs which encourage intra-EU cooperation and the formation of EU joint ventures. It also will be stimulated by monetary union and the growth of EU financial markets which will facilitate corporate takeovers - i.e. strengthen the role of capital markets.

A critical perspective of modern growth theory is to argue that structural change is poorly taken into account. Indeed, a two-sector (or n-sector) structural model would be quite appropriate to the problems at hand. There are indeed several models in the literature which emphasize the role of the investment goods sector and the consumption goods sector on the one hand, or on the other hand the role of the tradables and nontradables sectors. If trade unions are more influential in the nontradables sector and impose uniform wage rates across sectors excessive wage push will result in massive unemployment in the exposed sector. The productivity development in the nontradables sector strongly is influenced by the public sector. The importance of wage rigidity is affected by the degree of unionization as well as the dependence on export markets. Firms which have a large share of exports and are in a position of price takers will strongly resist wage pressures that exceed productivity gains. With the envisaged switch to a monetary union some EU firms will record lower export-output ratios (export here refers to non EMU-countries) so that wage restraint in the EU could become weaker.

One may note that the EU's unemployment problem partly is related to the high tax and social security burden which in turn are linked to low productivity growth rates in the public sector. One possible option to cope with unemployment is to actively measure and improve public sector productivity. Improved measurement would make it easier to impose wage increases in line with productivity growth so that relative prices for public sector services would not increase (hence tax burdens could remain stable), nor would excess wage pressure from the public sector spill over easily into the exposed sector in which productivity growth rates are traditionally relatively high. There could also be a reverse case in which an innovative and growing export sector stimulates high general growth which cannot be matches by adequate productivity growth in the nontradables sector.

2.2 R&D, Competitiveness and Employment

Private R&D expenditures and public R&D support are crucial for innovations and improved international competitiveness. Competitiveness has both the aspect of relative price positioning in the world market as well as an absolute price aspect. Most process innovations will lead to absolute price reductions worldwide which allow a higher absolute quantity of the goods to be sold; or there will be equivalent global real income effects which raise the demand for both the good produced with less costly technologies and the demand for all other products. The latter effects imply market growth as a consequence of process innovations which, of course, will also lead to redundancies in the innovative sector as long as there are strong increases in labor productivity growth. However, since process innovations are brought about by new machinery and sophisticated services they generate higher demand for investment and services which in turn raises demand for skilled labor (see Fig. 2). Investment also can replace low skilled workers, and indeed, there will be an incentive to replace unskilled labor with capital if relative wages of unskilled workers are rising.

Figure 2: R&D and Employment

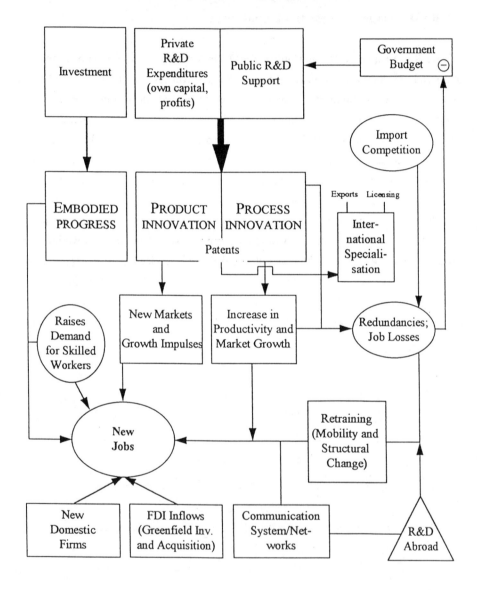

While competitiveness certainly has aspects of relative technological positioning in world markets - typically emphasized in the literature - one should not overlook the global real income effect of process innovations (the price reduction effect). Product innovations create new markets and stimulate the expansion of firms as diffusion of novel products and processes follow a logistical expansion path. In the context of an open economy it is crucial that EU firms specialize in a way that is consistent with their respective comparative technological advantage. This could be an actual comparative advantage or a potential advantage that relies on strong domestic market growth or R&D subsidies in the context of dynamic scale economies. Domestic market growth was impaired by high unemployment rates in the EU in the 1980s.

Those laid off normally can find new work in other firms after some time. This is obvious for cyclical unemployment. However, since the oil price shocks of the 1970s the EU has increasingly been characterized by structural unemployment. Structural change in Europe has been rather hesitant compared to the US and retraining or active labor market policies have had a thin foundation in the EU, except in Sweden. Moreover, in the 1980s and 1990s the rate of new firms which could offer new jobs was lower in the EU than in the US in the 1980s and 1990s (EUROPEAN COMMISSION, 1995b). It should be emphasized that new firms, investment of existing firms and foreign direct investment contribute to investment, growth and employment.

In the late 1980s and 1990s continental Europe also suffered from a lack of external FDI inflows, i.e. lack of greenfield investment from the US and Japan contributed to a reduced EU investment output ratio (the UK and the Netherlands being a partial exception in this respect) and hence a lower rate of capital embodied technological progress. More generally, if foreign acquisition of existing firms is increasing this could stimulate international technology transfer to the benefit of both the host and the source country. US FDI outflows have been found to cause job losses in the US and to create new jobs abroad where recent analysis confirms that workers in host countries have not suffered from reduced wages in the presence of foreign investors (PAPACONSTANTINOV, 1996).

New jobs in OECD countries have been created mostly in high-technology fields (see appendix I, Table A3). BROWN and HIRBAYASHI (1996) showed, based on US patent data, that the R&D process is internationalizing in the sense that important patent are from multiple inventors residing in different countries. Patent applications in Europe were dominated by the US, Germany and Japan (see appendix, Table A4).

In OECD countries relative annual employment growth was high in those sectors with relative high R&D expenditure growth in 1973-90. However, in the EU public budgetary appropriations for R&D - as a percentage of GDP - declined between 1983 and 1992; only Finland, Italy, Ireland, Portugal and Spain showed a slight increase (EUROPEAN COMMISSION, 1995b, p.7).

In the manufacturing sector the share of industrial R&D expenditure financed by the state was lower in EU-15 (13.5 %) than in the USA (29.3%). Slight reductions in the UK and France mainly reflect the fall in public military R&D expenditure in the 1990s which was rather high in the Cold War period. Germany where military R&D expenditures were of minor importance after 1945 also recorded falling public R&D-GDP ratios in the 1990s. Even after German unification there was no increase which is surprising given the fact that the collapse of the former socialist GDR R&D infrastructure and the need for eastern Germany to catch up with western Germany would have warranted extra public expenditures for R&D and special tax incentives to stimulate higher private R&D. This holds the more as the reunified Germany is quite exposed to rising exports of eastern Europe's transforming economies where the Visegrad countries are likely to raise the share of R&D- and skill-intensive exports in the long term, especially if high FDI inflows continue.

State aid for R&D does not necessarily require high government expenditures as is shown by the US where the share of tax relief (tax credits) dominated with a share of 88.8% in the late 1980s. A high share of direct subsidies was recorded in Sweden and Germany (37% in each), France (42.3%) and UK (55.4%). In Italy and the Netherlands subsidies plus soft loans accounted for more than 90% of state aid. Guarantees and equity financing played an important role in France and the UK (EUROPEAN COMMISSION, 1995b, p.10).

One may emphasize that subsidies are easier to obtain for big firms while tax credits have the advantage of providing incentives to both big and small profitable firms. This points to important policy options in the EU. The rate at which new firms are established fell in most EU countries in the decade after 1985, but it increased in the US (EUROPEAN COMMISSION, 1995b, p.15). Bankruptcy rates stabilized or increased slightly, except in the US, which together with the high rate at which new firms are established points to the outstanding entrepreneurial dynamics in the US and apparent deficits in the EU. The lack of EU small enterprise dynamics is worrying because the Community Innovation Survey found (for 1992) that total innovation expenditures divided by turnover are the lower, the larger the firm size. In Europe the share of non-R&D costs in innovation costs is, however, relatively high in small firms and declines as firms become bigger. While the propensity to patent is smaller for small firms than for large ones there is empirical evidence that technology-oriented small and medium firms are crucial for the overall innovativeness.

High unemployment rates and fear of further rationalization investment will increase the resistance of those employed against innovation. To improve EU competitiveness it is therefore of double importance to reduce unemployment in a sustainable manner: on the one hand, falling budgetary costs of unemployment will allow disposable private household income to be raised or government purchases of goods and services to be increased. On the other hand the resistance of workers against productivity-augmenting reorganization and investment will slow down and this should reinforce initial employment gains.

Technological Progress, Labor Supply and Services
Technology also affects labor supply (OECD, 1996b, p.11; OECD, 1996c) since modern durable products are often labor-saving households equipment which allow a rise in women's participation rates; and new technologies in the field of health control raise labor supply. New communication equipment facilitates long-distance work and global telecommunication networks could indeed increase effective labor supply in OECD countries from outside. There is the risk that EU unemployment could remain high.

Continental Europe's communications systems have not been conducive to employment growth because access to new information has been impaired by monopoly pricing of state monopoly telecoms operators. Interestingly, internet intensity in early telecom liberalizing countries - Finland, the UK and Sweden - is much higher than in Germany or France.

A much neglected field of EU innovations is the service sector whose importance has increased over the past decades both as a field of innovative activity and international technology trade (DEUTSCHE BUNDESBANK, 1996). After-sales services have become increasingly important. Computer and information technology services as well as tourism and health services are booming fields in OECD countries. R&D is indeed difficult to measure in the service sector - at the bottom line R&D intensity of OECD economies has gradually increased in the 1980s. One may assume that the level of required skills is gradually increasing if this trend continues. An important topic therefore is education as well as retraining activities in firms. In the future information society life-long learning could be organized on a very broad basis.

Labor Mobility Problems in a High R&D Sector

In R&D intensive sectors barriers to entry are rather high. This implies a high level of job security. At the same time highly specialized labor is quite vulnerable in the event of adverse technological and economic shocks - the shrinkage of the Californian defense sector in the 1990s is an example. It therefore is important in a society with high R&D and high skill intensities that regional and intersectoral labor mobility are high. Otherwise an adverse sectoral shock will cause continued mass unemployment. Hence, encouraging regional labor mobility via specifically designed income tax policies could be important from a labor market perspective.

The creation of new innovative firms is extremely important for competition, technological progress and growth as is amply shown by the success stories of Silicon Valley. Successive waves of new market entrants will help markets to expand and during this expansion process the most successful firms will grow strongly - this is the typical development identified by AUDRETSCH (1997). The creation of new firms certainly facilitates the shrinking of big firms which are no longer competitive in their respective sector.

With the declining significance of military R&D projects in the post-Cold War era and the privatization of part of the defense industry in many OECD countries there is a natural decline of government R&D programs which often are biased in favor of the military sector (two exceptions among the OECD countries were Japan and Germany in the 1970s and 1980s). There is nevertheless a need for national R&D subsidies to the extent that innovations have positive external benefits. In the EU the Maastricht fiscal criteria - among other indicators - emphasize the need for fiscal consolidation. This could mean that R&D budgets are sharply reduced in the context of a shrinking military sector. To the extent that military R&D projects have had important civilian technological spillover effects this could imply reduced economic growth. R&D subsidies have their own problems, with rent-seeking activities being one part of them. Small firms and newcomers are likely to be disadvantaged in a society in which large firms enjoy a superior political leverage.

Supranational R&D programs could be appropriate in some cases. However, even where economic reasons for such programs can be clearly identified one must ask the question whether political control at the supranational level is as efficient as at the national level, where it is already weak given the many imperfections of political competition. Hence one has to ask how the efficiency of political control can be improved in the EU. If the efficiency were to be improved the EU R&D budget could be much greater in the overall Community expenditures. However, appropriate evaluation procedures have to be developed to make sure that the political process is rather efficient. The role of appropriate labor market policies will be discussed with respect to EU countries, taking into account US experiences.

2.3 International Technology Trade, Multinational Companies and FDI

Continued downsizing by the existing large manufacturing firms has caused unemployment to ratchet higher throughout the 1990s to a level of nearly 11% by 1996. But unemployment is not an isolated economic problem. Two additional problems are a lack of innovative activity and deterioration of international competitiveness. The purpose of our analysis is to show how these three problems are interrelated and exacerbated by the increasing degree of globalization and to suggest policies that could be pursued to alleviate these problems.

The inability of Europe to create new jobs has not escaped policy makers. For example, as unemployment in Germany surpassed four million, and stood at 10.8%, it is not surprising that Chancellor Helmut Kohl would undertake some action to spur the creation of new jobs. Perhaps what is more surprising is the main emphasis announced by the Chancellor in the 30 January, 1996 Initiatives for Investment and Employment[1] on new and small firms. The first and main point of

---

[1] This was announced as the Aktionsprogramm für Investitionen und Arbeitsplätze („Soziale Einschnitte und Steuerreform sollen Wirtschaftswachstum anregen: Bundesregierung beschließt Aktionsprogramm für Investitionen und Arbeitsplätze", Der Tagesspiegel, 31 January, 1996, p. 1.

this program consists of a commitment to the „creation of new innovative firms"[2]. The rational underlying this commitment is stated factually by the Chancellor in the Program: „New jobs are created mainly in new firms and in small- and medium-sized enterprises."

The Weltanschauung apparent in the Kohl jobs program, as well as in a general trend in approaches throughout Europe to generate new jobs represents a sharp departure from that found in earlier years. For example, in his widely read, Le Defi American, SERVAN-SCHREIBER (1968, p. 159) advocated, „the creation of large industrial units which are able both in size and management to compete with the American giants ... The first problem of an industry policy for Europe consists in choosing 50 to 100 firms which, once they are large enough, would be the most likely to become world leaders in their fields". And as is clearly documented in the 1988 Cecchini Report, there were significant forces in Europe prepared to implement Servan-Schreiber's policy advice.

How could the Kohl Administration draw an inference about the links between the sources of jobs and innovation that is seemingly at odds with both the scholarship and policy thinking of just a few years earlier? In fact, the last decade has seen a virtual explosion of studies trying to identify the links between industrial organization, innovation and the creation of new jobs. These studies have been both theoretical and empirical, and have been undertaken across a wide spectrum of countries, industries and time periods.

According to the theory of the industry life cycle, the patterns of imports, exports and foreign direct investment should vary systematically with the evolution of an industry over the life cycle. During the introduction and growth stages the domestic industry in a leading industrialized country is predicted to be a net exporter and to engage in outward foreign direct investment. But by the time that the industry has evolved to the mature and declining stages, the theory predicts that the industry has become a net importer and engages in relatively little outward foreign direct investment.

What has occurred between the early and latter life cycle stags to trigger such reversals in flows of exports, imports and foreign direct investment? Diffusion, and in particular technological diffusion. As the technology becomes standardized and less uncertain, the cost of diffusing it across national boarders decreases. Just as the

---

[2] „Ein Kraftakt zur Rettung des Standorts Deutschland", Frankfurter Allgemeine Zeitung, 31 January, 1996, p. 11.

comparative advantage of the leading developed countries, which is certainly the case in Europe, lies in incurring the costs of innovation and establishing new produces and processes, it is the comparative advantage of less developed countries to adopt these products and processes once they have become proven viable commodities. The product-cycle theory is more applicable to economic flows, including foreign direct investment, between the so-called North and South countries, than between countries within any particular stage of development.

What is often overlooked is that the life cycle theory is as much a theory of the evolution of technological knowledge and its diffusion as it is about the life cycle of industries. At the heart of the evolution of technological knowledge over an industry's life cycle was the notion that the returns in innovative activity from a given effort of creating new technological knowledge diminish as the industry evolves. This means that the cost of innovating relative to the cost of imitating also diminish as the industry matures.

In perhaps the most famous version of the industry life cycle model, introduced by Raymond VERNON (1966), it was assumed that:
1. The United States was a sole technological leader and a sole economic leader;
2. There are follower developing countries, and
3. Industries evolve over a technological life cycle, which is technologically driven by a declining innovative output from a constant input of new technological knowledge.

As an industry matures, technological knowledge also tends to evolve where the content of that knowledge becomes increasingly based on information and less on knowledge and especially tacit knowledge. Thus, as the industry matures, the cost of imitating falls relative to the cost of innovating, so that it becomes more economical to transfer that technological knowledge to less costly locations of production – developing countries or newly emerging market economies – through outward foreign direct investment.

What was not anticipated and where the simple theory of the industry life cycle broke down is that the United States would not remain as the sole technological leader. As Europe and Japan recovered from the Second World War, not only did they achieve technological parity in many industries, but actually became innovative leaders, causing downward pressure on US living standards, just as European real wags and living standards expanded. A process of convergence across the leading industrial countries has taken place during the past forty years.

GIERSCH, PAQUE and SCHMIEDING (1992) point out that the German *Wirtschaftswunder*, or economic growth miracle, was fueled to a considerable extent by relatively low labor unit costs and an undervalued currency. Thus, technology developed in the United States could simply be adopted with the end result of lower unit costs of production and international competitiveness in Europe. But as the European countries caught up to the United States, and the unit cost of labor began to even surpass that of the United States in Germany and elsewhere in Europe, simply following a strategy of technology adoption is no longer sufficient to ensure international competitiveness in Europe. For example, the 1994 mean manufacturing employee compensation (including insurance and other employee non-wage benefits) was $25.71 per hour in Germany, but only $19.01 in Japan and $16.73 in the United States.

Many of the industries which have been the traditional strengths in Europe have evolved towards the mature and declining stages of the life cycle. This means that *Standort* Deutschland and Europe have become increasingly vulnerable, since the production of rather standardized technologies can be shifted to locations in central and eastern Europe, or in Asia, with lower production costs. For example, the average daily earnings of labor have been estimated to be $78.34 in the European Union, but only $6.14 in Poland, and $6.45 in the Czech Republic, $1.53 in China, $2.46 in India and $1.25 in Sri Lanka (JENSEN, 1993).

While labor cost disadvantages can be offset through productivity increases and technological change, innovative activity itself tends to become more incremental in nature as the industry evolves over the life cycle. Therefore, in mature industries it becomes increasingly difficult for European industries to maintain their international competitiveness through innovative activity. This tendency towards a loss of international competitiveness in western Europe has become the most pronounced in industries such as steel and shipbuilding.

By remaining locked in the same industry and technology it becomes increasingly difficult to maintain the international competitiveness of a high-cost *Standort*, even though the company itself may be able to retain competitiveness by shifting production out of the high-cost *Standort* to a lower-cost *Standort* through outward foreign direct investment. Consider the case of Sweden. Some 70% of Sweden's manufacturing employees work for large companies, most of them multinationals, such as Volvo, which have been constantly shifting production out of the high-cost *Standort*, Sweden, and into lower cost countries, through outwards foreign direct investment. Between 1970 and 1993 Sweden lost 500,000 private sector jobs, resulting in a 1995 unemployment rate of 13%. And Sweden is not an exceptional case in the European Union. For example, every third car that is manufactured by a German company is actually produced outside of Germany.[3]

While European companies themselves may be able to retain competitiveness by shifting production out of the high-cost *Standort* to a lower-cost *Standort*, new economic activity must be found to replace the loss of the old activity in order to maintain the high living standards. Especially in the high-cost countries, such as Germany, the innovation of new products and   processes must be constantly substituted for standardized ones in order to maintain international competitiveness.

The divergence in real living standards between the European Union and developing countries, combined with the maturation of Europe's traditional industries dictates that either foreign companies gain competitive advantage by adapting technological knowledge in mature industries, through transferring those technologies and applying them to cheaper location-specific costs, such as wages, or else the European companies maintain their competitiveness through outward foreign direct investment and shirting production to non-European locations.

The consequences of this dilemma become clear when it is considered what happens to the resources in the European *Standort* – particularly labor – that becomes displaced as standardized technological knowledge is more economically applied in lower-cost locations. More explicitly, the consequences are the massive downsizing of European companies, which has resulted in the greatest unemployment crisis in Europe since the 1920s.

The emergence of new economic knowledge as perhaps the most crucial input in the production process in the European Union has had a strong impact on multinational corporations. According to *The Economist*, "Multinational companies have been accused of many things in their time…But what has really hurt the men and (handful of) women who run the world's multinationals is new criticism that has emerged in recent years: that they are failures. The evidence is embarrassingly abundant. The list of companies that ended the 1980s in worse shape than they started reads like a Who's Who of leading multinationals."[4]

---

[3] "Globalisierung: Auslandsproduktion deutscher Autohersteller," Handelsblatt, 31 January, 1994.
[4] "Who Wants to be a Giant?" The Economist, 24 June, 1995, pp. 5-6.

One might have thought that the communications revolution combined with increased globalization would trigger even greater foreign direct investment activity (KINDLEBERGER and AUDRETSCH, 1983). On the one hand, governments around the world have been removing trade barriers and loosening restrictions on foreign direct investment. On the other hand, national capital markets have become increasingly interrelated, making it easier for multinational corporations to shift capital from one country to another.

Under this scenario, the increased globalization of business should have played to the strengths of multinational corporations. Presumably they would be able to manufacture products at locations around the globe where factor costs and quality are the most attractive. It had been typically predicted that inevitably "a handful of global firms would soon carve up the world between them."[5]

In fact, rather than reinforce the viability of multinational corporations, the trend towards increased globalization has generally weakened multinational corporations. In particular, deregulation and an overall reduction in trade barriers, both tariff and non-tariff, have generally reduced in some cases made irrelevant the value of carefully cultivated relationships with governments and expensively accumulated knowledge of local regulatory intricacies.

Thus, *The Economist* observes, "The trouble with many multinationals is that they are a legacy of a very different era. Many grew up in the heyday of command and control management, when strategy was made by a tiny elite at the top, work was broken down into its simplest component parts and workers were monitored by layer upon layer of managers. But today fashion is so fickle and markets so quicksilver that decisions are best taken by front-line workers rather than by lethargic middle managers."[6]

The economic challenges inherent in the new information revolution have triggered massive restructuring at multinational corporations. These organizational changes have involved the following aspects:

1. *Greater focus on core products and sticking to their knitting.* Production and services that do not belong to the core of the firm tend to be contracted out. PETERS (1992) observes that, "The Fortune 500 are madly de-integrating, selling off bits, subbing anything and everything, marketing subsidiary units." As a result of divestment alone, a number of leading multinational corporations have

---

[5] The Economist, 1995, p. 6.
[6] The Economist, 1995, p. 6.

reduced their size – Amdahl by 30%, J.E. Seagram by 17%, Digital by 17%, Eastman Kodak by 17%, Owens-Illinois by 16%, Union Carbide by 13%, IBM by 13%, Monsanto by 11%, BASF by 8%, and Data General by 8% (HAMEL and PRAHLAD, 1994).

2. *A decentralization of decision making.* Part of this decentralization in decisionmaking is directed towards linking the decision-making process to the groups actually performing specific tasks. A second dimension involves increasing the number of independent approaches being undertaken. Still, PETERS (1992, p. 22) warns that, "The central corporate culture casts a long, and long-lasting shadow." Examples abound of the decentralization of decision making taking place in multinational corporations. For example, when Jack Smith became the chief executive officer of General Motors in 1992, one of his first steps was to reduce the amount of corporate bureaucracy from 13,000 to 2,000. In addition he moved his office from the symbol of corporate America, the 14th floor of GM's headquarters in Detroit, to a new technical center located fifteen miles away in the suburbs. Similarly, Ford has reduced the number of its management levels from ten to seven. And Percy Barnevik, who is head of the Asea Brown Boveri (ABB) engineering firm, applies a *thirty percent rule* to the businesses acquired by ABB, where thirty percent of central staff is allocated to independent profit centers, thirty percent is allocated to operating companies, and another thirty percent are let go. Only ten percent of the original size of the central staff remain. The corporate headquarters of ABB in Zurich has a central staff of only about 70.

3. *Downsizing.* In order to restructure companies both in terms of emphasizing core products and the decentralization of decision making, large multinational corporations have generally pursued a strategy of employment downsizing.

4. *A shift in power and decision making away from the centralized offices to the regional level, particularly in Europe.* A number of multinational companies have been giving subsidiaries responsibility for global products and global functions. Part of the reason for doing this is to decentralize decision making. But the other reason is to take advantage of local expertise. Thus, IBM, AT&T, and Hewlett-Packard have moved their worldwide headquarters for certain products from the Untied States to Europe, In addition, Glaxo, Unilever, Siemens and Hoechst have all created what is called *global product groups*. For

example, Nestle has shifted its pasta business to Italy. And Johnson & Johnson has made its Belgian subsidiary responsible for the world market for pharmaceuticals.

5. The competitive advantage of multinational corporations may be shifting from scale economies to dynamic sources of knowledge. Multinational corporations are increasingly involved with international networks that involve the creation and dissemination of new economic knowledge. A natural competitive advantage of multinational enterprises is that knowledge gained in one part of the world can be used to gain advantage at a different location. For example, Nynex, and American telecommunications company, has used state-of-the-art cabling techniques in virgin markets such as Thailand, with an eye on drawing on that experience when faced with installing new cable in the home market.

2.4 Innovation Dynamics in New and Established Firms

The starting point for most theories of innovation is the firm.[7] For example, in the most prevalent theory found in the literature of innovation, the *model of the knowledge production function*, formalized by GRILICHES (1979), firms exist exogenously and then engage in pursuit of new economic knowledge as an input into the process of generating innovative activity.

The most decisive input in the knowledge production function is new economic knowledge. And as Kenneth ARROW (1962) concludes, the greatest source generating new economic knowledge is generally considered to be R&D. Certainly a large body of empirical has found a strong and positive relationship between knowledge inputs, such as R&D and innovative outputs.

The model of the knowledge production function has been found to hold most strongly at broader levels of aggregation. For example, the most innovative countries are those with the greatest investments in R&D. Little innovative output is associated with less developed countries, which are characterized by a paucity of production of new knowledge. Similarly, the most innovative industries also tend to be characterized by considerable investments in R&D and new knowledge. Not only are industries such as computers, pharmaceuticals and instruments high in R&D inputs that generate new economic knowledge, but also in terms of measured

---

[7] For reviews of this literature see BALDWIN and SCOTT (1987), COHEN and LEVIN (1989), SCHERER (1984 and 1992), and DOSI (1988).

innovative outputs (AUDRETSCH, 1995). By contrast, industries with little R&D, such as wood products, textiles and paper, also tend to produce only a negligible amount of innovative output. Thus, the model of the knowledge production function linking knowledge generating inputs to outputs certainly holds at aggregated levels of economic activity.

The model of the knowledge production function has also been found to hold at the desegregated microeconomic level of enterprises and establishments - but only among samples of large established enterprises. When small and new enterprises are included in the sample, the model of the knowledge production function becomes considerably less compelling. For example, a recent wave of studies has revealed that small and new enterprises serve as the engine of innovative activity in certain industries, both in North America as well as throughout Europe.[8] These results are startling, because as SCHERER (1992) points out, the bulk of industrial R&D is undertaken in the largest corporations; small enterprises account for only a minor share of R&D inputs. Thus, the model of the knowledge production function seemingly implies that, as the *Schumpeterian Hypothesis* predicts, innovative activity favors those organizations with access to knowledge-producing inputs - the large incumbent organization. The recent empirical literature identifying that small and new enterprises as well as large enterprises provide an important source of innovative activity raises the theoretical question, *Where do new and small enterprises get the innovation producing inputs, that is the knowledge?*

One theoretical answer, proposed by AUDRETSCH (1995), is that although the model of the knowledge production function may certainly be valid, the implicitly assumed unit of observation - at the level of the establishment or firm - may be less valid. The reason why the model of the knowledge production function holds more closely for more highly aggregated degrees of observation may be that investment in R&D and other sources of new knowledge spillovers over for economic exploitation by third-party firms.

A large literature has emerged focusing on what has become known as the *appropriability problem*.[9] The underlying issue revolves around how firms which invest in the creation of new knowledge can best appropriate the economic returns

---

[8] See studies by ACS and AUDRETSCH (1988 and 1990) for the United States, KLEINKNECHT (1989) for the Netherlands, SANTERELLI and STERLACCHINI (1990) for Italy, and ROTHWELL (1989) for the United Kingdom.
[9] See BALDWIN and SCOTT (1987).

from that knowledge (ARROW, 1962). AUDRETSCH (1995) proposes shifting the unit of observation away from exogenously assumed firms to individuals - agents with endowments of new economic knowledge. As J. De V. GRAAF (1957) observed, " When we try to construct a transformation function for society as a whole from those facing the individual firms comprising it, a fundamental difficulty confronts us. There is, from a welfare point of view, nothing special about the firms actually existing in an economy at a given moment of time. The firm is in no sense a 'natural unit'. Only the individual members of the economy can lay claim to that distinction. All are potential entrepreneurs. It seems, therefore, that the natural thing to do is to build up from the transformation function of men, rather than the firms, constituting an economy. If we are interested in eventual empirical determination, this is extremely inconvenient. But it has conceptual advantages. The ultimate repositories of technological knowledge in any society are the men comprising it, and it is just this knowledge which is effectively summarized in the form of a transformation function. In itself a firm possesses no knowledge. That which is available to it belongs to the men associated with it. Its production function is really built up in exactly the same way, and from the same basic ingredients, as society's."

When the lens is shifted away from focusing upon the firm as the relevant unit of observation to individuals, the relevant question becomes, *How can economic agents with a given endowment of new knowledge best appropriate the returns from that knowledge?* The appropriability problem confronting the individual may converge with that confronting the firm. Economic agents can and do work for firms, and even if they do not, they can potentially be employed by an incumbent firm. In fact, in a model of perfect knowledge with no agency costs, any positive economies of scale or scope will ensure that the appropriability problems of the firm and individual converge. If an agent has an idea for doing something different than is currently being practiced by the incumbent enterprises – both in terms of a new product or process and in terms of organization – the idea, which can be termed as an innovation, will be presented to the incumbent enterprise. Because of the assumption of perfect knowledge, both the firm and the agent would agree upon the expected value of the innovation. But to the degree that any economies of scale or scope exist, the expected value of implementing the innovation within the incumbent enterprise will exceed that of taking the innovation outside of the incumbent firm to start a new enterprise. Thus, the incumbent firm and the inventor of the idea would be expected to reach a bargain splitting the value added to the firm contributed by the innovation. The payment to the inventor – either in terms of a higher wage or some other means of remuneration – would be bounded between the expected value of the innovation if it were implemented by the incumbent enterprise on the upper end, and by the return that the agent could expect to earn if he used it to launch a new enterprise on the lower end. Or, as Frank KNIGHT (1921, p. 273) observed more than seventy years ago, "The laborer asks what he thinks the entrepreneur will be able to pay, and in any case will not accept less than he can get fro some other entrepreneur, or by turning entrepreneur himself. In the same way the entrepreneur offers to any laborer what he thinks he must in order to secure his services, and in any case not more than he thinks the laborer will actually be worth to him, keeping in mind what he can get by turning laborer himself."

Thus, each economic agent would choose how to best appropriate the value of his endowment of economic knowledge by comparing the wage he would earn if he remains employed by an incumbent enterprise, w, to the expected net present discounted value of the profits accruing from starting a new firm, p. If these two values are relatively close, the probability that the would choose to appropriate the value of his knowledge through an external mechanism such as starting a new firm, Pr(e), would be relatively low. On the other hand, as the gap between w and p becomes larger, the likelihood of an agent choosing to appropriate the value of his knowledge externally through starting a new enterprise becomes greater, or

$$Pr\,(e) = f\,(p-w)$$

As ARROW (1962) emphasized, new economic knowledge is anything but certain. Not only is new economic knowledge inherently risky, but substantial asymmetries exist across agents both between and within firm (MILGROM and ROBERTS, 1987). This suggests that the expected value of a new idea, or what has been termed here and in the literature as a potential innovation, is likely to be anything but unanimous between the inventor of that idea and the decisionmaker, or group of decision makers,[10] of the firm confronted with evaluating proposed changes or innovations.

---

[10] For example, as of 1993 a proposal for simply modifying an existing product at IBM had to pass through 250 layers of decision making to gain approval ("Ueberfoerdert und Unregierbar," Der Spiegel, No. 14, 1993, p. 127).

Combined with the bureaucratic organization of incumbent firms to make a decision, the asymmetry of knowledge leads to a host of agency problems, spanning incentive structures, monitoring, and transaction costs. It is the existence of such agency costs, combined with asymmetric knowledge that not only provides an incentive for agents with new ideas to appropriate the expected value of their knowledge externally by starting new firms, but also with a propensity that varies systematically from industry to industry.

HOLMSTROM (1989) and MILGROM (1988) have pointed out the existence of what they term as a *bureaucratization dilemma*, where, "To say that increased size brings increased bureaucracy is a safe generalization. To note that bureaucracy is viewed as an organizational disease is equally accurate" (HOLMSTROM, 1989, p. 320).

To minimize agency problems and the cost of monitoring, bureaucratic hierarchies develop objective rules. In addition, KREPS (1991) has argued that such bureaucratic rules promote internal uniformity and that a uniform corporate culture, in turn, promotes the reputation of the firm. These bureaucratic rules, however, make it more difficult to evaluate the efforts and activities of agents involved in activities that do not conform to such bureaucratic rules. As HOLMSTROM (1989, p. 323) points out, "Monitoring limitations suggest that the firm seeks out activities which are more easily and objectively evaluated. Authority and command systems work better in environments which are more predictable and can be directed with less investment information. Routine tasks are the comparative advantage of a bureaucracy and its activities can be expected to reflect that."

WILLIAMSON (1975, p. 201) has also emphasized the inherent tension between hierarchical bureaucratic organizations and the ability of incumbent organizations to appropriate the value of new knowledge for innovative activity outside of the technological trajectories associated with the core competence of that organization: "Were it that large firms could compensate internal entrepreneurial activity in ways approximating that of the market, the large firm need experience no disadvantage in entrepreneurial respects. Violating the congruency between hierarchical position and compensation appears to generate bureaucratic strains, however, and is greatly complicated by the problem of accurately imputing causality." This leads WILLIAMSON (1975, pp. 205-206) to conclude that, "I am inclined to regard the early stage innovative disabilities of large size as serious and propose the following hypothesis: An efficient procedure by which to introduce new products is for the initial development and market testing to be performed by independent investors and small firms (perhaps new entrants) in an industry, the successful developments then to be acquired, possibly through licensing or merger, for subsequent marketing by a large multidivision enterprise...Put differently, a division of effort between the new product innovation process on the one hand, and the management of proven resources on the other may well be efficient."

The degree to which agents and incumbent firms are confronted with knowledge asymmetries and agency problems with respect to seeking out new economic knowledge and (potential) innovative activity would not be expected to be constant across industries. This is because the underlying knowledge conditions vary from industry to industry. In some industries new economic knowledge generating innovative activity tends to be relatively routine and can be processed within the context of incumbent hierarchical bureaucracies. In other industries, however, innovations tend to come from knowledge that is not of a routine nature and therefore tends to be rejected by the hierarchical bureaucracies of incumbent corporations. Nelson and WINTER (1982) describe these different underlying knowledge conditions as reflecting two distinct technological regimes – the *entrepreneurial* and *routinized* technological regimes: "An entrepreneurial regime is one that is favorable to innovative entry and unfavorable to innovative activity by established firms; a routinized regime is one in which the conditions are the other way around" (WINTER, 1984, p. 297).

GORT and KLEPPER (1982) argue that the relative innovative advantage between newly established enterprises and incumbent firms depends upon the source of information generating innovative activity. If information based on nontransferable experience in the market is an important input in generating innovative activity, then incumbent firms will tend to have the innovative advantage over new firms. This is consistent with WINTER'S (1984) notion of the routinized regime, where the accumulated stock of nontransferable knowledge is the product of experience within the market, which firms outside of the main incumbent organizations, by definitions, cannot possess.

By contrast, when information outside of the routines practiced by the incumbent firms is a relatively important input in generating innovative activity, newly established firms will tend to have the innovative advantage over incumbent firms. ARROW (1962), MUELLER (1976), and WILLIAMSON (1975) have all emphasized that when such knowledge created outside of the incumbent firms cannot be easily transferred to those incumbent enterprises – presumably due tot he type of agency and bureaucracy problems described above – the holder of such knowledge must enter the industry by starting a new firm in order to exploit the value of his knowledge.

Thus, when the underlying conditions are better characterized by the routinized technological regime, there is likely to be relatively little divergence in the evaluation of the expected value of a (potential) innovation between the inventor and the decision making bureaucracy of a firm. Under the routinized regime, a great incentive for agents to start their own firms will not exist, at least not for the reason of doing something differently. When the underlying knowledge conditions more closely adhere to the entrepreneurial technological regime, however, a divergence in beliefs between the agent and the principal regarding the expected value of a (potential) innovation is more likely to emerge. Therefore, it is under the entrepreneurial regime where the startup of new firms is likely to play a more important role, presumably as a result of the motivation to appropriate the value of economic knowledge. Due to agency problems, this knowledge cannot be easily and costlessly transferred to the incumbent enterprise.

This theoretical model analyzing the decision of how best to appropriate the value of new economic knowledge confronting an individual economic agent seems useful when considering the actual decision to start a new firm taken by entrepreneurs. For example, Chester Carlsson started Xerox after his proposal to produce a (new) copy machine was rejected by Kodak. Kodak based its decision on the premise that the new copy machine would not earn very much money, and in any case, Kodak was in a different line of business – photography. It is perhaps no small irony that this same entrepreneurial startup, Xerox, decades later turned down a proposal from Steven Jobs to produce and market a personal computer, because the decision making hierarchy at Xerox did not think that a personal computer would sell, and, in any case, Xerox was in a different line of business – copy machines (AUDRETSCH, 1995). After seventeen other companies turned down Jobs for virtually identical reasons, including IBM and Hewlett Packard, Jobs resorted to starting his own company, Apple Computer.

Similarly, IBM turned down an offer from Bill Gates, "the chance to buy ten percent of Microsoft for a song in 1986, a missed opportunity that would cost \$3 billion today."[11] IBM reached its decision on the grounds that "neither Gates nor any of his band of thirty some employees had anything approaching the credentials or personal characteristics required to work at IBM."[12]

Divergence in beliefs with respect to the value of a new idea need not be restricted to what is formally known as a product or even a process innovation. Rather, the fact that economic agents choose to start a new firm due to divergences in the expected value of an idea applies to the sphere of managerial style and organization as well. One of the most vivid examples involves Bob Noyce, who founded Intel. Noyce had been employed by Fairchild Semiconductor, which is credited with being the pioneering semiconductor firm. In 1957 Noyce and seven other engineers quit *en masse* from Schockley Semiconductor to form Fairchild Semiconductor, an enterprise that in turn is considered to have constituted the foundation of what is today known as *Silicon Valley*. Although Fairchild Semiconductor had "possibly the most potent management and technical team ever assembled" (GILDER, 1989, p. 89), "Noyce couldn't get Fairchild's eastern owners to accept the idea that stock options should be part of compensation for all employees, not just for management. He wanted to tie everyone, from janitors to bosses, into the overall success of the company...This management style still sets the standard for every computer, software, and semiconductor company in the Valley today...Every CEO still wants to think that the place is run the say Bob Noyce would have run it". In fact, Noyce's vision of a firm excluded the dress codes, reserved parking places, closed offices, and executive dining rooms, along with the other trappings of status that were standard in virtually every hierarchical and bureaucratic corporation. But when he tried to impress this vision upon the owners of Fairchild Semiconductor, he was flatly rejected. The formation of Intel was the ultimate result of the divergence in beliefs about how to organize and manage the firm.

---

[11] "System Error," The Economist, 18 September, 1993, p. 99.
[12] Paul CARROL, "Die Offene Schlacht," Die Zeit, No. 39, 24 September 1993, p. 18.

3. R&D Policy and Employment in the Triade

3.1 R&D Policy in Leading EU Countries

Although ERGAS (1987, p. 206) concluded that „precise boundaries of technology policy are often difficult to identify", there are distinct technology policies which have been pursued in the European Union. Following the general notion in the literature, technology policy can be best defined as comprising the sum of all state measures promoting new or existing technologies for economic application in the broadest sense. An *explicit technology policy* is one in which economic goals are intended. An *implicit technology policy* is one in which there are no economic goals intended, but rather other types of goals, such as military research or environmental research. Included in technology policy are research activities of the state, research projects commissioned to private parties, financial aid and tax privileges to private research and activities and legal regulations, such as patent law.

In Germany, the most important approaches and instruments of technology policy include (KUHLMANN and MEYER-KRAHMER, 1995):
- regulative intervention, including technical norms and protective regulations,
- financial incentives, including the promotion of research and development and other innovative projects within enterprises by direct support or tax measures; in addition is the promotion of cooperation of enterprises with public or semi-public research institutions,
- the promotion of public demand for innovative products through procurement policies by the public sector,
- enhancing the public and semi-public infrastructure through the provision of research and development institutions, technology transfer institutions and advisory institutions,
- support for the formation of consensus on technical developments.

At the same time, these technology policy instruments have been anything other than consistent or coordinated. BECKER and KUHLMANN (1995, p. 5) refer to a „new order of non-transparency" in technology policy. As the summary of the German research landscape untertaken by the German Government (BUNDESMINISTERIUM FÜR FORSCHUNG UND TECHNOLOGIE, 1993) indicates, technology policy is both fragmented and segmented.

In 1982 technology policy underwent a basic reorientation in Germany. The basic principle underlying German innovation policy is to extend basic research and to maintain important long-run options while, at the same time, reducing R&D subsidies. In particular, this reorientation involves:

- reinforcing basic research;
- increasing the funding of preventative research, which includes environmental, health, and climate research;
- a continuation of funding market-oriented technologies where private initiatives are not sufficient, such as Airbus, information technology and biotechnology ;
- improving general conditions, particularly for innovative activity in small- and medium-sized enterprises;
- supporting R&D in fields with high long-term benefits, such as space, ocean research, and nuclear fusion;
- establishing research and fostering discussion on the assessment of technologies, and
- abandoning structural and institutional barriers to R&D, for example within the university system, and improving international cooperation.

Major changes in R&D subsidization have been a reduction in industrial targeting and in indirect R&D programs, such as the R&D research personnel subsidy.

An important part of German R&D policy includes a number of programs to support and stimulate innovative activity in small- and medium-sized enterprises. To encourage the innovative activity of small firms, the German government provides

- tax incentives for small-firms engaging in innovative activity,
- greater freedom for universities to cooperate with small firms,
- a reduction of regulations and bureaucratic costs imposed on small- and medium-sized enterprises,
- consulting assistance and access to technological information.

VAN PARIDON (1992, p. 108) points out that in the Netherlands, „Technology policy should be seen as an integral part of a deliberate government strategy aimed at realizing a sufficient level of welfare through realizing an adequate level of economic development... Economic development means structural change; it means the simultaneous rise and decline of products, firms, even sectors, through changes in demand, in technology (and in supply), and in international trade through the rise and decline of competitors. Such a broad government strategy should therefore be aimed at facilitating these changes, in the right volume, in the right direction, and with the right speed." In particular, technology policy in the Netherlands is viewed quite broadly.

ERGAS (1987) had emphasized that the difference between mission-oriented and diffusion-oriented technology policies is that mission-oriented policies are targeted towards basic research and projects associated with national priority, while diffusion-oriented technology polices are directed at increasing the capabilities of firms to absorb new knowledge and new applications and to translate them into new or improved products for which demand already exists. Ergas also argued that diffusion-oriented technology policies are more appropriate for smaller countries than are mission-oriented technology policies. Thus, it is somewhat surpassing that the Netherlands, in fact, have encouraged mission-oriented technology policies more than most other countries. The Netherlands spends the greatest share of its R&D budget on basic research.

What distinguishes technology policy in France form that in West Germany, the United Kingdom, and the Netherlands, is that the government has undertaken means of direct assistance and targeting through nationalization rather than indirect assistance. For example, the government has used technology policy to promote R&D expenditures in six „industries of the future", which include biotechnology, marine industries, robotics, electronic office equipment, consumer electronics and alternative energy technologies. To promote the acceleration of innovation and technological change and innovation in these key industries, the government merged the Ministry of Research with the Ministry of Industry. This Ministry was responsible for improving the technological performance of the high-technology industries. Similarly, the Technological R&D Orientation Act called for an annual increase in R&D expenditures approaching 10%. In addition, the Act established public Interest Groups in which private firms could engage in cooperative innovation projects. Finally, the Finance Act enabled firms to claim a tax credit which was the equivalent of one-quarter of the increase in the firm's R&D expenditures.

Like its counterparts in Germany, the Netherlands, and the United Kingdom, the French government has actively promoted joint R&D enterprises. Some of these projects have extended beyond national boundaries. The Concorde, for example, was the result of a joint venture with the United Kingdom, and the Airbus was the result of a joint venture with Germany.

3.2 R&D Policy and Employment in the US

Investment in R&D in the US has averaged a little over 2.5% of GDP since 1960. As can be seen in Figure A6 in appendix I, the industry-funded component of R&D spending has risen over time while the federal share has declined. A lower bound estimate of the contribution of R&D to the growth in productivity between 1963 and 1992 is 0.2% (ECONOMIC REPORT OF THE PRESIDENT, 1995, p. 106). The decline in productivity after 1972 has of course stimulated much discussion of R&D policy, to which we return below.

Added detail on R&D spending is contained in Table 9. The table indicates that the lion's share of total R&D is performed by industry - $123 billion out of $172.5 billion in 1994, of which federal funds contributed just under 20%. Since the proportion of overall R&D undertaken by the private sector has not changed materially over the period - around 70% - the major change here is the larger contribution of industry funds, first noted in the figure. Universities and university associated federally-funded R&D centers accounted for just under 15% of all R&D outlays in 1994, as compared with 13.3% in 1980 and 11.8% in 1970 (the corresponding proportions for universities alone are 11.9, 9.7, and 8.9%, respectively). Again, the federal share of R&D performed in the universities has declined through time while the contribution of industry has risen - from 3.9% of funding in 1980 to 7.1% in 1994. The table also indicates that basic and applied research currently account for 41.8% of all R&D, with basic research representing 43.2% of non-development outlays. Basic research expenditures have grown relatively since 1980, from 13.5% to 18.1% of all R&D. Overall, the Federal contribution of R&D funding has fallen from 57% in 1970 through 47.2% in 1980 to 36.1% today.

Not shown in the table is the industrial composition of R&D, which is highly concentrated. Eight industries account for 80% of the total and the top two industries (aircraft and missiles and communications) are intimately related to defense.

Table 9: R&D Funds by Performance Sector, 1980–94

(In millions of dollars, except percent)

Performance Sector	1980	1985	1989	1990	1991	1992	1993	1994
Total R&D[1]	**62,596**	**113,818**	**140,981**	**151,544**	**160,096**	**166,697**	**169,515**	**172,550**
In 1987 dollars[2]	87,649	120,599	130,025	134,135	136,385	138,099	137,397	137,025
% Federal as source	47.2	45.8	42.5	40.7	37.7	36.2	36.3	36.1
% of gross domestic product	2.3	2.8	2.7	2.7	2.8	2.8	2.7	2.6
Federal Government	7,632	12,945	15,121	16,002	15,238	15,690	16,556	17,200
Industry	44,505	84,239	102,055	109,727	116,952	121,314	122,000	123,800
Federal funds	14,029	27,196	28,554	28,125	26,372	24,660	24,000	24,000
Industry funds	30,476	57,043	73,501	81,602	90,580	96,654	98,000	99,800
Universities & colleges	6,063	9,686	14,975	16,283	17,577	18,794	19,911	20,500
Federal funds	4,098	6,063	8,988	9,634	10,230	11,090	11,957	12,200
Industry funds	236	560	995	1,128	1,205	1,291	1,374	1,450
University & college funds[3]	1,326	2,369	3,921	4,329	4,835	5,018	5,111	5,300
Other nonprofit institutions funds[3]	403	694	1,071	1,192	1,307	1,395	1,469	1,550
Universities & colleges, assoc. federally funded R&D centers	2,246	3,523	4,730	4,832	5,079	5,249	5,298	5,100
Other nonprofit institutions	2,150	3,425	4,100	4,700	5,250	5,650	5,750	5,950
Federal funds	1,450	2,400	2,500	2,900	3,300	3,550	3,600	3,700
Industry funds	200	375	550	650	700	750	750	800
Other	500	650	1,050	1,150	1,250	1,350	1,400	1,450
Total research, basic and applied	**22,045**	**39,537**	**53,525**	**57,144**	**65,342**	**68,422**	**71,060**	**71,190**
In 1987 dollars[2]	27,513	41,046	51,018	53,144	59,813	61,762	63,411	63,744
Percent Federal as source	54.8	50.8	46.5	47.9	45.2	44.4	45.4	45.2

Table 9: R&D Funds by Performance Sector, 1980–94 (cont.)

Performance Sector	1980	1985	1989	1990	1991	1992	1993	1994
Total basic research	**8,435**	**14,210**	**21,248**	**22,322**	**27,985**	**29,579**	**30,676**	**31,150**
In 1987 dollars[2]	11,902	15,064	19,620	19,860	23,906	24,563	24,901	24,788
Percent of total R&D	13.5	12.5	15.1	14.7	17.5	17.7	18.1	18.1
Percent Federal as source	70.1	64.7	61.9	61.9	57.9	57.1	58.3	58.3
Total development	**40,551**	**74,281**	**87,456**	**94,400**	**94,754**	**98,275**	**98,455**	**100,360**
In 1987 dollars[2]	56,669	78,698	80,635	83,453	80,650	81,353	79,761	79,643
Percent of total R&D	64.8	65.3	62.0	62.3	59.2	59.0	58.1	58.2
Percent Federal as source	42.9	43.1	40.0	36.1	32.4	30.4	29.6	29.5

Notes: [1]Basic research, applied research, and development.
[2]Based on GDP implicit price deflator.
[3]Includes state and local government funds earmarked for R&D.
[4]Includes estimates for nonprofit hospitals and voluntary health agencies.

Source: *Statistical Abstract of the United States 1995, Table No. 981*
(Taken from US National Science Foundation, National Patterns of R&D Resources, annual)

Table 10: Scientists and Engineers in R&D by Industry, 1975-92
(Data are estimates on full-time-equivalent (FTE) basis)

Industry	1987 SIC code	1975	1980	1985	1987	1988	1989	1990	1991	1992
Average FTE of scientists and engineers (1,000)[1,2]		363,9	469,2	646,8	702,2	714,4	725,6	717,5	741,7	783,2
Chemicals[3]	28	44.8	53.1	73.5	75.5	76.7	78.3	78.9	82.2	87.4
Machinery	35	54.3	65.7	85.7	97.1	99.1	106.1	109.8	103.3	99.4
Electrical equipment[4]	36	81.5	100.7	115.6	131.5	136.6	139.3	137.9	114.8	91.2
Motor vehicles	371	25.7	36.7	31.3	46.9	46.6	47.8	47.6	45.0	44.9
Aircraft & missiles	372,376	67.2	90.6	137.5	136.4	139.4	135.4	123.2	105.4	94.0

Notes: [1]Prior to 1992, 1972 SIC; beginning 1992, 1987 SIC.
[2]Includes industries not shown separately.
[3]Includes allied products.
[4]Includes communication

Sources: Statistical Abstract of the United States 1995, Table No. 992.
(Taken from US National Science Foundation, Research and Development in Industry annual.)

Table 11: Scientists and Engineers Employed in **R&D,** 1970–91

(**Data are estimates on full-time-equivalent basis**)

	1970	1980	1982	1983	1984	1985	1987	1989	1991
Total[1] (1,000)	**543.8**	**651.1**	**711.8**	**751.6**	**797.6**	**801.9**	**877.8**	**924.2**	**960.5**
DISTRIBUTION (%)									
Industry	69.1	72.1	73.8	74.8	75.6	80.9	80.0	79.3	80.8
(excl. social scientists)									
Federal Government	12.4	9.0	8.4	8.2	7.8	6.5	6.2	6.4	6.1
Other[2]	18.5	18.9	17.8	17.0	16.6	12.6	13.8	14.3	13.1

Notes: [1] Data beginning 1985 not strictly comparable with prior data.
[2] Includes professional and R&D personnel employed in universities and colleges, other nonprofit institutions, and federally funded R&D centers administered by organizations in these sectors, and graduate students engaged in R&D in universities and colleges.

Sources: Statistical Abstract of the United States 1995, Table No. 993.
(Taken from US National Science Foundation, National Patterns of R&D Resources, annual)

Table 10 and 11 provide data on R&D employment in industry and in all sectors, respectively. The all-sector total still represents less than 1% of civilian employment, although the numbers of R&D personnel have risen much faster than overall civilian employment since 1970 - 76.6% versus 48.6%, 1970-91. (The values given in these tables are of course considerably smaller than the total of scientists, engineers, and technicians in employment. There were 2.673 million such employees in 1992 - see MONTHLY LABOR REVIEW, 1993). The ratio of R&D scientists/engineers for every 10,000 people in the labor force stood at 75.6 in 1989, as compared with 73.6, 59.3, 49.7, 36.3, and 31.4 in Japan, (West) Germany, France, the UK, and Italy, respectively.

There is little concrete evidence on the relation between R&D and employment. The OECD Jobs Study (OECD, 1994a, Part 1, Chapter 4) has however presented a fairly comprehensive examination of the relation between technology and employment. This suggests that the income generating effects of new technologies have proved more powerful than the labor-displacing effects, which is of course not to deny the pronounced compositional shifts in labor demand that have been linked in the US with technological change (see section 1.3). Between 1970 and 1991 employment in high-tech (science-based) manufacturing industries in the US grew at an annual rate of 0.7% (1.4%), while employment in low-tech industries declined by 0.6% per year. But this growth has not been sufficient to arrest the overall decline in manufacturing industry employment, and is perhaps even less likely to do so in the future. Employment growth has been restricted to the service sector and it is precisely here that our understanding of the effects of technology and R&D is most opaque. This is because of the considerable problem of measuring output and productivity in the service sector (see GORDON, 1996). One obvious problem is that much of computer software is treated as an intermediate good in the national income and product accounts rather than an investment good. It has been argued that measured R&D in the service sector is underestimated by a factor of three or four in services. Yet even so one study concludes that the growth in R&D expenditures in this sector grew at twice that of manufacturing between 1986 and 1988 (POLLAK, 1991). And there are indications that increasing amounts of R&D funding are being committed to the service sector. Such investment has been identified by the OECD as a crucial determinant of future growth in service sector employment. In the US this development appears to have been achieved by the sector itself with little government intervention other than through deregulation. As a source of jobs, of course, the service sector is projected to add 23 million jobs between 1990 and 2005 as compared with a loss of 600,000 jobs in manufacturing. A corollary of the ongoing growth in service sector employment is that white-collar jobs today make up a larger component of permanent layoffs than in the 1980s (GARDNER, 1995), although such workers continue to have higher reemployment rates than their blue-collar counterparts.

Finally, Table 12 presents comparative data on R&D as a percent of GDP for the US and five other countries. Proportionally the US spends more on R&D than any other country with the exception of Japan. However, both Germany and Japan have higher ratios of nondefense R&D. In dollar terms, and despite 1995 levels of R&D spending that are 2% lower in real terms than in 1990, the US still spends more on R&D (the most recent estimate, for 1995, is $171 billion) than do Japan, France, Germany, and the UK combined.

Nevertheless, there is no small dissatisfaction with the US R&D performance. In part this is linked to the post-1973 decline in productivity. Note, however, that R&D is only one input into total factor productivity and that the slowdown in R&D is in fact a post-1985 phenomenon. The real link is rather that declining productivity growth first prompted concerns about America's technological leadership that the recent slowdown in R&D has done nothing to assuage. Today Americans are much preoccupied with the dramatic closing of the economic and technological gaps between themselves and the major industrial powers. The erosion of the US lead in high-technology industries and the declining share of patents taken out in the US assigned to Americans are cases in point - the latter declined from 62.4 to 52.0% between 1978 and 1988. (The labor market aspects of this "decline" have been touched on in section 1.3.)

US policy toward R&D has mirrored these concerns but in examining current policy it would be unwise to suggest that there is real consensus as to the causes of the erosion of leadership and hence the road to be taken by policy. Expressed a little differently, recent moves toward a techno-nationalistic approach are unlikely to survive a change in administration.

With these preliminaries behind us, we turn to review recent changes in R&D policy in the US The starting point is of course defense R&D. National security has long commanded the largest share of Federal R&D funds. The defense share of post 1960 federal R&D spending peaked in 1987, when it accounted for roughly 69% of the total. This subsequently declined from approximately 59% to 56% between 1992 and 1994. The Clinton administration's goal is to achieve a balance between civilian and defense expenditures by 1998.

Table 12: National R&D Expenditures as a Percent of GDP by Country, 1975-93

Year	Total R&D						Nondefense R&D					
	US	Japan	Germ.	France	U.K.	Italy	US	Japan	Germ.	France	U.K.	Italy
1975	2.22	1.91	2.24	1.79	2.05	0.84	1.61	1.90	2.10	1.44	1.42	0.83
1980	2.31	2.01	2.45	1.82	--	0.75	1.76	2.00	2.33	1.41	--	0.74
1985	2.82	2.58	2.72	2.25	2.27	1.13	1.98	2.56	2.58	1.78	1.68	1.06
1990	2.73	2.89	2.75	2.42	2.19	1.30	2.01	2.87	2.61	1.85	1.81	1.25
1991	2.80	2.87	2.65	2.42	2.13	1.32	2.11	2.84	2.53	1.92	1.73	1.26
1992	2.77	2.80	2.53	2.36	2.12	1.38	2.10	2.77	2.42	1.92	1.71	1.33
1993	2.67	--	--	--	--	1.40	2.02	--	--	--	--	1.25

Source: Statistical Abstract of the United States, Table No. 985
(Taken from National Science Foundation, National Patterns of R&D Resources, annual; and Organization for Economic Cooperation and Development)

Defense priorities have also shaped support for much industrial and university-based R&D. As was noted earlier, although Federal funds currently amount to just 24% of the contribution of industry to R&D, this proportion is very much higher for some industries than others, and three-quarters of Federal support still goes to aerospace and communications equipment firms primarily for the military systems. Also, as is well known, the Defense Department has historically provided much of the funds for academic engineering research.

The attempt to realign Federal spending to produce a more equal balance between civilian and military priorities has evidently some very considerable way to go, and is by no means an article of faith across the political spectrum. One interesting transitional aspect of this ongoing process is the development of "dual-use" R&D programs that exploit goods with both military and commercial uses, under the so-called Technology Reinvestment Program (TRP). Examples include the National Flat Panel Display Initiative and the development of microwave and millimeter wave monolithic and integrated circuit technology (MIMIC). The latter seeks to facilitate the production of components for commercial applications (e.g. portable telephones and satellite communications devices) and military goods on the same production line. And part of the former will involve joint development of dual-use technology in future products and manufacturing processes by the Pentagon and those firms which demonstrate a commitment to build current generation displays. All of this has to do with providing cost effective development of new technologies for national defense and to create an integrated civilian military industrial base through flexible manufacturing systems.

The larger part of the flat panel initiative is to meet a need for a good currently largely controlled by foreign producers. Military reasons were also the stated basis for the earlier (and continuing) SEMATECH initiative. This was created in 1987 with half its budget from the Department of Defense and the remaining half contributed by a consortium of 14 civilian semiconductor firms. The goal was to restore the ability of US semiconductors to compete with their Japanese counterparts. Staff in the SEMATECH laboratory were to work collaboratively on the production of state-of-the art memory chips in near-commercial quantities and thereby advance integrated circuit manufacturing technology; later the mission shifted to support US equipment makers' design efforts (SCHERER, 1996, 232).

The military rationalization for funding technology R&D programs with direct civilian applications might seem a little forced and indeed a number of projects administered the Department of Defense have more recently been justified on overtly more commercial grounds. An example here is the Maritime Research Project (MARITECH) shipyard R&D program, based on SEMATECH, the goal of which is to assist in the development of new commercial tankers, bulk carriers, and container vessels.

The move toward supporting pre-competitive projects of commercial relevance through the provision of Federal R&D resources is typified by the new role of the Commerce Department and its Advanced Technology Program (ATP). ATP is a funding mechanism for technology projects performed by industry. Its initial budget was just $70 million but this was quickly raised by the Clinton administration to $200, and current proposals seek to expand this to $700 million in 1997. ATP is a policy experiment to test whether government-industry partnerships can overcome market failure associated with supposed industry specific public goods. An example of one such ATP partnership is a $28 million five-year research program to achieve technical improvements in materials and manufacturing processes for printed wiring boards, the nervous system of all electronic products. The project, jointly financed by an industry consortium and ATP, is reported to have saved the commercial parties around $13.5 million by averting redundant research, and by allowing the more rapid dissemination of results and improving access to specialized know-how and facilities (ECONOMIC REPORT OF THE PRESIDENT, 1995, p. 168).

A feature of public-private partnerships under current policy initiatives is the allocation of such resources to specific technology areas held to be critical to the nation's competitiveness. Of these the High Performance Computing and Communications Program is perhaps the best known example but other such focuses include environmental technology, advanced manufacturing technology development, and transportation (e.g. smart highways and high-speed rail).

An additional important aspect of present R&D strategy is technology transfer. Thus the Department of Energy laboratories (e.g. Lawrence Livermore, Los Alamos, and Oak Ridge) have been charged with transferring their technologies and technical expertise to the private sector as well as cooperating on joint research projects with commercial firms. The goal for all laboratories managed by the Department of Energy, NASA, and the Department of Defense that can make a positive contribution to the civilian economy is to devote at least 10 to 20% of their budgets to R&D partnerships with industry. More important perhaps in this connection is the dissemination of expertise via the National Institute of Standards and Technology (NIST) at the Department of

Commerce, established in 1988 under the Omnibus Trade and Competitiveness Act. (The ATP program discussed above is part of NIST.) NIST is engaged on setting up a number of Technology Extension Service centers - note the patterning on the Agricultural Extension Service Program, which absorbs one half of the Agricultural Department's R&D budget - to share expertise gained through government R&D and study to the broadest range of manufacturing firms (SCHÄFER and HYLAND, 1994, p. 604). For example, the Manufacturing Extension Partnership (MEP) provides small- and medium-sized manufacturers with access to public and private resources, information, and services to increase their use of appropriate technologies and modern manufacturing processes. Note that MEP includes assistance on so-called "high-performance work structures" focusing on improvements in workforce skills and changes in the working environment. Here one observes signs of an embryonic policy link between technology and training at the workplace.

Another and some would say the most fundamental aspect of R&D policy is regulatory reform, geared to improving the climate for technological development. (Early regulatory reform, specifically the 1984 National Cooperative Research and Development Act, created an exception to the anti-trust laws in allowing appropriately registered research and development joint ventures. Some 350 multifirm collaborative ventures, many of them R&D consortia, have been created since 1985.[1] Further antitrust legislative reform to cover joint production ventures is envisaged.) A major example is the reform of telecommunications regulations through the National Information Infrastructure initiative. Here the principal advantages will accrue from rationalizing a plethora of regulatory regimes covering the various mediums such as telephone, cable, and satellite communications into a coherent whole. The basic result should be to encourage industry to invest in the new technologies sooner than would otherwise be the case.

The remaining policy elements have to do with R&D tax credits and patent protection. Currently the federal government allows a tax credit for the increment of domestic research expenditure over a certain threshold level. The present system allows a 20% income tax credit for research and experimentation - and also allows most R&D expenses to be deducted immediately rather than spread over several years. As far as patent protection, the main innovation is a proposal to permit greater third-party

---

[1] There are also in excess of 1,000 university-industry research centers, the large majority of which were established with either Federal or state support.

participation in patent reexamination proceedings to facilitate innovation in follow-on innovations.

In sum, recent years have seen a number of innovations in R&D policy in the form of technology reinvestment (in defense), new national initiatives, enhanced technology transfer mechanisms, and new public-private partnerships. These essentially incremental developments are associated with the end of the Cold War and a perception that US technological leadership is under challenge (SCHÄFER and HYLAND, 1994). The new commercial orientation of policy has also to be qualified. First, funding realities are such that major expansion of programs favored by the Clinton administration is precluded. Second, the notion of a national R&D policy outside the classic public good of defense (and basic research) remains highly controversial in the US, where many still hold that commercial R&D is best left to the market - which is of course not to deny the lure of procurement outlays. Third, the cost effectiveness of programs is a nagging worry and one would be hard pressed to attribute the renaissance of the US semiconductor industry to SEMATECH or other interventions such as the Japan-US Semiconductor Agreement(s). A substantial body of opinion in the US would see the best R&D policy as one that removes distortions such as regulation and the budget deficit rather than interventionist domestic industrial policies. These attitudes are of course shaped by the American history of aggressive start-up firms. Finally, and relatedly, there is the ongoing debate over globalization: in a nutshell might not international tie ups be more rewarding than national endeavors? Or are the former only likely to be effective if there is in place a set of government policies to build upon existing nation state technological advantages? The debate in the US over R&D policy has been less engaged by these particular controversies given its rather late adoption of a commercial technology program.

3.3 R&D Policy and Employment in Japan and Asian NICs

At first glance, research appears to be strongly supported and to have provided impressive results in Japan. The ratio of total research expenditures to gross domestic product is higher in Japan than in any other developed country. Japan has continued to dominate high-technology trade in global markets in the 1990s.

However, concern in Japan about research policy has been growing. The ratio of public research expenditures to total research expenditures is the lowest among the developed countries. Perhaps of even greater concern, research expenditures by the private sector have decreased in the last several years. As a result, in 1992 the Cabinet set a goal for doubling expenditures on public research. The 1996 national budget reflects this goal. Grants-in-aid of the Ministry of Education, Science, Sports and Culture (*Monbusho*) exceeded 100 billion yen, with 11 billion yen being allocated to the Japan Society for the Promotion of Science, which commissions new research projects to universities. In addition, five ministries, including the Science and Technology Agency, and the Ministry of International Trade and Industry (MITI) were granted large increases in research budgets to be managed by their affiliated quasi-governmental organizations. This budget amounts to 21 billion yen, most of which is allocated to research undertaken at universities.

The *Science and Technology Basic Law* was enacted by the Japanese Diet in November 1995. While the government usually proposes new laws, the level of concern in Japan concerning national science and technology policy motivated the Japanese Diet to take the initiative. In fact, the Japanese Government had placed a high priority at enhancing Japanese research competence and had made special increase in the science and technology budgets in recent years, even in the face of severe budgetary constraints. The *Science and Technology Basic Law* paved the way for a massive five-year plan to promote science and technology.

One of the key policy initiatives being undertaken in Japan is the recruitment and training of young scientists. The Ministry of Education, Science, Sports and Culture (Monbusho) has committed itself to upgrading the quality and scale of scientific training at postgraduate schools, which until now, have remained smaller than programs in other developed countries. These initiatives include increased attention to the support of young scientists, both at doctoral and postdoctoral levels. Under the current plan, a wide array of fellowship schemes will be expanded to support as many as 10,000 young scientists by the turn of the century, which is a more than two and a half times as great as the number of 1995 fellowships.[2]

There is also concern in Japan that the quality and applicability of university research needs to be enhanced. The *Science and Technology Basic Law* provides provisions to upgrade both the quality and applications of research. The Science Council of the Ministry of Education, Science, Sports and Culture (Monbusho) has implemented a new series of research evaluation systems, measures to establish centers of excellence, and mechanisms to promote university-industry cooperation

---

[2] HAYASHIDA, HIDEKI, "Science Policy in Japan," Science, Vol. 272, No. 14, June 1996.

and exchange.

One of the aspects of Japanese Science policy that is most effective is what *Science* magazine characterizes as "a planning process that lets the community set its priorities without outside interference and a steadily increasing science budget that accommodates new capital projects once an earlier generation of facilities goes on line. That benign and orderly process is remarkable in the scientific world."[3] The key element to the Japanese Science policy is the process under which scientists are funded. Scientists in Japan typically receive funding from either the Ministry of Education, Science, Sports, and Culture (Monbusho) or the Science Technology Agency (STAA). Research projects are approved by the Ministry of Education, Science, Sports and Culture on the basis of building a scientific consensus. For example, the process begins with the Nuclear Physics Committee or the High-Energy Physics Committee in physics. By contrast, consensus building plays less of an important role in obtaining funding from the Science and Technology Agency.

The relatively small, newly industrialized countries in Asia are generally confronting with three different policy options for enhancing research and technological capabilities through foreign direct investment - serving as a regional business services hub for other nations with close geographic proximity; niche specialization; serving as a home base and R&D hub to global firms. These three options are pursued differently to compensate three major disadvantages:

1. A small domestic market;

2. Extremely limited natural resources;

3. Limited supplies of indigenous human resources.

In contrast to the more developed industrialized nations, small newly industrialized economies are characterized by a shorter history of industrial development, which has resulted in a limited accumulation of technological assets and a lower level of infusion of scientific-technical infrastructure upon which to base innovative activity.

To compensate for these three inherent size disadvantages, small newly industrialized economies typically respond by adapting the three policy responses listed above:

• The Model of the Regional Hub:

This strategy is based on positioning the country to perform complementary value-

---

[3] "Big Science is Booming in Japan," Science, Vol. 271, No. 23, February 1996, pp. 1046-1048.

added services for the larger geographic region in which the country is located. To accomplish this, the country must be in a position to exploit either some geographic or locational advantage, or superior labor force skills and infrastructure involving transportation, communications, and ancillary services. Examples of countries which have succeeded by pursuing this strategy include Hong Kong and Singapore, which have established hubs for regional trading, distribution, marketing and technical support.

- The Model of Niche Specialization:
  Under this strategy the small economy concentrates its limited resources in selected clusters of niche industries, or even only certain aspects within the vertical chain of production and distribution within these niche industries, with the hopes of attaining competitiveness through specialization and economies of agglomeration.

    As PORTER (1990) has emphasized, such a strategy of niche specialization typically involves not just a single industry, but rather a host of related complementary industries, linked either upstream or downstream, but generally co-located in the same geographic region. The competitive advantage stems from the dense network of closely related industries that yields spillovers and positive knowledge externalities.

    BECKER has even argued that this niche strategy has become so attractive that, "Small nations are proliferating because economies can now prosper by producing niche goods and services for world markets."[4] According to Becker, on reason that the number of nations has almost doubled in the past fifty years, to 191 independent countries, is that the economic cost of independence has been sharply lowered by the globalization of markets: "In fact, small nations now have advantages in the competition for international markets. Economic efficiency requires them to concentrate on only a few products and services, so they often specialize in niches that are too small for large nations to fill."[5]

- The Model of the Home Base and R&D Hub to Global Firms:
  Under this model, the small country provides a home base to domestic companies that have evolved into becoming multinational enterprises. While the country continues to serve as the corporate headquarters of these multinational corporations, and is likely to retain some of the higher value-added activities, such

---

[4] Gary S. BECKER, "Why So Many Mice Are Roaring," Business Week, 7 November, 1994, p. 11.
[5] Gary S. BECKER, "Why So Many Mice Are Roaring," Business Week, 7 November, 1994, p. 11.

as R&D and product development, most of the production activities are likely to be located overseas.

One major distinction between the model of niche specialization and the home base hub model is that in the latter situation the small economies no longer have the competitive advantage in retaining most of the high value-added activities of these firms, but instead only provide the home base to the corporate and perhaps some of the R&D functions. The advantage of a home base and R&D hub is based either on national identification, or other complementary factors, such as first mover advantages in developing a superior scientific and human capital infrastructure, close and long-term linkages to universities, and tax incentives. Examples of small countries that have developed a home base and R&D hub to many global companies include Switzerland and Sweden.

A country typical of the Asian Tigers, Singapore, has established a regional business services hub in Southeast Asia. This has been a very important factor in its high economic performance during the 1970s and 1980s. Today a large part of Singapore's gross domestic product continues to derive from being a regional marketing and technical support center, a regional and business services center, and a regional headquarters for multinational corporations with considerable outward foreign direct investment. Much of this outward foreign direct investment is devoted towards small- and medium-sized businesses throughout Southeast Asia. At the same time, Singapore has generally pursued a strategy of niche specialization, so that the major industries include shipbuilding and maintenance, computers and industrial electronics, and aerospace maintenance and repairs.

The Singapore Government has aggressively pursued increased competitiveness through promoting outward foreign direct investment, especially by high-technology firms. According to Pom-Kam Wong, Director of the Centre for Management of Technology (CMT) of the National University of Singapore, "Besides the strategic thrusts to make Singapore a high technology hub, the government has also started promoting the transformation of home-grown companies into globe-trotting transnational corporations. Under the slogan of developing a 'second wing' for the economy, the government has proposed a set of policies to encourage local firms to venture abroad, and a number of government-linked companies have taken the lead to internationalize. The volume of outward directed foreign investment coming out of Singapore, which has already increased rapidly over the last few years, will be expected to accelerate further in the future. Besides assisting local firms to internationalize, the government is also actively assisting multinational corporations, whether they have existing operations or are new in the region, to invest in the ASEAN region and in China. In this case the Singapore is leveraging its good business and political contacts with the countries in the region to act as a business architect for transnational corporations entering or expanding in the region" (WONG, 1993).

Under the *New Strategic Plan*, announced in 1991, the government of Singapore announced its strategic intent to move aggressively into high-technology industries and knowledge-industries while encouraging the less knowledge-intensive industries to locate into neighboring countries. In fact, what is termed as a *growth triangle strategy* has been implemented to support the shifting of labor-intensive production from Singapore to the nearby regions of southern Malaysia and the Riau Islands of Indonesia through outward foreign direct investment. According to WONG (1993, p. 10.), "The promotion of Singapore as a regional manufacturing platform for transnational corporations will continue and even intensify, but with greater selectivity emphasizing in particular various high-tech industries that are technology and knowledge-intensive. The major industry clusters that Singapore will particularly emphasize include electronics and computers, software development, petrochemicals, aerospace and precision engineering, biotechnology and environmental engineering."

The technology policy deployed by Singapore seems to be co-ordinated with the policy to promote outward foreign direct investment in order to enhance the global competitiveness of the country. For example, under one of the current technology policies, the *National Automation Masterplan*, which is designed to promote the adoption of advanced manufacturing technologies, particular emphasis is devoted towards encouraging outward foreign direct investment in the high-technology and high-information industries which are based on high levels of human capital and labor skills. As part of this shift towards more technology-intensive industries, Singapore is emerging as a manufacturing process engineering and transfer center to assist multinational corporations based in Singapore to deploy their manufacturing operations over the region. When a new product is launched, Singapore is often picked as the first site to get the production line operational. Singaporian engineers are typically involved in jointly (and often concurrently) developing the manufacturing process for the new product line. After the manufacturing processes are successfully implemented and the operations become stabilized, they are then typically transferred to another location, such as Malaysia or Thailand, with the Singaporian engineers responsible for the entire transfer process.

As in other countries, most of the research and development in Korea is undertaken by large firms. Only around 16% of small firms are formally engaged in R&D (REGNIER, 1993). Most of the technology learning stems from various subcontracting contracts with larger firms, which are becoming increasingly numerous. Still small firms in Korea have been the recipients of about 44% of all technology transfers from abroad. The majority of small firms asking for technology support from the state run Small and Medium Industry Promotion Corporation (SMIPC), which is the major stage agency charged with promoting the small- and medium-sized firms.

4. The Global Economy: R&D, Structural Change and Employment Shifts

4.1 Dynamic Innovation Fields: High Technology and Sustainable Growth

Whither science and technology in the decades ahead? All leading industrial nations have been looking for plausible answers to this question. Government agencies and industry - particularly in Japan and the United States - have been carrying out technological studies in recent years to marshal facts and arguments for their research planning. The key studies undertaken in Japan and the US so far have provided important clues for respective work in Europe. Meanwhile, several European foresight studies are available. They highlight the structural changes which technology itself has undergone. They attest to integrational trends in what used to be separate branches of knowledge, the emergence of new disciplines and their growing interpenetration. The technology sectors fall under headings such as advanced materials, nanotechnology, microelectronics, photonics, microsystems engineering, software and simulation, molecular electronics, cellular biotechnology, information, production and management engineering. The technology of the early 21st century will defy any attempt at demarcation in the traditional sense. However different the various lines of development may be, they are all bound to converge and interact.

There is a constant temptation for technical observation to restrict itself to describing the potential supply of scientific and technical solutions. However, it must do far more than depict the supply factors. The importance of technology in the future depends just as much on the pressure of social, ecological and economic problems which are expected to arise, and which will make important demands on science and technology in the future. For this reason, any discussion of problems must focus increasingly on factors relying to demand. The issue of how to determine which *basic values for innovation activities* may be adopted worldwide in the medium and long-term perspectives and how to forecast the resulting problems is naturally a prognostic and synthetic question to which there is no definite answer based in fact. It is justified to take as a basis in the European Union the current fundamental legal (state founded on the rule of law), social (social market economy) and political (parliamentary democracy) conditions for innovation activities.

The innovation cycle now beginning could cursorily be described as that of the 'intelligent technologies'. The long-term scientific and technological developments on which the planning and technological policy may be based arise from the interplay between what is technically feasible and what is required from a political and economic point of view. It is precisely on this crucial point that some of the mentioned studies show poor forecasting ability and make ill-founded assertions (GRUPP, 1994a). In terms of taking account of factors relating to demand, the documented state of knowledge is poor. At international level, it is only now that initial attempts are being made to achieve a more comprehensive assessment of technologies. It is obvious that opinions in Europe concur in this respect, overseas countries and markets may differ more in demand than in technology.

Although great care has been taken in forecasting a context for new technologies at the start of the 21st century, such foresight is really nothing more than plausible indication. Each argument may readily be expanded, analyzed, divided into smaller problems and explored at greater depths. The arguments should therefore be regarded as well-founded foresight on future development, but not as an authoritative assessment of developments which will take place in the future. Technical forecasting would not be possible if the expectations were for guaranteed, consistent pieces of evidence. Rather, the studies represent a rational, comprehensible database comprised of information ascertained in a systematic manner.

Initially euphoric expectations of a new technology (mostly on the part of the scientific community) tend to be followed by increasingly cautious developmental phases before the market is finally penetrated. The use or rejection of innovative products often leads to new demands on research and technology, which is why it generally makes sense to speak of feedback processes.

Pure research will continue to dominate the innovative development of some of the dynamic innovation fields (e. g. bioinformatics, mounting and connecting technologies in microsystems engineering, manufacturing processes for high-performance materials, surface materials, behavioral biology) over the next ten years. Many areas have developed erratically in the past and will continue to do so in the future, with no significant progress to show for their existence during the past ten years. Such areas nevertheless remain worthy of monitoring. However, it is true that those aspects of new technology which are currently still the subject of scientific exploration cannot achieve their full potential for economic penetration in a mere, say, ten years. It is only where prototypes or initial technical realizations have already been produced that it will be possible to witness the full economic potential of such technologies soon after the year 2000.

These findings also call in question the possible expectation that a technology needs no more than a single incentive to see its full potential realized at the start of the 21st century. Any hopes of being able to drop the accompanying pure research within the next ten years once the applied objectives have been achieved will meet with disappointment; tomorrow's science-based technology requires continuous support through targeted basic research (see also section 5.2).

Without claiming to be comprehensive, let us consider some dynamic innovation fields discussed in several foresight studies in greater detail (compare GRUPP, 1994a). *Advanced materials* play a key role in growth in many sectors of the economy and also have an effect which extends far beyond the techno-economic aspects. They make it possible to satisfy the ever increasing demands for safety, environmental protection and comfort and, in so doing, to extend creative possibilities in work and leisure as well as in science and technology. As in medical technology, innovations in information technology are causally dependent on the possibility of using new materials with specifically developed optimal characteristics. The materials sciences have now established themselves as independent branches of research. No longer to be excluded from this inter-disciplinary research field, next to physics and chemistry stand the engineering sciences and applied mathematics, which brings in computer simulation and modeling. The trend is however towards producing materials with characteristics which can be increasingly precisely predetermined in accordance with a previously defined need. Development of materials by the 'trial and error' principle is increasingly giving way to tailor-made materials. This ability to tailor materials precisely to their application profile means that technology can now be defined less and less frequently in terms of the category of substance used.

The new technological field now emerging, which deals with the manufacture, examination and use of two- and three-dimensional structures, laminates, molecular units, internal boundary layers and surfaces in terms of nanometres, is known as *nanotechnology*. It is a challenge to engineering science at atomic and molecular level. Inter-disciplinary collaboration with electronics, information technology, materials science, optics, biochemistry, biotechnology, medicine and micromechanics is an important prerequisite if the new basic technologies are to give birth to future innovation processes and new technical developments across the whole spectrum. Applications of nanotechnology - as far as can be predicted today - will reach into the field of tailor-made materials and biological technical systems, but above all they may be seen in electronics. Nanotechnology has an affinity with both the materials sector and the microelectronics of the future. Nanotechnology is still in an early stage of development, with all the resulting uncertainties which affect the reliable assessment of its various implications.

Microelectronics is also a technology for the twenty-first century. Although there can be no doubt as to the historic advance made by microelectronics before the new biotechnologies and nanotechnologies came along, a national economy must master the most modern microelectronic processes in order to be able to adapt to subsequent developmental advances. Silicon continues to dominate most microelectronics applications. The so-called compound semiconductors are systematically being made available; the transition to nanoelectronics may also take place with compound semiconductors. Silicon microelectronics is exerting a strong influence on other microtechnologies (micromechanics, microsensors, microsystems engineering, multifunctional systems). An overview of the selected segments of microelectronics and their momentum shows that even such a traditional area still offers considerable development opportunities. In the early twenty-first century, microelectronics will - with high temperatures, high frequencies, high data transmission rates and superconduction - present quite a different picture from today.

Photonics is the combined use of microelectronics, optoelectronics, integrated optics and micro-optics, in which particular consideration is given to the requirements of parallel signal processing. In view of the large number of technologies combined in photonics, it is understood as a general concept, even though the segments operating together are not strict sub-divisions of photonics. Behind this lies the conviction that by the start of the twenty-first century the subject matter, the use of the concept and the economic aspects of photonics will increasingly come to the forefront. Beams of light can cross in a plane or in space without affecting each other. This can produce parallel and highly networked systems, so that photonics is particularly well suited to all types of pattern recognition, associative storage, parallel search procedures etc as well as, and especially, artificial neural networks. The individual subjects in the field of photonics are closely related and are classed in the immediate neighborhood of microelectronics, microsystems engineering, nanotechnology and materials technology.

Systems technology relates less to a concrete technology but rather refers to an integrative procedure (process technology), which brings various technological fields together in a systematic manner. The challenge here is found not only in dealing with the complex and expensive achievements of individual technologies which have reached different stages in their development, but also in the fact that new problems may arise when such technologies are combined to produce new solutions. Because of the increasing use of miniaturization in many areas (microelectronics, nanoelectronics, molecular materials, molecular biotechnology etc), the systems technology of tomorrow will be the *microsystems engineering* we are already working with today. Microsystems technology brings together subject-based disciplines in the natural and engineering sciences which until now have functioned separately: physics and biology with electrotechnology, precision engineering with micromechanics. The technological elements of microsystems engineering consist of procedures and strategies from the fields mentioned and their combination, and in that way create the conditions for the dramatic miniaturization of systems technology and the integration of many functions in the smallest possible space.

Over the next ten years there will be a high level of demand from all sides for improvements to *software and simulation* technologies. None of the technological fields considered here will escape from this. This must be said all the more clearly in Europe, since in software development a specific weakness in Japanese research and development systems has occurred recently for cultural and educational reasons (according to Japanese self-diagnosis sources). High levels of education and creativity will possibly enable Europe to recover more ground specifically in software than in other areas of modern information technology. The analysis of technical similarities has shifted software and simulation between biotechnology and molecular electronics on the one hand and systems engineering and microelectronics on the other. While the proximity of software to information technology hardware conforms to the current analysis, its immediate proximity to molecular electronics and biotechnology will become even clearer by the start of the twenty-first century, if the significance of life processes and their study to software and simulation is fully recognized. Even the relevant terminology (bioinformatics, neurobiology, neuroinformatics, artificial intelligence, bionics etc.) suggests this context by association.

Molecular electronics has for a number of years been a topical research field, which attempts to create highly complex systems whose switching elements and networks operate on a molecular basis. Organic materials are used in production. More recently, biological materials have increasingly been used. The relatively established and frequently synonymous concept of bioelectronics denotes an area which deals in molecular processes in biosystems and to that extent is a sub-division of molecular electronics. However, the concepts are in flux; there are considerable differences of understanding and different schools of thought. For example, bioelectronics can also be understood to mean a research field on the border between biology and electronics, such as the broad areas of biosensors, the similarity processes between the brain and electronics and the imitation of the human brain and its processing procedures (neural networks), which cannot for the most part be understood as a sub-division of molecular electronics. To that extent bioelectronics extends beyond molecular electronics. Since it does not appear possible to classify this research field definitively in a hierarchy, molecular electronics was introduced for understandable reasons as a general term for the technology which will be used at the start of the twenty-first century, in order to shift molecular access to electric processes to Centre stage alongside microtechnology and nanotechnology.

Another large area could simply be labeled 'biotechnology'. Why then we term it *cellular biotechnology*? Behind this lies the conviction that the biotechnology of tomorrow will be based essentially on the application of a knowledge of cell biology. Cell biology covers the elucidation of structural functional relationships both at the level of the integration of whole cells and of that of biological macromolecules, which are the most important cell components. Over the next few years cell biology will establish itself increasingly as an independent subject with the biological sciences and incorporate an important, if not the most important, bridging function between molecular genetics, biochemistry and medicine. In the early twenty-first century the general title 'cellular biotechnology' may sound less surprising than it does today. It should also be said however that the introduction of sub-divisions in biotechnology is quite arbitrary and even in the future no elucidation is foreseeable. The heading 'cellular biotechnology' should therefore be accompanied by a note to the effect that at the start of the twenty-first century biotechnology cannot be reduced to the concept of 'genetic engineering' but will be considerably more diverse and more complex. For that reason too, the emphasis on cellular biotechnology in this study must be consciously applied. The essential bridge between cellular biotechnology and molecular electronics runs through medical applications and biosensors; the materials sector is opened up by catalysts and biocatalysts. Bionics and biomimetic materials point in the direction of simulation and systems technology. Altogether biotechnology has enormous potential for the future. If we try however to measure the impact in the medium term, that is just to the start of the twenty-first century, we shall find we cannot yet unreel the measuring tape. This should not lead to the conclusion that there is time enough to bring on the relevant technological activities (in addition to research activities).

After running through the list of subjects, important areas are set out which escape from the usual classification into subject areas in the natural and engineering sciences. These are here given the title *information, production and management engineering*, but do not relate to production and management as a sub-division of business economics in the narrow sense. It becomes clear from the study that the mastery of technology at the start of the twenty-first century means more than carrying out laboratory work. Questions of acceptance, organizational innovations, the bringing together of previously disparate research, development and production divisions, the redefinition of the significance of software and simulation to laboratory research and production and many other subjects form an indivisible part of it.

The above observations apply to technical applications at the start of the twenty-first century as they relate to consumer and capital goods of a general nature. In this case, the task of public research and technology policy is restricted, in accordance with the European States' conception of itself, to the provision of basic functions in research and education. There is additionally a series of problem areas in which the provision of solutions is seen as a public task (such as transport or energy problems). Conceivable solutions are to some extent of an organizational nature or consist of persuading society to renounce certain claims (educational task). Frequently however there are also technical methods available to tackle these important future tasks. In particular, in energy and transport, 'infrastructure technology' has an as yet inexhausted potential. In Europe, 'preventive research' is being carried on especially to prevent additional stresses arising in the first place and to reduce them immediately they occur.

If the real challenges for a particular policy in the area of high technology originate from increasing social, economic, and environmental problems, the aim of the respective policy is to make the innovation system adaptive enough to meet those challenges. Some important questions remain largely open. Does the traditional notion of high technology competitiveness meet - in addition to growth and employment goals - the goals of protection of natural resources and the environment, supplementary challenges for implementing sustainable growth in the further development of the economy? The new research questions are of the following sort (GRUPP, MÜNT, GEHRKE AND LEGLER, 1996): Is structural change heading in the right direction of sustainable growth? Do we observe a reduction in the use of natural resources at the 'cost' of better utilization of human capital? Does the science and technology system offer the necessary potential in terms of scientific knowledge, technological inventions and innovations, and highly educated and qualified personnel?

4.2 Technometric Analysis of Innovation in a Comparative Perspective: EU-US-J

The ability to develop and exploit new business opportunities, i. e., the *economic competence*, is generally difficult to determine quantitatively. As '(e)conomic competence is a scarce and unequally distributed resource whose quality and quantity is an important determinant of the degree to which successful innovation will take place (...)'(CARLSSON and STANKIEWICZ, 1991, p. 94), one is tempted to 'measure' economic competence by its outcomes - successful innovation. In modern science-driven markets, the firm's competences in various areas of activities, such as R&D, engineering, production but also general administration (CARLSSON and STANKIEWICZ, 1991., p. 10), have to be extended to monitor scientific achievements, coordinate learning from science and scientists outside the firm or to communicate problems to them, and to organize knowledge accumulation by appropriate risk taking.

But how to measure successful science-based innovation? In the framework of the emerging 'new economics of science' (DASGUPTA and DAVID, 1987), codification of knowledge is a step in the process of reducing *complexity* for markets and firms. Scientific papers may represent quantified knowledge on science, patents codified knowledge on technology. For measuring the tacit (POLANYI, 1966), embodied knowledge included in innovative products, measurement of technological characteristics is also required. Here, the newly established technometric concept (GRUPP, 1994b) may be embarked upon. It requires the consultation with technology experts and thus the handling of multi-disciplinarity in industrial economics.

In very general terms, technological innovation is problem-solving. The technological paradigms which relate to products' attributes are progressively developed by socio-economic uses or requirements (e. g. for overcoming dangerous conventional operations using stilettos by laser surgery). Companies pursuing innovative activities are strongly selective and cumulative and direct the appropriation of the scientific and technical opportunities towards their (future) markets. Because this creates inertia, technological trajectories (NELSON and WINTER, 1982, and DOSI, 1988) bring about dominant product design configurations (UTTERBACK and ABERNATHY, 1975).

A dominant design usually takes the form of a new product with given characteristics (in the sense of LANCASTER, various works, refer to 1991) that is synthesized from individual technological innovations introduced cumulatively in prior product variants. A dominant design has the effect of enforcing or encouraging standardization so that production economies can be achieved (UTTERBACK and SUÁREZ, 1993). The variety of possible new products is narrowed to few realized products or innovations. Dominant design configurations can be identified in many product lines. These often have the result of drastically reducing the number of performance requirements to be met by a product by making many features implicit in the dominant design and increasing its acceptance by business rivals.

At the beginning of the eighties a series of 'metrics' for evaluating and comparing technological sophistication and quality were proposed. What was coined 'technometrics' in 1985 (GRUPP and HOHMEYER, 1986; an overview of other approaches may be found in GRUPP and HOHMEYER, 1988) is a procedure designed along Lancaster's consumer theory and is based on the observation that every innovative product or process has a set of key attributes that defines its performance, value or ability to satisfy customer wants. Many can be quantified, for instance, in the case of lasers, such attributers as coherent light output, beam divergence and diameter, directional stability, standard power supplies, mode selection or warranty time can all be defined and measured in physical units (GRUPP, 1997). Each of these attributes has a different unit of measurement. Problems then arise in aggregating attributes to build a single quality index. Mathematical details of the general procedure are not discussed here as they may be found elsewhere (GRUPP, 1994b). Suffice to say that the technometric indicator surmounts this difficulty by converting each measured attribute into a [0,1] metric, enabling construction of weighted averages, etc., and permitting comparisons across products, firms, industries and countries. The '0' point of the metric is set as the technologically standard attribute; the '1' point is set as the most technologically sophisticated attribute in existence at a given point in time.

From the micro-level, single-item definition, a technometric profile may be aggregated on the level of all specifications per product if functional characteristics or (revealed) preferences are defined. The preferences may be derived from utility functions, by introspective or market observation, from expert knowledge or via hedonic prices. Technometric profiles may be used for measuring the economic competence through the proxy firm-specific technological performance or quality level, one of the important determinants for innovation, which includes the tacit knowledge. Yet, the compilation of technometric data is time-consuming as the specifications are not accessible in data banks. In particular, technometric time series data are very difficult to obtain and rather costly. The measure also does not differentiate between the sources of know-how. It may be created within the firm by R&D, in the science system, by learning by doing or learning by using or by adoption of innovative solutions developed by other industries or firms and embodied in capital equipment and intermediate inputs (PAVITT, 1984).

To our knowledge, the latest technometric comparison between the European Union, the United States and Japan is rather dated and relates to the year 1982 (GRUPP and HOHMEYER, 1988). Japan was a catching-up nation then. In Europe, the aerospace industry was just beginning to develop and the Single Market not yet established. We think, these data do not represent the relations in the 1990s. More actual data apparently do not exist.

Besides technometric measurement, therefore, the combined use of *patent indicators* is suggestive. As patent data represent a widely accepted proxy measure for firm's own technology output (GRILICHES, 1990), and as, compared with technometrics, patent statistics are relatively easy to compile, and further, as patents are always assigned to the first innovator, but not to the imitator, the adopter or the learning company, it may be assumed that patent data are a good proxy for the explicit and codified firm-specific technology generation process. In the analysis of global technology appropriation and to do justice to a balanced EU-US-J comparison only the part of the inventions for which patent protection has been applied for in several important markets, in particular the triade countries, may serve as a good measure of technology. The superiority of external patents is undisputed (GRILICHES, loc. cit., SCHMOCH et al., 1988, among others). Thereby, effects originating from the corporate strategy and advantages of companies on domestic markets are corrected. This type of patent search must be based on data from more than one patent office. Together with the more recent patents, also the stock of existing intellectual property determines the actual technology levels achieved as technological knowledge acquisition is a cumulative procedure.

In this paper, out of the many possible patent indicators proposed, the triade patent productivity index (patents per employment) is used. It is determined at the European, the United States and the Japanese patent offices and consists of this part of all patent documents being registered at all three patent offices. The 'production function' for technology as measured by the sophistication levels of innovative products can be modeled as follows:

$$Y(i,k) = \alpha_i \, P(i,k)^\beta \, \varepsilon_k,$$

with i for products, k for countries, Y for technology output and P for triade patents as before. The elasticity parameter β is assumed to be constant, whereas α_i may vary with the technology (e. g. patent propensity). Competition for intellectual property, however, forces the competing firms in the countries (or regions) k in the market i to follow about the same patent strategy, hence α is not a function of k. Other inputs like tacit knowledge including external science sources and managerial competences are all covered by the residual as there is no way to quantification.

Figure 3:   Triade Patent Productivity Since 1980 (By region of origin)

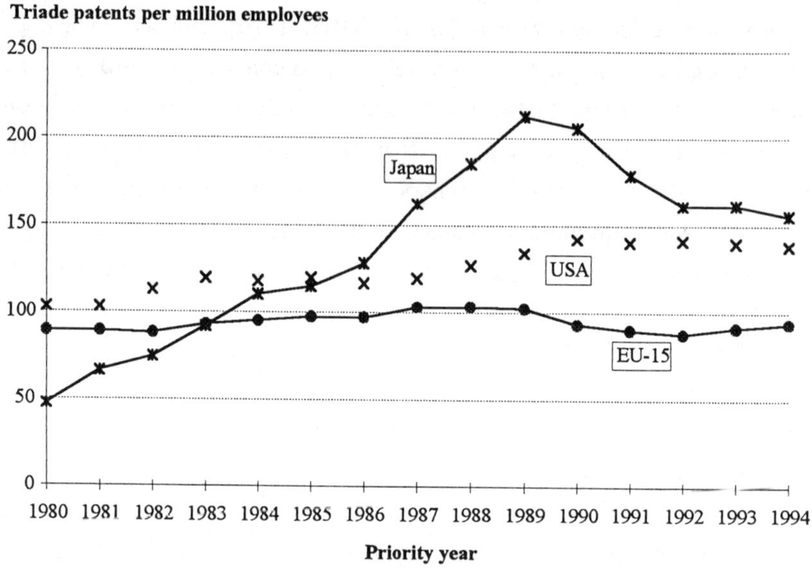

Triade patents per million employees

A patent is often applied for long before the invention ever sees the market. In this respect, such inventions are the result of innovative processes. To simplify and generalize: Patents that were applied for in 1994 are the result of research and development conducted around 1991/2 and are targeted for markets in 1995 to 2000. Europe (EU-15 by artificially adding up the then non-members and East Germany) was unreservedly one of the world's two leading economic regions in terms of the number of patent applications filed annually at the beginning of the 1980s. During the 1980s, patent productivity and technological competition both increased. However, the number of European patents with world market relevance has been on the decline since the early 1990s, largely due to diminishing patent activity on the part of major EU nations. This trend parallels the drop in R&D activity in some European countries. On the other hand, among Europe's smaller nations, Belgium, Finland and Spain have increased their patent activity to such an extent that the approximate overall EU level could be maintained, or, after 1992, even improved a bit.

In terms of patents, Germany holds a strong position in the research-intensive manufacturing sector within the EU. Germany does remain the world's third most important single country producer of technology, following Japan and the USA; it is also the most productive technology producer within Europe. However, in Germany in particular and in the EU in general, technological dynamism is increasingly concentrated on a few technologies. This trend clearly distinguishes the EU from the US. Although the degree of concentration is also increasing in the USA, the increase is only gradual. Despite this, the USA still has the world's most technologically diversified economy. Japan on the other hand is slowly dismantling a certain one-sidedness. As a result, patent activity is generally more broadly spread throughout various technologies. The degree of specialization in both Japan and Europe is distinctly higher than in the USA (REPORT, 1995).

A country's structural patterns change only in small increments. In Europe, technological strengths and weaknesses have remained approximately the same since the early 1980s. The technological know-how that has been accumulated over the course of many years and the experience gained in developing individual technologies ('technological accumulation') are presumably the reasons for the stability and parallelism of focal technological fields and the economic structures in major economies. Foreign trade structures in various sectors often parallel technological accumulation patterns as well: An above-average number of patents is often linked with comparatively high export volume (see section 4.3).

In comparison, Japan and the USA continue to specialize in R&D-intensive fields, whereas the share of patents generated by the R&D-intensive sector is below average in France, Great Britain, Germany, Italy and even in Sweden - just as it is in the EU in general.

The relative strengths in Europe's technology activity are clearly to be found in the automotive engineering, mechanical engineering and chemical sectors. These strengths reflect the international division of labor in R&D and foreign trade - how could it be otherwise? The microelectronics and instrument engineering industries report below-average 'R&D output'. The almost complementary structure of specialization patterns found in Japan and Europe is striking; Japan has weaknesses in those areas in which Europe shows its strength - and vice versa. Accordingly, the areas automatic data processing, telecommunications, instruments and consumer electronics head the list of technological strengths in Japan. Plastics is the only technological field from the chemical industry to be included on this list. Also worthy of note are the comparatively low shares in patents with global market-relevance for vehicles, machine tools (metal processing), machines for specific industries, service equipment and mechanical handling equipment, which still comprise major components in Japanese exports. This does not mean that Japan would not be in a position to manufacture technologically outstanding products and sell them on world markets. It does however mean that more recent Japanese technology does not comprise the fundamental basis for Japan's foreign trade position. The number of Japanese patents in aviation and aerospace technology is virtually negligible; Japan's patent and foreign trade structure patterns match each other well in these areas (compare section 4.3). The tremendous increase in technology productivity in the past 15 years has to be noted with an 'overshoot' around 1989-90 (see Figure 3).

Aviation and aerospace technology, certain areas in the chemical industry and modern microelectronics - with the exception of consumer electronics - are undoubtedly among the USA's technological strengths. Invention activity is low in electrical circuit technology and in mechanical and automotive engineering (excluding railway vehicles). A glance at the US portfolio also seems to indicate a striking similarity between the country's patent and foreign trade positions. Exceptions are however to be found in pharmaceuticals and turbines where a large number of patents is contrasted by less impressive world trade shares. On the other hand, the low patent shares in cutting-cdge electrical engineering and service equipment offer no indication of these product groups' relatively high world trade shares.

A different way to replace the unavailable technometric assessment is to ask for subjective ratings of experts. In the second round of the German as well as in the French Delphi surveys (CUHLS and KUWAHARA, 1994) it was asked for the international comparison of the level of research and development regarding 1147 specific topics. Figure 4 shows German and French experts' assessments about R&D levels. Percentages for 'USA', 'Japan', 'Europe' show the extent to which each country or country group is estimated to be a world leader in the various technological areas. It has to be noted that the survey differentiated between 'Germany', 'France' and 'other countries', whereby 'other countries' were identified to be EU countries in nearby all cases.

Overall, the R&D level of the United States and Europe is far above Japan. The survey seems to be biased in favor of Europe. Areas in which Europe is assessed as having a high level of R&D are mineral and water resources, urbanization and construction, agriculture and food, environment, energy, and transportation. In these six areas, Europe's R&D level is assumed to be the most advanced in the world. In contrast, areas in which Europe's R&D level is assessed as low are information and electronics, as the lowest, followed by communications. Even if the overall ratings may be biased in favor of Europe's position the sectoral breakdown seems to be reasonable and coincides with other data.

The United States have an R&D level far in excess of all others in the two advanced technological areas of life sciences, and information and electronics, as well as showing an overwhelming capability in space. Japan is assumed to be more advanced than the United States in production, and is also rated quite highly in communications, information and electronics, and materials and processing.

Figure 4:   Estimation of Current R&D Levels by Technology Area (German and French Delphi Surveys)

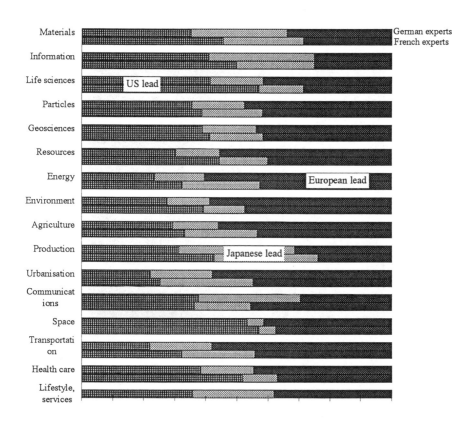

In Figure 5, the R&D level in the various triade regions for each technological stage combining all sectors is compared. Europe's R&D level seems to be lowest in development, and rises through successive stages of innovation and widespread use. The United States' R&D level is, according to the Delphi surveys, extremely high in basic research, then lower in the successive stages of development, innovation, and widespread use. Japan's R&D level in basic research is assumed to be quite low, while it is assessed as higher in all subsequent stages.

This clearly reflects the well developed basic science system in the US and Europe as compared to Japan and points to a specific transfer problem in Europe between the science and the 'developing', i. e. the business sector. In *using* technology, including overseas technology, Europe is stronger than in *developing* it.

Figure 5: R&D Level by Innovation Phases (German and French Delphi Surveys)

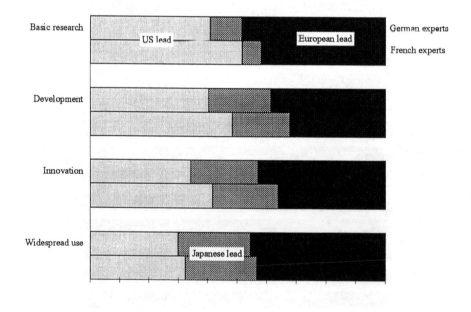

4.3 Implications of Technology Position for International Trade Dynamics

International competitiveness is an elusive concept. It is not the same as the micro-economic notion of competition between firms on markets. Whereas economic growth and subsequent welfare gains are illustrated in detail by various economic indicators, the impact of high technology production cannot yet be accounted for analogously. In the more recent literature comparative national advantages are regarded as being dominated by *absolute advantages*. These advantages result in different rates of macro-economic or sectoral activity which are caused by processes of cumulative causation. Thus, instead of looking at an international equilibrium of factor prices one has to focus on *persisting* differences in the rates of technological and economic development.

The measurement of international technological activity is almost entirely reduced to foreign trade vis-à-vis patent statistics. With the contributions of PAVITT and SOETE (1980), SOETE (1981, 1987), DOSI et al. (1990), LEGLER et al. (1992), GRUPP (1995) and MÜNT (1996) there is, however, a lot of evidence at hand that indicates that a strong relationship between an economy's technological and trade *specialization* exists. As far as the effects of *technological specialization* on economic growth - and, thus, a nation's competitiveness - are concerned, evidence is scarce, so far. Although we know about the overall positive relationship between the levels of innovativeness and economic activity as shown in the contributions of FAGERBERG (1988), DOSI et al. (1990), LEGLER et al. (1992) and AMENDOLA et al. (1993), we lack an exact understanding and evidence about the relationship between a nation's distribution of technological activity on selected technology fields and the induced effects on international trade and economic activity in *other* sectors. That means, our knowledge about what lures R&D funds away from some products into other technological fields, what brings about innovation in the latter fields and what are the implications this has on growth and competitiveness is, at best, incomplete.

Although we know that specialization in international trade is made up amount of resources spent on R&D and production. Thus, economies have to specialize economically and technologically - that is, select some areas and skip others. Which technological or product fields a country chooses for specialization depends on a variety of different factors. 'Natural' abundance of production factors, accumulated technological knowledge and skills in production, and the realized specialization of competitors on world markets rank among the most important.

According to theoretical literature, the basic drive for economic *change* is the country-specific adoption of different technological and economic paradigms which are adapted to the already existing national innovation structure. In comparison, radical structural change which opens totally new opportunities is a rather seldom phenomenon. Technical change is neither a free good or nor is it costlessly transferred between different countries but is shaped and generated in differing country-specific ways. Especially, it is the cumulative process of learning that gives a country the possibility to acquire technological knowledge that is distinct from that of other nations. Following the accumulation of this specific knowledge in single technological fields, an economy is able to allocate R&D funds to areas of built-up national advantages, more or less independent of any endowment with natural resources. The structural approach applied here (cf. GRUPP and MÜNT, 1996) - whereby structure is defined as distinct from the traditional sectors either as product groups or technological fields - allows for different technological potentials built up in a process of continuous technological learning in innovation and production. Note, that the accumulation and path-dependence of changes in trade pattern is called 'trade hysteresis' by KRUGMAN (1981) and GROSSMAN and HELPMAN (1991).

Most interestingly, the German Bundesbank (see DEUTSCHE BUNDESBANK, 1994), in an edition of its Monthly Report, published a macro-economic test of several monetary indicators which are supposed to reflect the price competitiveness of countries in changing world trade structures. Contrary to common belief, neither the terms of trade nor the wage rate in industry proved successful in testing against German dynamics in world market shares - a result which may not be very robust under alternative specifications. Thus, the Bundesbank's economists concluded, if the concept of price competitiveness should be of any use at all, it is not determined by the relative price of labor costs. Almost in line with this argument is the study of AMENDOLA et al. (1993) who showed convincingly that technology and investment variables are more pertinent to explain trade dynamics than other factors. Their most general result concerns the *long-term* effect of technical change both in its disembodied form as captured by patents, and embodied into fixed investments upon export dynamics. Thus, the approach used here seems to be justified both from theory and from empirical evidence.

As was argued in section 4.2 above, patent statistics are an accepted output indicator for codified knowledge from strategic and applied research and industrial development. As patent applications are legal documents that are valid in only one country, many foreign 'duplications' of domestic priority patent applications are generated. The selection of patent data from only one patent office, therefore, does not always yield an indicator that is representative of the world output of inventions. As duplications of patents can be traced and matched to each other, so-called patent families may be defined centering around one invention and bringing together the foreign property rights in all countries of the world. The selection criteria in the investigation which follows (see also Figure 3 above) was that only those inventions are taken into consideration where a foreign duplication at least in the United States, in Japan and at the European Patent Office was filed. By this selection criteria, the *'triade' model* is again applied as it is in section 4.2, requiring protection of industrial property in each of the triade blocs USA, Japan and Europe. The patents were assigned to product categories by a respective patent-to-sales concordance.

Following the above considerations, the technological know-how that has been accumulated over the course of many years and the experience gained in developing individual technologies ('technological accumulation') are presumably the reasons for the stability and parallelism of focal technological fields and the economic structures in major economies. Foreign trade structures in various sectors parallel technological accumulation patterns, indeed: An above-average number of patents is linked with comparatively high export volume (Figure 6).

Figure 6: Relation of Triade Patent Productivity to World Trade Share for High Technology in Major OECD Countries

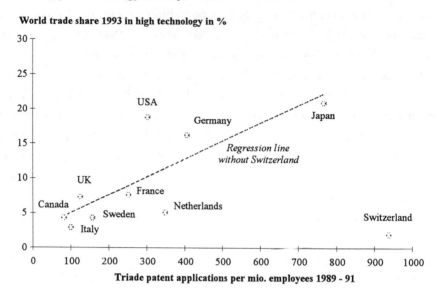

World trade share 1993 in high technology in %

Triade patent applications per mio. employees 1989 - 91

In addition to the overall treatment of technology *relative patent activity* and *relative world trade share* indexes may be used to compare technology and export structures. A country has a positive technology specialization irrespective of overall performance when her patent share in a specific technological area is larger than the average for all other countries. Specialization is negative when the country reports a below-average level of activity in the area under consideration. The exports specialization works in a similar fashion: it compares a country's share in overall world trade volume for a specific product group with her share in total exports of manufactured goods. Trade specialization rises when the product group's share in the respective country's basket of export commodities increases in comparison to the product's world market share. A positive specialization high export orientation: The respective country has had relatively greater success in penetrating foreign markets with this product group than suppliers of other goods. Analogously, the reverse applies for a negative specialization of exports (cf. LEGLER et al., 1992, among other sources for the respective formulae).

In terms of world trade shares, Japan has been the world's largest export nation for years (21% of all R&D-intensive goods exported by all western industrialized nations), followed by the USA with nearly 19% and Germany with

16% (compare Figure 6). Compared to previous years, the USA and Canada, as well as Japan to a lesser extent, were able to improve their positions - mainly through an intensified exchange coupled with an economic upswing in the USA, and through their proximity to growing markets in Southeast Asia. By contrast, most of Europe's industrialized nations - which are much more dependent on foreign trade than are either Japan or the USA - were in a recession. Consequently, it was scarcely possible for them to enlarge their world trade shares. (The Netherlands constituted the only exception, particularly in the field of information technology.)

The USA has massive comparative advantages throughout the entire range of leading-edge technologies in the narrower sense. The lover overall average for R&D-intensive products is due to the unfavorable balance reported for cars and consumer electronics. As is also the case in France and Great Britain, the USA's stable position in leading-edge technologies is strongly dependent upon substantial R&D activity in military-related areas which are not likely to enjoy the same preferential treatment in future government R&D budgets as they have in the past. Japan has unusually strong advantages arising from its specialization in advanced technologies *and* leading-edge technologies. Imports of research-intensive products have a much lower share in the domestic market in Japan than in countries of comparable size, while there is a dependence on leading-edge technology imports. This would indicate that barriers to market entry continue to exist. All in all, a review of the national portfolios of major economies reveals a large degree of similarity in technological foci and world trade advantages. The distribution of comparative advantages and disadvantages in foreign trade often corresponds to a country's 'technological accumulation'.

Comparatively seen, Germany's export-import ratios for R&D-intensive products, as well as those of the USA, have continually fallen over a longer period. Japan's ratios rose rapidly until 1988 but have since edged downward. Japan has apparently already passed its peak with regard to specialization in research-intensive products. Great Britain and France tend to concentrate on leading-edge technologies. They also commit a large portion of their industrial R&D resources to these areas. The high-level technology field remains Germany's domain. In this area, Germany is the only country to show above-average market results, even vis-à-vis the USA and Japan. Germany's relatively robust position in international competition is due primarily to its strength in this area. France and Great Britain distinctly trail in these market segments.

Although less specialized than Japan, Germany has approximately the same level of specialization as Switzerland and an even greater level than the USA. Other industrialized nations such as Belgium, Great Britain and the USA follow at some distance. The research-intensive sector in France, Sweden and Spain represents approximately an average share in the world market. No other country has comparative advantages in these markets. In this context, 'specialization' and 'comparative advantages' mean that the ratio of exports to imports is better than the average for the respective industry. Great Britain - and the USA in particular - would rank considerably higher if export performance were the only factor taken into consideration, as is done when calculating specialization values. These countries are relatively open to technological imports. On the other hand, Germany, and Japan in particular, have strong import-substitution sectors as well.

Special comments on Ireland are called for. Given its level of R&D endowment, the country has an unexpectedly high specialization ranking. Ireland benefits especially from intensive interrelations with the UK and from the trend among multinational corporations toward separating research facilities from production plants wherever possible. Ireland has repeatedly succeeded in attracting 'mobile' production facilities in R&D-intensive industries. The share of industries that are R&D-intensive in name only is correspondingly high in Ireland. Evaluating data from threshold nations often involves similar problems. The necessary know-how is imported together with the production facilities.

4.4 The Role of Small Firms for Innovation and Employment

AUDRETSCH (1995) suggests that divergences in the expected value regarding new knowledge will, under certain conditions, lead an agent to exercise what Albert O. HIRSCHMAN (1970) has termed as *exit* rather than *voice*, and depart from an incumbent enterprise to launch a new firm. But who is right, the departing agents or those agents remaining in the organizational decision making hierarchy who, by assigning the new idea a relatively low value, have effectively driven the agent with the potential innovation away? *Ex post* the answer may not be too difficult. But given the uncertainty inherent in new knowledge, the answer is anything but trivial *a priori.* When a new firm is started, its prospects are shrouded in uncertainty. If the new firm is built around a new idea, i.e., potential innovation, it is uncertain whether there is sufficient demand for the new idea or if some competitor will have the same or even a superior idea. Even if the new firm is formed to be an exact replica of a successful incumbent enterprise, it is uncertain whether sufficient demand will prevail in the future. Tastes can change, and new ideas emerging from other firms will certainly influence those tastes. Finally, an additional layer of uncertainty pervades a new enterprises. It is not known how competent the new firm really is, in terms of management, organization, and workforce. At least incumbent enterprises know something about their underlying competencies from past experience. Thus, a new enterprise is burdened with uncertainty as to whether it can produce and market the intended product as well as sell it. In both cases the degree of uncertainty will typically exceed that confronting incumbent enterprises.

The initial condition of not just uncertainty, but greater degree of uncertainty vis-à-vis incumbent enterprises in the industry is reflected in the theory of noisy firm selection and industry evolution proposed by JOVANOVIC (1982). Jovanovic presents a model in which the new firms, which he terms *entrepreneurs*, face costs that are not only random but also differ across firms. A central feature of the model is that a new firm does not know what its cost function is, that is its relative efficiency, but rather discovers this through the process of learning from its actual post-entry performance. In particular, JOVANOVIC (1982) assumes that entrepreneurs are unsure about their ability to manage a new-firm startup and therefore their prospects for success. Although entrepreneurs may launch a new firm based on a vague sense of expected post-entry performance, they only discover their true ability – in terms of managerial competence and of having based the firm on an idea that is viable on the market – once their business is established. Those entrepreneurs who discover that their ability exceeds their expectations expand the scale of their business, whereas those discovering that their post-entry performance is less than commensurate with their expectations will contract the scale of output and possibly exit from the industry. Thus, Jovanovic's model is a theory of noisy selection, where efficient firms grow and survive and inefficient firms decline and fail.

The role of learning in the selection process has been the subject of considerable debate. On the one hand is what has been referred to as the *Larackian* assumption that learning refers to adaptations made by the new enterprise. In this sense, those new firms that are the most flexible and adaptable will be the most successful in adjusting to whatever the demands of the market are. As NELSON and WINTER (1982, p. 11) point out, "Many kinds of organizations commit resources to learning; organizations seek to copy the forms of their most successful competitors."

On the other hand is the interpretation that the role of learning is restricted to discovering if the firm is viable in terms of the goods it is producing as well as the way they are being produced. Under this interpretation the new enterprise is not necessarily able to adjust to market conditions, but receives information based on its market performance with respect to its *fitness* in terms of meeting demand more efficiently vis-à-vis rivals. The theory of organizational ecology proposed by HANNAN and FREEMAN (1989) most pointedly adheres to the notion that, "We assume that individual organizations are characterized by relative inertia in structure." That is, firms learn not in the sense that they adjust their actions as reflected by their fundamental identity and purpose, but in the sense of their perception. What is then learned is whether or not the firm is viable, but not necessarily how to make it viable.

The theory of firm selection is particularly appealing in view of the rather startling small size of most new manufacturing firms. For example, the man size of more than 11,000 new-firm startups in the manufacturing sector of the United States was found to be fewer than eight workers per firm (AUDRETSCH, 1995). A similarly small start-up size for new manufacturing firms has been found by MATA (1994) for Portugal and WAGNER (1994) for Germany. While the minimum efficient scale (MES) varies substantially across industries, and even to some degree across various product classes within any given industry, the observed size of most new firms is sufficiently small to ensure that the bulk of new firms will be operating at a suboptimal scale of output. Why would an entrepreneur start a new firm that would immediately be confronted by scale disadvantages?

An important implication of the dynamic theory of firm selection and industry evolution (AUDRETSCH, 1995) is that new firms may begin at a small, and even suboptimal, scale of output. Then, if merited by subsequent performance, they will grow. Those new firms that are successful will grow, whereas those that are not will remain small and may ultimately be forced to exit from the industry. A recent wave of studies has determined not only is the likelihood of a new entrant surviving quite low, but that the likelihood of survival is positively related to firm size and firm age. These relationships have been found to hold for Portugal (MATA, 1994), Germany (WAGNER, 1994), and Canada (BALDWIN and RAFIQUZZAMAN, 1995).

Some fifteen years ago, David Birch revealed some startling findings from his study of job generation in the United States. Despite the prevailing conventional wisdom at that time, BIRCH (1981, p. 8) reported that, "whatever else they are doing, large firms are no longer the major providers of new jobs for Americans. Rather, Birch claimed to have discovered that most new jobs emanated from small firms. Birch's findings triggered a storm of controversy that has only intensified in the 1990s. Perhaps in response to the controversy triggered by Birch's study, a wave of studies emerged during the 1980s examining the links between firm size and age on the one hand, and job creation on the other. In a 1989 article on "The Disciples of David Birch," INC magazine reported that "The debate keeps raging: How important are small, growing companies to the US economy? Do they really create most of the new jobs? There's a lot of bad information on the subject being bandied about – but increasing numbers of researchers are assembling hard evidence, even going out and counting companies themselves."[1]

Such job generation studies were also undertaken outside of the United States. For example, a study for Italy (INVERNIZZI and REVELLI, 1993) found that overall job creation and destruction accounted for 8% of annual manufacturing employment during the 1980s. The entry and exit of firms accounted for between one-third and one-quarter of gains and losses in employment. As in the case of the United States, small firms were found to contribute positively to net employment, while large firms were found to be net job destroyers.

GALLAGHER, DALY, and THOMASON (1991) used Dun and Bradstreet credit rating data to measure job generation in the United Kingdom over the 1980s. They found that between 1985 and 1987 small firms provided 48% of all new jobs, greatly exceeding their share of employment, which was 21% in 1985. By contrast, the largest enterprises, defined as having at least 1,000 employees, provided only 13% of all new jobs, although they accounted for 37% of 1985 employment. Their results were generally consistent with two previous studies they had undertaken for the 1971-81 and 1982-84 periods.

---

[1] "The Disciples of David Birch: A New Generation of Researchers is out to Discover How the U.S. Economy Really Works," INC, January 1989, pp. 39-45.

While the propensity for large and small firms to create jobs was clearly found to vary across sectors of the economy, countries, and time periods, Birch's results seemed to hold up qualitatively, in that most studies found that new and small firms generate more than their share of new jobs. Still, there was no consensus. For example, and OECD study "expresses skepticism about the assumption that small enterprises will be the motor of job creation."[2] What has become known as the *OECD Jobs Study* (OECD, 1994a) stresses that, "the large claims made for the job creation ability of small enterprises are often based on faulty statistics...a more correct statement is that small establishments are disproportionately responsible for both gross job gains and losses."[3]

Still, the findings in most of the job generation studies (LOVEMAN and SENGENBERGER, 1991) show that when rates of job creation, job destruction, and net employment changes are calculated by size class, smaller plants and firms are generally found to have the highest rates of job creation and job destruction. Most strikingly, while the rates of net job change, or job creation minus job destruction, tend to be the greatest in small producers and the lowest in large producers, small firms tend to exhibit a positive rate of net job change, while their larger counterparts tend to exhibit a negative rate of net job change.

Just when the debate seemed to be converging towards a consensus – that small firms provide the engine of job creation – DAVIS, HALTIWANGER and SCHUH (1996a) injected considerable doubt by arguing that the findings of most job generation studies are based on a statistical fallacy. According to DAVIS, HALTIWANGER and SCHUH (1996a), "Most longitudinal studies of the relationship between employer size and job creation suffer from a statistical pitfall known as the regression fallacy or regression-to-the-mean bias. The potential for bias arises whenever employers experience transitory fluctuations in size, or whenever measurement error introduces transitory fluctuations in observed size. Both phenomena are important features of longitudinal data on employers." They show that when various corrections are made for regression-to-the-mean, it is the large firms and not the small enterprises that account for higher rates of net job change (measured as gross job creation minus gross job destruction).

The regression-to-the-mean objection to the job generation studies was first made by LEONARD (1986), who pointed out that if plants and firms have a long-

---

[2] "Skepticism on Job Creation Role of Small Business," Financial Times, 20 July, 1994, p. 7.
[3] "Skepticism on Job Creation Role of Small Business," Financial Times, 20 July, 1994, p. 7.

run equilibrium size that is different from their current level, due to a stochastic shock or random shock, they will tend to adjust intertemporally towards their long-run equilibrium level. Large firms will tend to have grown as a result of such stochastic fluctuations, and small firms will tend to have been adversely influenced by such random shocks. An implication is that employment statistics will tend to identify small producers growing on average and large producers declining.

Based on United States Census Bureau data for manufacturing plants between 1972 and 1988, DAVID, HALTIWANGER and SCHUH (1996b) find that small firms and plants dominate the creation and destruction of jobs in the United States manufacturing sector. Smaller manufacturing firms and plants were found to exhibit sharply higher *gross* rates of job creation but not higher *net* rates of job creation.

However, after correcting for the regression-to-the mean problem, BALDWIN and PICOT (1995) find that the net job creation for smaller establishments in Canadian manufacturing exceeds that of large establishments. In a related paper, PICOT and DUPUY (forthcoming) correct the longitudinal data base for the influence of the transient component of employment change and find the same results.

WAGNER (1995) also corrected for the regression-to-the-mean problem in analyzing the relationship between firm size and job creation in the German federal state of Lower Saxony between 1978 and 1993. As in the American and Canadian studies, Wagner fund that gross job creation and destruction rates tend to appear to be systematically related to the size of the firm, as measured by average employment in the base and final year. Most recently, a government study found that between 1997 and 1994 establishments with fewer than 20 employees created 1.2 million new jobs, which accounted for two-thirds of all new jobs created.[4]

Does creative destruction, as captured by the extent of market turbulence, lead to higher job creation, in the manner posited by Joseph Schumpeter in 1911? While some preliminary evidence for the United States does provide evidence for the *Schumpeterian* Thesis (AUDRETSCH, 1995), AUDRETSCH and FRITSCH (1996) find no evidence that job creation is associated with a turbulent environment, at least in the case of West Germany during the late 1980s. In fact, in both the manufacturing and service sectors a high rate of turbulence in a region tends to lead

---

[4] "Studie: Kleinbetriebe schaffen mehr neue Jobs," Die Welt, 15 March, 1996, p. 11.

to a lower and not a higher rate of growth. This negative relationship is attributable to the fact that the underlying components – the birth and death rates – are both negatively related to subsequent job creation. That is, those regions with higher rates of new-firm startup activity tend to experience less job creation in subsequent years. Most strikingly, the same is true for the exit rates. Those regions that experience higher exit rates also tend to experience less job creation in subsequent years.

KONINGS (1995) uses the Workplace Industrial Relations Surveys of 1980, 1984 and 1990 of plant level employment data to analyze the relationship between establishment size and gross job creation and destruction in the United Kingdom during the 1980s. Konings finds that the gross job creation rate is higher in small establishments and lower in large establishments. By contrast, the gross job destruction rate is lowest in the small plants and highest in large establishments. Thus, in contrast to the American, Canadian and German studies cited above, Konings finds that, in absolute numbers, the larger plants create most jobs but also destroy the most jobs.

BROERSMA and GAUTIER (forthcoming) use longitudinal data from the Netherlands Central Bureau of Statistics between 1978 and 1991 to identify the link between firm size and job flows. They find that both job creation and job destruction tend to be negatively related to firm size in the Netherlands. However, the evidence still suggests that small firms contribute the most to *net* job growth.

BROWN, HAMILTON and MEDOFF (1990) draw a number of economic welfare conclusions regarding the recent shift in job creation away from large enterprises and toward smaller enterprises. After documenting the systematically lower wages and poor working conditions associated with smaller enterprises, in terms of hours worked and the safety and health environments, they conclude that there is a net economic welfare loss associated with such a shift in economic activity. Thus, BROWN, HAMILTON and MEDOFF (1990, pp. 88-89) conclude that, "Workers in large firms earn higher wages, and this fact cannot be explained completely by differences in labor quality, industry, working conditions, or union status. Workers in large firms also enjoy better benefits and greater job security than their counterparts in small firms. When these factors are added together, it appears that workers in large firms do have a superior employment package."

The positive relationships between wage and non-wage benefits on the one hand, and firm size on the other, have been confirmed to hold across a wide spectrum of countries. For example, OOSTERBEEK and VAN PRAAG (1995) found that the positive relationship between firm size and employee compensation holds in the Netherlands. WAGNER (forthcoming) similarly finds along with wages, quality of job training apprenticeships tend to be positively related to firm size in Germany.

However, the conclusions by BROWN, HAMILTON and MEDOFF (1990) and others are generally based on a static analysis. AUDRETSCH, VAN LEEUWN, MANKVELD and THURIK (1995) examine the link between employee compensation and firm size through the dynamic lens provided by a longitudinal data base of Dutch manufacturing workers. They find that firm age exerts a positive impact on productivity and employee compensation. As firms mature they become more productive and raise the level of employee compensation, even after controlling for the size of the firm. This new finding suggests that not only will some of the small and sub-optimal firm of today become the large and optimal firms of tomorrow, but that there is at least a high tendency for the low productivity and low wage firm of today to become the high productivity and wage firm of tomorrow. Thus, the links between firm size on the one hand, and productivity growth and wages on the other appear to be very different when viewed through a dynamic lens rather than through a static lens.

4.5 Foreign Direct Investment and Labor Market Problems

Since 1985 international direct investment has been growing much faster than trade (SIEBERT, 1991; UNCTAD, 1996). An increasing share of employment, R&D and investment of industrial firms in OECD countries is taking place abroad. At the same time multinational companies' activities have become increasingly important in these fields for host countries (see appendix I, Table A2). Foreign direct investment as a two-way flow between countries certainly is economically beneficial. From an EU perspective the adjustment problems which occur in partner countries with major outflows are of minor importance if such outflows are going to other EU countries. For example, if German foreign investment outflows increase and mainly go - at the margin - to France, the UK or the Benelux countries one may anticipate limited macroeconomic problems for Germany as a higher stock of German FDI given that the countries are Germany's main export destinations will stimulate higher German exports. This holds because of two effects, namely the positive effects of FDI on the production potential and hence on real income abroad and because German subsidiaries abroad are likely to have a strong preference for using machinery and equipment from German (and other EU) producers. Since FDI outflows are motivated by net returns on investment exceeding that in the source country one may expect that FDI outflows remaining in the Community contribute to a higher Community marginal product of capital Y_K.

However, even with positive income effects in other EU countries a major EU source country with rising FDI outflows will face the problem that its aggregate domestic investment output ratio I/Y (I/Y times Y_K equals the growth rate of output) will fall to the extent that there are large FDI outflows not compensated by FDI inflows from EU partner countries or from outside source countries. For the EU as a whole high FDI inflows from the US and Japan (plus Asian NICs) would be quite crucial. One may note, however, that US outflows in 1995 were very unevenly concentrated within the Community: the Netherlands ($12.3), Sweden ($9.6) and the UK ($8.7), trailed by France, Belgium and Germany with $4.8, 3.6 and 3.4 billion respectively, received the bulk of US direct investment abroad in Europe in 1995 (DEPARTMENT OF COMMERCE, 1996, p.48). On the basis of the Dutch figures Germany and France should have received some $50 billion and 40 billion of inflows from the US alone while the actual figure was just 1/10. Hence a low investment output ratio in the EU can partly be attributed to insufficient extra-EU FDI inflows into Germany and France. The falling investment-output ratios in the EU-9 in the 1980s imply - compared to the more stable US investment-output ratio - a capital shortage. In this light high EU labor productivity growth rates observed in the EU seem surprising. However, a considerable part of this productivity growth is due to redundancies which raise average labor productivity. Insufficient EU capital formation can be partly explained by high public budget deficits (and insufficient infrastructure investment) and insufficient profitability of investment.

European societies apparently find it more difficult to accept high income dispersions between capital owners and workers - a traditional perspective which might be quite dysfunctional for a future European high tech society. If globalization requires a new international division of labor in which the EU, the US and Japan move strongly toward an expansion of services and high technology manufacturing, investment and innovation projects in the EU will become more risky. This implies a (higher) risk premium for capital owners or entrepreneurs and therefore tends to accentuate gross income dispersion. To correct this via a system of progressive income taxation will be quite difficult in an era of increased global capital mobility. Instead one could reduce income dispersion across households by government-promoted savings plans for workers investing in EU or other investment funds. Such funds typically are superior to employee ownership programs (disregarding exceptions) because they reduce income risk due to the pooling of different assets and their liquidity is relatively high.

4.6 Telecoms Liberalization and Employment Growth in the Information Society

Telecommunications is among the fastest growing economic activities in OECD countries and eastern Europe. The telecom network does not only allow people to talk to each other but is also the basis for communication within and across firms. Learning about new technologies, product innovations and business options for new profitable joint ventures or mergers & acquisitions is facilitated by the use of telecommunications. Modern telecoms networks are typically used by firms for voice telephony but even more for data transmission and, increasingly, for video conference applications and multimedia services. The European Commission already emphasized in a 1984 paper the importance of modern telecommunications networks and services in the EU, namely as a contribution to international competitiveness. This indeed follows from the perception that an expanded telecommunications infrastructure is a catalyst for technological progress since users will learn faster about new technologies, profitable business partnerships and new market trends. To date it was rather unclear how important the contribution of telephony really is.

A study by JUNGMITTAG and WELFENS (1996) gives a first estimate of the contribution of telecommunications to economic growth for western Germany in the period of 1961-90. Based on the estimation of a production function with labor, capital, patents, real license expenditures (representing mainly licenses imported) and telephone connections - as a proxy for telephone use - the authors obtain a remarkable result: telecommunications explains more than 1/4 of economic growth in Germany's enterprise sector which comprises all sectors except the housing rent sector and agriculture. The following table gives the estimated and actual growth rates in the enterprise sector in the two bottom rows, while the rows above inform about the absolute contribution of capital (k), labor (l), patents (pat), real license expenditures (la) and telephone connections (tv). According to these results the growth of the capital stock is most important for economic growth, while the use of telecommunications comes second; the latter explains between 0.7 and 1.7 percentage points.

Table 13: Explaining the Growth of Real Gross Value-added in the Enterprise Sector

Source of growth	Average annual growth rate						
	61 - 90	61 - 65	66 - 70	71 - 75	76 - 80	81 - 85	86 - 90
k_t	1,5	2,5	1,9	1,8	1,1	0,8	1,0
l_t	0,2	0,7	0,1	-0,6	0,5	-0,6	1,1
pat_{t-2}	0,1	0,3	0,2	-0,3	0,2	0,1	0,3
la_t	0,3	0,4	0,3	0,3	0,0	0,0	0,8
tv_t	1,1	1,2	1,7	1,2	1,3	0,7	0,7
Total:							
Estimated	3,3	5,2	4,3	2,3	3,2	0,9	4,0
Actual	3,3	5,2	4,4	1,7	3,6	1,1	3,8

Note: The sum of the individual growth rate components may diverge from total estimated growth rates due to rounding.

Source: JUNGMITTAG, A. and WELFENS, P.J.J. (1996), Telekommunikation, Innovation und die langfristige Produktionsfunktion: Theoretische Aspekte und eine Kointegrationsanalyse für die Bundesrepublik Deutschland, EIIW Discussion Paper No. 20, Potsdam University, p. 25.

The EU-wide deregulation of telecommunications will stimulate economic growth in Europe. With the liberalization date of 1998 the European Commission gave an important starting date for the full liberalization of voice telephony and network operation. Dominant operators will face increasing competition from domestic and foreign newcomers which will rely on internal networks (energy companies, railway networks) or dual use of existing cable TV networks, or even satellite networks. Value-added services were already liberalized in the early 1990s in the EU.

One may anticipate that cheaper telecom user rates will encourage firms to optimally pursue the gathering of information about technology and market trends as well as facilitate the cooperation among new partners - sometimes even creating a virtual company. In countries in which competition in the telecoms sector was introduced relatively early (US and UK since 1984, Scandinavia, Australia and New Zealand in the 1990s) cheap network user prices have encouraged the increasing professional use of telecommunications networks. Since EU liberalization is coupled with the privatization of telecoms companies one may expect a double growth impulse from telecoms deregulation: (1) In the face of competition private telecoms companies will develop new product varieties and productivity enhancing services, (2) cheaper services will stimulate more widespread application of new services and more sophisticated network capacity. Dominant operators will have to reduce their workforce after liberalization but the overall employment impact of deregulating telecommunications is expected to be positive since cheaper and more innovative telecoms services are expected to generate additional employment as are newcomers in network operation (OECD 1995a).

While it is clear that slow EU growth ultimately can be overcome only if there is a sustained rise in capital formation the modernization of telecommunications in a more competitive framework will support economic growth. Full privatization of existing dominant operators and asymmetric regulation to encourage the market entry of newcomers are required in Europe. Virtual firms, research centers and universities could be created on the basis of modern cheap EU telecom networks.

4.6.1 Specifics of High-Technology Industry and the Information Sector

The stock of knowledge - including basic research - share basic characteristics of a public good and can be considered as a nonrival input. Since the costs of R&D are largely financed by private firms (and since benefits are difficult to fully appropriate by the innovator) while the benefits of R&D progress could accrue to all firms in a region, a market economy is unlikely to come up with a socially optimum R&D budget. While this argument of the literature is valid for competitive markets it is less relevant in the oligopolistic markets where firms face strong rivalry and interdependency; the latter could imply excessive patent racing.

Given the new mix of cheap telecoms networks, powerful computer technology and international service providers in the information society, knowledge can be transferred across firms, sectors and countries in an unprecedented manner. The liberalization and internationalization of the telecommunications sector will stimulate economic growth in OECD countries (WELFENS and GRAACK, 1996). In the information society technological progress of the unembodied type could become increasingly significant. Skilled personnel which is able to use technologically relevant information will then become more important. Indeed in the modern service society capital intensity could fall. The information intensity, by contrast, will increase; as will the skill requirements in the labor markets. This could have serious implications for training and education in information societies.

4.6.2 Displacement Effects of Telecoms Liberalization and New Employment Opportunities

The important question regarding the development of the telecommunications sector and job growth has been analyzed in several studies, e.g. SEUFERT (1996). In these analyses the focus is mainly on three aspects of the European information society: (1) The fact that there will be structural changes in European labor markets as a consequence of the new information and communication technology (ICT). Since mass media utilization and communication behavior change only gradually, the process of multimedia diffusion is expected to be faster in the business sector than in the private household sector - with process innovations dominating in the medium term over product innovations. On the one hand, a changing employment structure will result from the development towards the information society: the share of information jobs increased from 18% of the German labor force in 1950 to 51% in 1995. On the other hand, there will be growth in the ICT producing industries. (2) The prospects for additional jobs, which are considered as rather limited because new jobs are accompanied by the melting away of old jobs. (3) The steps required by economic policymakers in order to generate employment growth in the European information society, where specific steps are necessary to nurture the expansion of information related employment opportunities. At the bottom line often stands a rather skeptical view with emphasis on productivity gains stimulated by ICT and on aggregate growth effects that are generated by improved international competitiveness.

While the analysis gives a clear and well-founded picture of the main impacts of the information and communication industry one might point to a more optimistic long-term perspective if one takes into account several changes in both the regulatory area in Europe and in the structure of industry since the 1990s. In anticipation of the liberalization of telecommunications services and network operation in the EU in 1998 deregulation, privatization and internationalization processes are characterizing Europe (WELFENS and GRAACK, 1996). Deregulation will allow new market entrants to enter highly profitable segments of the telecommunications market which will become more competitive, while prices for equipment and transmissions will fall under this new pressure. This will facilitate the entry of newcomers in the services market, who will also benefit from the fact that the service sector is less capital-intensive than industry. Privatization will expose dominant telecoms operators to stock market pressure and thereby stimulate productivity-enhancing reorganization and revenue-generating product innovations. With dominant operators in each EU country facing newcomers in the home market there exists a natural incentive for internationalization. Thus, large international networks could be built at falling international communication costs. This has the effect of reinforcing the integration of all markets in Europe. These pro-competitive effects could help European firms improve their global competitiveness. Thus, the lead of the US in telecommunications and computer technology could be eroded if European companies follow the successful strategy of GSM mobile telecommunication.

A specific feature of the information society will probably be network sharing, in the sense that firms and individuals can use powerful software - and hence productivity raising - via various computer networks. Improved opportunities to organize part-time work is likely to stimulate labor supply. New technological options to store information will gradually expose part of the service to stock-building cycles and to cyclical changes in general (WYCKOFF, 1996).

The rapid progress scenario of METIER assumes that interactive communication services with up to 34Mbits/s will be available to almost 90% of all EU businesses by 2003. A more optimistic vision is that by 2005 the majority of EU firms will have access to ATM switches with a speed of 155Mbits/s. For both the telecommunications network and equipment, the Bureau of Labor Statistics predict employment increases of 2% annually, but these figures seem somewhat over-optimistic (NOAM, 1993). Crucial for a more optimistic scenario will be the development of cable TV networks in Europe. US cable TV companies, which until 1996 were not allowed to enter the US telecoms market, have contributed to the expansion of telecoms services via cable TV network. If cable TV networks on the continent are quickly liberalized and - in the case of Portugal and Germany demonopolized and fully privatized - one may expect a boom in telecoms services in the context of falling prices.

A sector which will particularly benefit from a more competitive telecoms sector is international banking (WIELAND, 1995). EU financial market integration could be much stimulated by reduced transaction costs and greater transparency in financial markets. With investors facing a richer set of investment opportunities the pressure on firms' management to maintain efficiency and a strong innovation record will increase. A high marginal product of capital will stimulate economic growth. While the overall employment impact of ICT is likely to be positive due to induced price reductions creating new demand, it is unclear which EU countries will benefit most (GRAACK, 1996). Given its underdeveloped service sector Germany is likely to benefit strongly from productivity growth in the service sector.

Cheaper and innovative services can be crucial for the international competitiveness of industry. Moreover, cheaper and faster networks in Europe will facilitate the organization of pan-European companies, which in turn will stimulate the formation of EU multinational companies that will be more active competitors in world markets. Innovative and cheap networks plus services should facilitate the rationalization of government and, thereby, the reduction of government expenditures as well as taxes. Lower wage tax rates will raise employment. An important development in OECD countries after 1985 concerns the fact that foreign direct investment flows in services have outpaced those in manufacturing. The long-term rise in foreign direct investment supports the expansion of the information and communication sector which provides vital service for MNCs.

A more optimistic scenario founders on problems of venture capital financing in the information and communication industry. Given the low capital intensity of this sector, banks often find it difficult to provide loans for newcomers since there is insufficient collateral. Innovative venture capital financing in continental Europe is urgently needed to overcome this bottleneck for the expansion of the service sector. As the service sector in advanced OECD countries increasingly accounts for innovations, government support for the expansion of this sector is crucial. Hence, the role of stock markets, which provide risk capital, needs to be strengthened in Europe. Adequate tax incentives for new service firms and industrial newcomers - and less favorable treatment for investment in the housing sector - are required in the EU.

With the further development of the information society one should expect a rising share of employees working in the information sector. This sector can be seen as a distinct sector within a four sector model of structural change (see Fig. 7). A recent analysis by NEFIODOW (1991) contains arguments for the occurrence of a new long wave of innovation and growth where expansion is based on the increasing use of information technology. The sectoral composition of employment growth will, therefore, continue to change.

With rapidly growing public and private networks worldwide and falling network user costs the diffusion of new knowledge will accelerate. Leading OECD countries face prospects of declining first mover advantages in all industries. In eastern Europe and the developing world the skill level of employees and the endowment with hardware plus software are appropriate for efficient retrieval and adaptation procedures. Countries in the EU, however, have a new advantage in the information society, namely the creation of virtual firms and universities which link know-how and expertise across countries in an innovative way. Moreover, the global information highway will create new opportunities for EU firms to team up with partners in eastern Europe, the US or Asia.

Figure 7:   Employment Developments in a Four-Sector-Model (1800-2010)

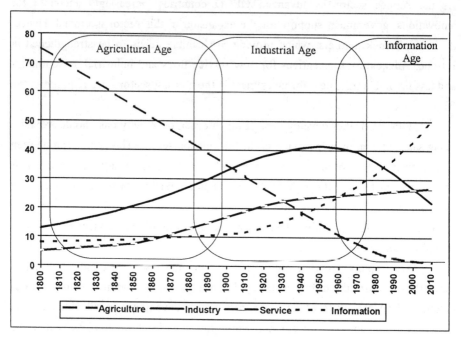

Source: EU Informationen (1995), February 1995, No. 2, p. 5.

5. European R&D Policy

The legal basis for supranational research and technology policy in the Community is laid down in specific articles of the ECSC Treaty (steal and coal union), the EAEC Treaty (nuclear research) and the EC Treaty, the Single European Act and the Treaty of Maastricht on European Union. According to the latter there are framework programs for R&D policy which have to be adopted unanimously by the Council (Art. 130i) and specific programs which require a qualified majority. The main objectives of the common R&D policy is to provide impulses for welfare-increasing progress in important technological fields (e.g. energy saving, new technologies, environment) and to stimulate the diffusion of new technologies. The idea is to develop coordinated national policies as well as supranational research activities, where the concrete aims are (PALINKAS, 1994):

- improving the efficiency of projects by task and cost sharing or use of pooling resources;
- supporting the single market by helping to achieve common standards;
- promoting research projects that referring to transfrontier problems (e.g. environment and public health);
- eliminating unwarranted duplication of national R&D programs;
- helping to reduce unemployment in the Community through new technologies and product innovations. International cooperative R&D ventures - such as Eureka (the Eureka initiative of 1985 is not a Community program, but a program in which the EU participates) - are designed to reinforce technological progress;
- strengthening the scientific and technological bases of Community industry and encouraging it to become more competitive at the international level (Art. 130f of the Maastricht Treaty). "The Community and the Member States shall coordinate their...activities so as to ensure that national policies and Community policy are mutually consistent" (Art. 130h).

The EU very much emphasizes the coordination of national programs. While this may be useful in many fields the time-consuming coordination procedures are neither necessary nor useful over the whole range of projects. Each member country should have a few "wild card projects" which require no coordination ex ante so that competing concepts of R&D can be pursued in some fields. There should be an optimum balance between coordination and conceptual competition. Market forces in the single market later often act later as a catalyst for coordination.

Political Basis and Economic Analysis of Research and Technology Development
EU countries no longer face the common threat of the USSR, so that the search for common economic benefits within the (enlarged) Community becomes increasingly important in the future. While the Common Agricultural Policy is losing economic and political weight, EU innovation policies become increasingly important as countries face the challenge of globalization and enjoy new opportunities to organize international R&D projects in an enlarged Community with rising intra-EU foreign direct investment (Europeanization of firms in the EU). One would expect EU countries' R&D expenditures relative to GDP to rise in the long term and reach the high levels prevalent in Japan and US. However, rising civilian R&D expenditure-GDP ratios were recently only observed in France, while Germany's ratio clearly declined after 1989 (STIFTERVERBAND, 1995; OECD, 1995b; NIW et al., 1996). The R&D orientation of the UK and the US (and France) - until the end of the Cold War markedly shaped by military R&D - changed in the early 1990s towards a higher share of civilian R&D. Together with the rising technology orientation of Asian NICs this implies sharply intensified competition in tradable civilian products, shorter innovation cycles and new impulses for joint R&D projects. It is unclear whether the EU's international competitiveness can be quickly reinforced in a period in which industry in the UK is at the end of a sharp structural contraction (with a parallel expansion of the service industry), while Germany and the Netherlands as well as other EU countries are recording falling R&D-GDP figures. Are there fewer technological opportunities for process or product innovations or are other factors at work? For example, problems in financing R&D projects by the private sector due to a more competitive single market - with a high number of privatized firms - and by the public sector due to budget consolidation based on the Maastricht criteria. It will be important to identify the present and future constraints of RTD in Europe.

There could be contradictions between the goals of EU RTD cooperation (listed below):

• a global approach for individual framework program participation to advance the EU's competitiveness;

- a regional approach with a focus on targeted improvements in S&T in selected regions;
- a bilateral approach to shape science and technology relations with particular countries;
- a multilateral approach for Community science and technology endeavor at world level.

Support for central and eastern European countries in the pre-adhesion phase could be particularly difficult if the EU itself experiences sustained and serious regional economic disparities. The new growth theory points to potential mechanisms that reinforce regional economic strengths during periods of intensified innovation and growth. If rising regional disparities are not to be associated with desirable higher economic growth in the Community one might have to look for specific new orientations of EU structural policy.

Clearly, the issue of overcoming the east-west income gap is even more pressing than reducing regional disparities within western European countries. Those countries which have introduced competition and privatization might also face the problem that desirable R&D cooperation undermines domestic competition and, thus, to some extent also international competitiveness. The analysis of the institutional organization of science and technology policy in the transforming countries is quite important as is the statistical analysis of key figures on RTD.

An important political basis for innovation policy in the EU is the Communication from the Commission "Perspective for International Cooperation in Research and Technological Development" [COM (95 489 final)]. Above all it sets out the new international context, changes in the conditions of RTD, global problems (S&T topics) of the 21st century as well as objectives, guiding principles and goals etc. The globalization of the economy, the economic opening up of eastern Europe and the emerging information society in OECD countries - in the EU much fostered by the liberalization of the telecommunications sector - are the main international trends identified by the Commission.

More intense technology trade in Europe will contribute to higher economic growth and employment which is urgently needed in both eastern and western Europe. The growing role of the service sector for technology-intensive sectors and innovation dynamics has also been neglected in the traditional literature and most policy analysis, although employment growth in the US clearly was dominated by job growth in the service sector in the 1980s and early 1990s. One important aspect of a growing innovative service sector is that it allows - due to a relatively low capital intensity - high employment and output growth to be achieved at a given savings rate. Prudent deindustrialization could, therefore, generate additional employment since a given investment output ratio could endow more service jobs with adequate capital.

5.1 Coordination Between National and EU R&D Policy

The coordination between national and EU R&D policy is naturally difficult. From an economic point of view it would be rational to allocate R&D competences at the supranational level only for those fields with a clear international dimension and cross-border technology spillovers. Such fields could be transeuropean networks, basic technologies, air pollution control and solar as well as climate research.

R&D Policy Implementation and Strategic Reform Options
EU policy implementation takes place in various forms. There are direct projects which are carried out by several Joint Research Centers (e.g. ISPRA); and indirect projects, which are organized by groups of research workers, labs and universities of EU member countries, where the EU gives partial financing. Finally, there are concerted projects which are carried out by participants from several EU member countries but for which the EU finances only coordination. In 1994 the fourth R&D framework program for research and technological development and demonstration was adopted (1994-98) and the Euratom Framework Programme for research and training. ECU 11 billion and ECU 1.25 billion were adopted for the two programs. After the accession of Austria, Sweden and Finland to the EU, the budget was increased to a maximum of ECU 13.1 billion for both programs. Additional funds will be allocated across the four topics of the framework programs: (1) research, technological and demonstration programs (10.045 billion); (2) cooperation with third countries and international organizations (0.575 billion); (3) dissemination and optimization of results (0.352); (4) stimulation of the training and mobility of researchers (0.795). Main headings under research topic 1 are information and communication technologies (0.3626), industrial technologies (2.125), and the

environment (1.150), life sciences and technologies (1.674), non-nuclear energy (1.067), and transport (0.256).

While in the early 1990s in Germany, France and the Benelux group about 2/3 of R&D expenditures were financed by the private sector, in the early 1990s the private sector percentage in Italy, Spain and France was about 45% (in Portugal and Greece even lower than this). In the US about 50% of R&D expenditures come from the private sector and in Japan the private percentage is even higher. Higher R&D tax credits which are the dominant state aid instrument in the US could play a more important role in the future in the EU. Subsidies which tend to be biased towards big firms with political connections should be reduced correspondingly.

High private sector shares in R&D financing are appropriate because otherwise the incentive for optimum innovation processes - geared towards marketable profitable products - will be undermined. Strengthening the role of capital markets and adequate tax reforms in certain EU countries could stimulate the share of private R&D financing. In addition to higher private R&D expenditures more training and retraining is required in Europe. The analysis of BOYER (1996, p. 126) shows that the frequency of training of employees was relatively high in Japan, the US and Sweden while - except for people with a basic educational level - it was low in Germany and France. This points to urgent reform needs in EU countries.

On a per capita expenditure basis - at purchasing power parities - US expenditures were more than twice as high as that in the Community, while Japan reached 178% of the Community level in 1990. In Japan and the US the number of scientists and engineers per 1000 working population is about twice as high as in the Community. One might consider introducing special technical universities which could be co-financed by the Community, regional government and industry. This would reinforce high technology research in the EU. According to the new growth theory such strong efforts could stimulate R&D, economic growth and exports in the long term. There is no need to tailor a selective (sectoral) industrial policy, rather a supranational university network and multinational training initiative could be appropriate. In certain regions (low income or with a declining industry) high tech training centers could be partly financed by regional policy funds with a focus on innovation.

The apparent Community deficit in R&D activities could be reduced by new research convergence policies of EU member countries and a new Community R&D

initiative. National governments should achieve R&D expenditures of at least 3.5 % of GDP in the long term, except for countries with a low share of industry. Supranational funds could be directed much more towards R&D financing. Only about 3% of EU funds (less than 5% of funds are spent on R&D at the national level) are spent on R&D. A figure of at least 20% would be appropriate in the long term, while the corresponding share of EU agricultural policy should strongly fall in turn.

Improved Reporting

The Community would have a difficult role to play if it wanted to assume any major political responsibility for employment developments. However, the Community can generate adequate national policy impulses by regular comparative reporting on national R&D efforts, employment effects and the global success (or failure) of EU innovations. It will be crucial to analyze regularly in which fields EU patenting is particularly intense and to which extent rising global and extra-EU export market shares correspond to relative patent positions.

There is a need for improved policy evaluation. Standardized national R&D reports - based on a minimum set of indicators - should be published annually as a means to improve the transparency and efficiency of innovation policies in the future. The Community and the European Parliament should also publish a comparative global R&D report every two years. Regular scientific evaluation of R&D policies should be undertaken at both the national and supranational level.

Strengthening Competition and New Agenda

Strengthening competition can often be a relatively cheap way to stimulate innovativeness and price or tax responsiveness of the economy. Traditional energy R&D policy support could be reduced in the medium term if liberalization of EU energy markets reinforces the pressure on companies to cut costs and increase efficiency. In a more competitive market new energy taxes would also have a stronger impact than in the present regional or national monopoly setting in which electricity companies in effect face a soft budget constraint. Privatization will also help to produce more flexible and innovative firms; e.g. the number of patents by Deutsche Telekom AG rapidly increased in the 1990s after the outlines of a liberalized global telecoms markets became clearer in 1991/92 and privatization was envisaged.

Given the ongoing internationalization and globalization of R&D the Community might encourage virtual R&D networks (of labs, firms and universities) by a special Network Program. Given the rapid growth of traffic volume in the single market R&D in the transport sector could be a new R&D focus of the Community. This would improve overall resource productivity in the capital-intensive transportation sector.

Employment can be created via cost cutting (i.e. technological progress) and product innovations which will stimulate the emergence of new markets. One might consider encouraging such innovations by allowing big firms in certain industries in the EU to merge and, at the same time, by stimulating the entry of newcomers in high-technology markets. Supporting newcomers should be a priority of an employment-augmenting R&D policy.

Full employment can be achieved in the EU within a decade if an appropriate mix of reforms were to be adopted. Improved R&D financing and R&D project efficiency will be important steps towards a new international division of labor and capital in Europe. Following WELFENS (1997a) a series of institutional innovations would help to achieve full employment in the EU. Wage dispersion should increase if the tendency of the 1980s in most continental EU countries were to be reversed and moderate wage growth for low skilled workers adopted. Lower gross wage increases will be more acceptable for low skilled workers if income tax rates for low income groups were to be reduced. Such tax reform should, however, be conditional on wage moderation for unskilled workers. More efforts have to be undertaken in the field of education, retraining and virtual university networks. Furthermore, in the future capital markets should play a much more prominent role in the EU (see also WELFENS, 1997e).

Finally, contributions to unemployment insurance should be regionally - possibly also sectorally - differentiated in order to provide an incentive compatible arrangement; i.e. if regions with above average unemployment rates had to anticipate above average contribution rates, regional and local political authorities as well as collective bargaining actors would have an incentive to avoid regulations and wage patterns that impair full employment. Such a reform of the unemployment insurance system might be politically feasible only after full employment (almost) has been regained, because in such a situation there exists a rational "veil of ignorance" as to which regions will be particularly hard hit in the future. Under such a system there would be a tendency for higher regional income differentials and higher migration rates, but this is indeed required in the EU - especially in the future EMU (WELFENS, 1997b). Attracting higher foreign direct investment might be important for several continental EU countries in the future, most notably Germany which had a poor record in the late 1980s and early 1990s. Better anticipation of technology trends could also be useful, although our report argues that this is difficult to achieve. Encouraging small firm dynamics is of particular importance in the EU and so is deregulation of labor markets.

5.2 Strategies for Basic Research

The term *science* is understood to cover the creation, discovery, examination, classification, reorganization and dissemination of knowledge on physical, biological or social subjects. *Technology* is science application know-how. As such, it belongs to a larger group of like activities which embrace the creation and use of artifacts, crafts and items of knowledge as well as various forms of social organization. The 'technology' concept is often used indiscriminately and carelessly. In languages other than English, the equivalent of 'technology' only refers to the doctrine (or the science) of application knowledge; in this generic meaning the term has no plural. Per contra, in English the concept for technology has the secondary meaning of artefacts, sometimes in a generational sense and certainly in the plural form. Other languages such as German or Japanese use a distinctly different word here. Thus *technology* does not only signify the *application* of scientific results, but any *purposive treatment*, method, working method and skill in the exploitation of scientific knowledge together with the products of so doing.

Viewed in terms of the social science system theory (LUHMANN, 1988), the society consists of autonomous sub-systems which respond respectively according to their own particular systemic rationality. The system theory examines the respective system-environment differences, whilst the respective sub-systems are reciprocally the environment. Systems have as their goal their own reproduction or survival. STANKIEWICZ'S (1992, p. 23) contention that technology represents an autonomous socio-cognitive sub-system, is therefore significant; the technological sub-system *can* come into conflict with the scientific or economic. In fact, European history confirms that there has been a long-standing tradition of a strict division between science and technology. Scientists are regarded as intellectually and morally superior to technologists, an attitude which is directly attributable to Plato's differentiation between the superiority of the intellectual over manual work. SKOLIMOWSKI (1966) counters with the idea that science is concerned with what is, whereas technology strives for what ought to be, i. e., it has a creative and organizational function. Consequently, LENK (1979, p. 140) perceives technology as equivalent to science. It is certainly characterized by a different assessment pattern. It remains to be shown to what extent this difference still applies within the field of science-based innovation.

The significance of the research process in the materialization of innovations nowadays is uncontested. According to the rules of present day research statistics, a distinction must be made between fundamental research, applied research and experimental development (OECD, 1993a; the concepts refer back to earlier definitions formulated in 1980 and before and were revised in 1992). The three subsequently differentiated concepts are often combined under the heading *research and development (R&D)*.

Basic research refers to experimental or theoretical work geared 'primarily' to the acquisition of new knowledge about the basic origin of phenomena and observable events without targeting a particular application or use. *Pure basic or fundamental research* is not initiated 'primarily' but exclusively with the aim of advancing knowledge without in so doing raising expectations of an economic or social increase in prosperity, not even as a long term prospect, nor is it dedicated to solving practical problems. The term *application oriented fundamental research* is used in situations where basic research targets certain areas of general interest or is focused in their direction. For this gray area between pure basic research and applied research, other concepts such as *strategic* or *long term application-oriented* concepts have also been formulated (see IRVINE and MARTIN, 1984, KRUPP, 1984 and particularly BROCKHOFF, 1994) which are however not component parts of the set of conventions specified above.

Research and development are perceived as the driving force for the innovation event which chronological dimensions also shape. In early projects, research or more accurately *basic research* was equated to *science*. However, a distinction needs to be made between the two. Scientific activity is characterized, amongst other things, by adherence to specified methodological practices and working standards which have materialized as essential rules of play in the scientific community. However, these practices can also govern oriented basic research, applied research and experimental development. It is important to establish the various *functions* of R&D.

Science and technology (S&T) are often distinguished from research and development by institutional demarcations and then designate the place at which R&D occurs. In this guise, *scientific research* is that particular R&D which is completed outside the company, i. e., in the public domain. *Industrial R&D* denotes corporate activities.

The term *science* includes college instruction, while R&D activity adds of the generally available 'state of the art' knowledge. It represents *knowledge production*. Unlike college instruction, i. e. caring for the knowledge base and its transmission, knowledge production was ascribed the status of an economic activity by economist Machlup as far back as 1962, as it was obvious what impact research processes could have on economic growth. Thus the concepts 'science' and 'technology' should be kept separate from R&D (an economic activity) and not be demarcated by the institutional approach. For is it not science for which an industrial researcher is awarded the Nobel Prize? And surely virtually everything that a college does is therefore already science? *Basic research is not identical to science and experimental development is not identical to technology.*

Therefore, owing to the partial overlaps between the science and technology sub-systems, these are only clearly distinguishable in archetype. Also, R&D activities can only be sub-divided into various types analytically but not always in practice. As is evident from the respective definitions, however, often work in pure basic research can be assigned to the scientific, and work in experimental development to the technical sub-system. *Oriented basic research* and applied research straddle the two.

Contemporary R&D policy has moved away from the inappropriate idea that the State could direct basic research over technological developments right down to individual national innovations. Equally outmoded is the idea that the State could be satisfied with the role of a subsidiary supporter of basic research and leave the control of technology in the future to anonymous market processes. R&D policy for the start of the twenty-first century requires a middle way, an active role for the

State as an intermediary between social players (companies, associations, interest groups, science communities, consumers, media, employers' and employees' representatives etc.).

This intermediary role must also take account of the fact that European R&D policy is restricted in its scope from below. The activities of the European Communities must always be seen in context with the efforts of national policies and, in addition in some member countries, with below-national policies as in federal states to promote research on a regional basis.

The new role of R&D policy as active moderator necessitates a policy process which is co-ordinated with industry, science and society. Cooperation does not however occur of itself since there are too many divergent interests in the foreground. If there is to be agreement over the possibly selective eligibility for support of basic research with implications for technology at the start of the twenty-first century, dialogue with other social players must be initiated and pursued on a permanent basis. It cannot otherwise be expected that lasting cooperation can be achieved and that the platforms to be created for a subject-specific understanding will become more than simply forums for the exchange of information.

It follows from these general trends in R&D policy, that European support for oriented basic research, in so far as it is concerned with technology at the start of the twenty-first century, cannot be replaced by other, for example indirect, instruments of R&D policy. In the field of preventive research in particular, selective project support continues to be of the greatest importance. One new task will be that R&D policy in basic research should in future not only examine technological options but also indicate creative perspectives. This relates to research-related evaluation of the consequences of basic research.

5.3 Improving the Links Within Research and Between Research and Industry

While the organization of production was centered upon mass-production for more than half of this decade (PIORE and SABEL, 1984), an alternative system of industrial organization, *flexible specialization* has seen something of a re-emergence during the last several decades, particularly in Europe. Flexible specialization consists of producing smaller series of specially designed goods of a specific quality for a niche market. Such goods typically are higher value and command a greater price (DIJK, 1995). The organization of industrial activity centered around flexible specialization typically contains five key elements:

1. *A reliance upon multi-purpose equipment.* General purpose equipment enhances the flexibility to rapidly change the product specifications to meet demands of customers. This requires high levels of human capital, skilled labor and technical know-how.
2. *Continual innovative activity.* Both the nature of the product(s) as well as production and organization methods are continually improved upon.
3. *Clustering.* Groupings of enterprises, in both a product as well as a geographic dimension provide a seedbed for the exchange of new ideas. Not only does physical proximity tend to facilitate the transmission of knowledge, but it also enhances the development of institutions and makes them more effective.
4. *Networking.* Formal and informal links between enterprises, including subcontracting relationships facilitate both increased economic specialization to the firm as well as superior access to knowledge.
5. *Spillover Effects.* Knowledge created within an enterprise spills over for use by other enterprises. Conversely, enterprises and individuals have access to external knowledge.

There is considerable evidence supporting the hypothesis that not only does flexible production provide a viable alternative to mass production as a system of industrial organization, but also that such systems are more conducive to enhancing knowledge links between firms and individuals, both within the same industry and across different industries. One of the most striking examples is provided by Emilia Romagna, a mixed agricultural-industrial region located in north central Italy, with a population of around four million. Through a structure of flexible production, small- and medium-sized enterprises have created impressive knowledge links by creating specialized industrial districts where an agglomeration of producers in one industry work in close physical proximity.

Perhaps it was the prominence of such innovative clusters that motivated KRUGMAN (1991) to propose a new theory of economic geography. In particular, KRUGMAN (1991) poses the question, "What is the most striking feature of the geography of economic activity? The short answer is surely concentration...production is remarkably concentrated in space." Perhaps in response to Krugman's concern, a literature in economics has recently emerged which focuses on the implications of the geographic concentration of economic activity for knowledge linkages and ultimately economic growth. Theoretical models posited by ROMER (1986 and 1990) and LUCAS (1993) link increasing returns to scale yielded by knowledge externalities within a geographically bounded region to higher rates of growth. And the empirical evidence clearly suggests that R&D and other sources of knowledge not only generate externalities, but studies also suggest that such knowledge linkages tend to be geographically bounded within the region where the new economic knowledge was created (AUDRETSCH and FELDMAN, 1996; and AUDRETSCH and STEPHAN, 1996). That is, new economic knowledge may spill over across firms and economic agents but the geographic extent of such knowledge linkages tends to be bounded.

The importance of location to innovative activity in a world increasingly dominated by E-mail, fax machines, and electronic communications superhighways may seem surprising and even paradoxical at first glance. The resolution of this paradox lies in the distinction between knowledge and information. While the marginal cost of transmitting *information* may be invariant to distance, presumably the marginal cost of transmitting *knowledge*, and especially *tacit knowledge*, rises with distance. VON HIPPLE (1994) persuasively demonstrates that high context, uncertain knowledge, or what he terms as *sticky knowledge*, is best transmitted via face-to-face interaction and through frequent contact. Proximity matters in transmitting knowledge because, as ARROW (1962) pointed out some three decades ago, such tacit knowledge is inherently non-rival in nature, and knowledge developed for any particular application can easily spill over and be applied for different purposes. Similarly, GRILICHES (1992) has defined knowledge spillovers as "working on similar things and hence benefiting much from each other's research." Thus, GLAESER, KALLAL, SCHEINKMAN and SHLEIFER (1992) have observed that "intellectual breakthroughs must cross hallways and streets more easily than oceans and continents."

That knowledge linkages tend to be geographically localized is consistent with frequent observations made by the press, business community, as well as by policy makers. For example, *Fortune* points out that, "Business is a social activity, and you have to be where important work is taking place."[1]

In addition, systematic econometric evidence suggests that location and

---

[1] "The Best Cities for Knowledge Workers," Fortune, 15 November, 1993, pp. 44-57.

proximity clearly matter in generating knowledge linkages. Not only have JAFFE, TRAJTENBERG and HENDERSON (1993) found that patent citations tend to occur more frequently within the geographic region in which they were patented, but AUDRETSCH and FELDMAN (1996) found that the propensity for innovative activity to cluster geographically tends to be greater in industries where new economic knowledge plays a more important role.

Despite the general consensus that knowledge linkages within a given location stimulates innovative activity, there is little consensus as to exactly how this occurs. In fact, there are three different general types of theories found in the literature. The first, which could be termed the *Marshall-Arrow-Romer* model, suggests that an increased concentration of specialized economic activity promotes knowledge linkages between firms and therefore is more conducive to innovative activity. This type of spatial concentration is also known as *industry localization* and dates back at least to LOESCH (1954).An important assumption is that knowledge externalities with respect to knowledge linkages among firms exist, but only for firms within the same industry. Thus, the relevant unit of observation for analyzing economic organization is extended from the firm to the region in the theoretical tradition of the Marshall-Arrow-Romer model, and in subsequent empirical studies, but knowledge linkages are limited to occur only within the relevant industry, but not across industries. The transmission of knowledge across different industries is assumed to be non-existent or at least trivial. In fact, Michael Porter has explicitly argued that *regional specialization* within an industry best promotes innovative activity.

Restricting externalities from knowledge linkages to occur only within the industry may ignore an important source of knowledge linkages – inter-industry knowledge spillovers. Jane JACOBS (1969) argues that the most important source of knowledge linkages are external to the industry in which the firm operates and that cities are the source of innovation because the diversity of these knowledge sources is greatest in cities. Thus, Jacobs develops a theory that emphasizes that the variety of industries within a geographic region promotes knowledge linkages and ultimately innovative activity and economic growth. According to Jacobs' theory, *diversity* rather than *specialization* is the operative mechanism driving economic growth.

In studying the networks of California's Silicon Valley, SAXENIAN (1994) emphasizes that it is linkages between individuals that facilitates the transmission of knowledge and ideas across agents, firms and even industries, and not just the high endowment of R&D, that has promoted the high degree of innovative activity: "It is not simply the concentration of skilled labor, suppliers and information that distinguish the region. A variety of regional institutions – including Stanford University, several trade associations and local business organizations, and a myriad of specialized consulting, market research, public relations and venture capital firms – provide technical, financial, and networking services which the region's enterprises often cannot afford individually. These networks defy sectoral barriers: individuals move easily from semiconductor to disk drive firms or from computer to software makers. They move from established firms to start-ups (or vice versa) and even to market research or consulting firms back into start-ups. And they continue to meet at trade shows, industry conferences, and the scores of seminars, talks, and social activities organized by local business organizations and trade associations. In these forums, relationships are easily formed and maintained, technical and market information is exchanged, business contacts are established, and new enterprises are conceived...This decentralized and fluid environment also promotes the diffusion of intangible technological capabilities and understandings.

The diversity thesis raises the question of what types of diverse linkages best promote innovation.[2] That is, firms have different absorptive capacities that will shape their ability to make useful applications, and realize the potential value of knowledge spillovers. Implicit in the literature on networks and supplier linkages is the assumption that firms must have some basis for interaction and knowledge transfer. According to the theories developed by David Teece and others (TEECE, RUMMULT, DOSI and WINTER, 1994), the expected economic value of new knowledge to a firm is shaped by what is termed as the *core competency* of the firm. As COHEN and LEVINTHAL (1990) point out, the costs associated with innovation, such as learning new techniques and absorbing new research results, are less if the new knowledge is relevant to the firm's on-going activities and existing expertise. In general, it is science-based knowledge that presumable provides a shared language, an appreciation of a common set of problems and applications and a collective stock of techniques and procedures. In fact, SAXENIAN (1994) claims that even the language and vocabulary used by technical specialists is specific to a

---

[2] Too much diversity may create a *Tower of Babel* effect where there is not enough of a common knowledge base so that externalities can be absorbed, limited any positive benefit that can accrue.

region: "...a distinct language has evolved in the region and certain technical terms used by semiconductor production engineers in Silicon Valley would not even be understood by their counterparts in Boston's Route 128."

5.4 R&D and Reforms in European Capital Markets

Capital markets have played an important role in the financing of industrial expansion once before when 120 years ago most industrial ventures were considered to be rather risky. Facing globalization, many newcomers in world markets and high technology competition there is again a fundamental role for stock markets in the OECD countries. With eastern European countries and Asian (plus Latin American) NICs moving increasingly into medium and high technology markets there is a need for western Europe to restore its economic vitality with the help of massive high technology investment.

R&D projects have to be financed if they are to be realized (and jobs to be created). Sectors characterized by high R&D intensity face a special problem of asymmetric information as regards the evaluation of innovation projects. Since the innovator knows best about his particular field of technology, financing projects by bank loans could be particularly difficult. Few banks have strong technological expertise on which loan decisions could be based, so in reality most banks require collateral for credits and those are then given only at interest rates incorporating a high risk premium. Innovative firms like IBM, INTEL or SIEMENS nevertheless face few problems in financing innovation projects since they have built a reputation to be successful innovators: as joint stock companies they therefore can tap capital market.

In the start-up period many innovative newcomer firms hire skilled personnel at low wage costs coupled with generous stock option packages. Due to a functional venture capital market in the US innovative newcomers can finally be transformed into a public joint stock company. The lack of venture capital markets on the European continent - except for the Netherlands and Denmark - has been a major problem for innovative EU newcomers. With the new markets in Frankfurt and Paris and the London AIM stock market plus the EASDAQ (modeled after the US NASDAQ), stock markets will play a stronger role in the financing innovative firms in Europe. Moreover, stock options could play a much larger role in management remuneration in Europe in the future. National regulations as well as tax laws should encourage venture capitalism strongly in Europe.

Taking into account the findings of the McKINSEY (1996) study about the relative lag of EU capital productivity, one might also consider establishing a special research focus on increasing capital productivity. There exists an obvious need for stronger specialization in innovative activities in western Europe considering the insufficient specialization of the EU in patenting. A more clear-cut innovation profile can be mainly expected due to a rising role of capital markets. Tax benefits for workers investing in investment funds could support both a strengthening of capital markets and help to share benefits from globalization between firms and workers. This could also help to bring about the required higher wage dispersion in continental EU countries assuming that the government will tie tax benefits for low-skilled workers to the condition that their wages do not exceed average wage growth - after rebalancing. This requires a one-off-reduction in the wages of unskilled workers.

5.5 Optimizing Regional EU Policies

EU Structural Funds are available for six categories under the new system. The budget amounts to an overall volume of ECU 155,2 billion in 1994-99, on top of which comes the EU cohesion fund for countries with a per capita income of below 90% of the EU average. In addition to these regional policy measures the EU influences regional development via the European Investment Bank (EIB), which according to the 1994 annual report financed roughly 4% (ECU 18 billion) of EU gross capital formation. While the EIB is not giving subsidized loans, the matching funds that typically are mobilized by national governments often contain a subsidy element. The overall amount of direct and indirect Community funding thus is considerable, and it is quite important that funds are allocated in a way consistent with the stated policy goals (economic catching up, employment creation and structural change) and do not impair other goals of the Community or interfere with major policy principles. Whether goals have been achieved and funds been spent in an efficient way can only be assessed:

a) if recipient regions are defined wide enough, i.e. beyond the scope of a municipality and - except for the cohesion funds - below the scope of a national economy. Otherwise policy responsibilities become blurred.

b) if impacts are measured by an appropriate set of indicators - based on standard economic theory - and if regional macroeconomic models allow the assessment of the regional impact at the (sub-) macroeconomic level.

c) if incentives for policy makers to maintain the disadvantaged status of the respective region are weak.

d) if negative national and international spillovers as well as external effects are small.

e) if overall "consistency of objectives" is achieved in the sense that measures for promoting catching-up and structural change do not impair employment creation or reduce overall EU competitiveness.

What is most difficult in the evaluation process is that there is no common and comprehensible set of indicators which would allow the policy impact to be measured. A major problem is that recipients give only a selective and incomplete set of indicators to cover the impact effects of policies. Some multiplier figures for employment created and secured are implausible.

Without an appropriate macroeconomic model, assessing the efficiency of a single politico-economic measure in a world influenced by a large number of factors with different and partly unknown impacts is a difficult task. A recent evaluation of the impacts of structural policies on the economic and social cohesion of the EU points to these problem resulting from various factors influencing demand and supply of labor (ZENIT, 1996). The pure effect of a politico-economic bundle of measures such as EU structural policy is, therefore, hard to estimate. Any positive impact can easily be outperformed or at least distorted by the country's overall economic situation. Thus, non-standardized, soft indicators render the task even more difficult.

A new international division of innovation and labor has to be achieved in Europe. This requires a high degree of structural and regional change. Raising R&D efforts can only be one element in a strategy that aims at restoring full employment. An improved infrastructure is quite important in bringing about structural change and higher economic growth. It is clear that macroeconomic stability in a future monetary union would support economic growth. Transitory high growth - as a basic strategy to reduce the unemployment overhang in the EU - requires the combination of macroeconomic stability, labor market reforms and new innovation efforts (including the encouragement of small and medium enterprises). If growth policies were to be directed primarily at the service sector and high technology fields negative side effects of growth would be limited. Within a transitory high growth strategy it is, however, necessary to increase wage dispersion and share extra profits fairly. Encouraging worker participation in investment funds could be one possible way of achieving this. Finally, a high growth strategy requires that environmental side effects are minimized and that opportunities for creating new jobs through pro-ecological policies are fully exploited.

Figure 8: Key Variables Leading to Economic Growth, Structural Change and Employment

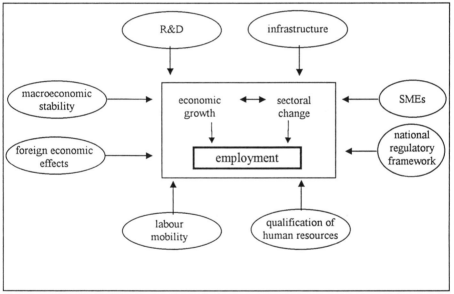

Source: ZENIT (1996), Evaluation of the impacts of the structural policies on the economic and social cohesion of the Union: Germany, Final Report, p. 221.

The above figure displays some of the key parameters that directly or indirectly - via economic growth and sectoral change - influence the demand for labor and hence the rate of employment. However, only some of those variable could be efficiently affected by active structural policies. With regard to the instruments of structural policy, options for supply side oriented interventions are: promoting of founding small- and medium-sized enterprises, subsidizing R&D-projects, expanding and modernizing the infrastructure and training unskilled or less qualified people.

5.6 Reform Requirements at the National Policy Level

Among the most cited sources of evidence for the existence of an *Innovations-Krise* in Europe is the declining share of patent and R&D activity vis-à-vis Japan and the United States exhibited by Europe. But a more careful inspection reveals that the relative technological advantage of European companies in the industries that Europe has traditionally held a comparative advantage, such as chemicals, specialized machine tools, and automobiles, has not greatly deteriorated greatly over the last decade.

The continued technological leadership of European firms in these industries is evidenced by their sound and profitable recovery out of the recession and rapid recovery in global export markets.[3] The companies in these industries have not exhibited a loss in either innovative capacity or the capacity to adopt innovations made abroad, at least within their narrowly defined industries.

The problem in these industries may have less to do with an *Innovations-Krise* and more to do with a *Standort-Krise*, as reflected by the continued transfer of production facilities out of Europe into lower-cost countries, along with corporate restructuring, which has left large numbers of displaced workers unlikely to be re-hired, even once the economic recovery has taken hold. That is, substituting technology and organizational innovations for labor has resulted in substantial productivity gains in these European industries, which has had a positive impact on firm efficiency. But at the same time it places downward pressure on the number of jobs available in these traditional industries. how and under what conditions can these displaced workers, as well as new entrants be absorbed into productive economic activity?

The innovation challenge in Europe does not seem to exist in the industries in which Europe has traditionally held a comparative advantage. Rather, the innovation challenge confronting Europe apparently lies in new industries. For example, a recent cover story of *Newsweek* is devoted to "Why Europe is Losing the Technology Race."[4] As the lead article of this issue points out, "The problems at Siemens are far

---

[3] "European Economies: Gloom to Boom," The Economist, 24 December 1994, pp. 35-36.
[4] "Why Europe is Losing the Technology Race," Newsweek, 31 October, 1994.

from unique. They are, instead, spread throughout much of Europe's high-tech landscape, and in particular what the Germans like to call 'telmatik': the rapidly converging fields of computers, telecommunications and television...With only a handful of exceptions, in nearly every segment of the so-called information-technology industry, there is a rout underway. European competitors are all but invisible."

Similar sentiment can be found in Germany, where *Der Spiegel* observed recently that, "Global structural change has an impact on the German economy that only a short time ago would have been unimaginable: Many of the products, such as automobiles, machinery, chemicals and steel are no longer competitive in global markets. *And in the industries of the future, like biotechnology and electronics, the German companies are barely participating."* [5] And *The Wall Street Journal* recently warned that in Germany, "If you look at the chip industry, it's a disaster. And the computer industry has been for many years. Energy technology as such is a disaster."[6] This echoes the concerns of one of Germany's leading politicians, Lothar Spaeth, and the chairman of the McKinsey & Co. Germany, Herbert A. Henzler, who argue in their best-selling book, *Can the Germans Still Be Saved?* that, "Germany's greatest structural crisis in the postwar period" has been the result of "missing the boat on cutting edge technologies."[7]

Europe apparently has not been at a disadvantage in producing basic knowledge. As *The Economist* observes, "Western Europe has no shortage of capital or educated people."[8] At the same time, it has proven difficult for Europe to apply that new knowledge in creating new industries. As *The Economist* also points out, "Yet Europe is not creating enough entrepreneurial firms."[9]

For example, a software firm that was founded in Bavaria, FAST, needed more capital to fund product development. But after being continually refused from financial institutions and non-financial institutions, the founder Matthias Zahn is not only planning an Initial Public Offering on the NASDAQ in the United States, but also to move the company's headquarters from Bavaria to Redwood City,

[5] Der Spiegel, number 5, 1994, pp. 82-83.
[6] "Some Germans Fear They're Falling Behind in High-Tech Fields," The Wall Street Journal, 27 April, 1994, p. 1.
[7] Quoted from The Wall Street Journal, 27 April 1994, p. 1.
[8] "Small But Not Yet Beautiful," The Economist, 25 February, 1995, pp. 88-89.
[9] "Small But Not Yet Beautiful," The Economist, 25 February, 1995, pp. 88-89.

California.[10] This is no isolated example. Scores of entrepreneurs in newly emerging industries, ranging from computer software and hardware to biotechnology and visual reality have engaged in a kind of *Auswanderung*, or emigration, in order to appropriate the expected value of their technological knowledge.

Economists speak of static economic welfare loss, but this is a type of dynamic economic welfare loss in the form of forgone technological knowledge and the economic externalities that would otherwise have been accrued. That such technological knowledge in its early stage flows from Germany to selected locations in North America may reveal differences in institutions. These institutions make it either relatively easier or more difficult for people to pursue new innovative ideas. It may be that the institutions of European countries like Germany, ranging from finance to the labor market, and even to education were developed to excel in the transfer and application of technological knowledge in traditional industries but not in emerging industries. The traditional industrial policy of European countries has been oriented towards channeling resources into economic activities where it is more or less known what is to be produced, how it should be produced and who should produce it. This traditional approach to industrial policy is essentially *restraining* in nature, in that it restrains the actions of individuals and firms. But a new industrial policy approach is required to shift economic activity into new industries. This new industrial policy approach needs to be *enabling* in nature, in that individuals and firms are encouraged to pursue the production and implementation of new ideas. Such an enabling industrial policy is appropriate when the comparative advantage of a region lies in economic activity where it is no longer known what should be produced, how it should be produced and who should produce it.

For example, a proclaimed virtue of the German banking system and financial system in general is that by allowing bank ownership of private companies, the companies avoid the types of liquidity constraints more commonly experienced by their counterparts on the other side of the Atlantic. While this may be true, it is also a double-edged sword, because it tends to be the large, incumbent companies - which are typically tied to existing technological trajectories - that receive a generous flow of cash from the banks. What has been overlooked is the difficulty outsiders and entrepreneurs, with new and different ideas, encounter in procuring founding. At the same time there have been only negligible venture capital and

---

[10] "German Innovation: No Bubbling Brook," The Economist, 10 September 1994, pp. 75-76.

informal capital markets developed to channel finance into projects involving new and different technological trajectories. It is not surprising that one of the most repeated phrases on the pages of the business news over the last few months has bee what Helmuth Guembel, who is research director of the Gartner Group in Munich observed,[11] "Put Bill Gates in Europe and it just wouldn't have worked out."[12]

Equity investment in small firms in new industries is scarce. Although the stock market established a "regulated bourse" for small firms in 1987, only seven small companies floated shares in 1993 and just four in 1994. Venture capitalists are rare, in part because they cannot sell their stakes on the stock market."[13]

Labor market institutions also may tend to impede the development of new firms pursuing different ideas. As *The Economist* observes, "SPEA Software is the sort of company Germany wants to create. Based near Munich, this developer of multimedia equipment boosted its sales by 60% last year to about DM 180 million and got Germany's biggest-yet injection of venture capital. SPEA's success will, however, worry one group: Germany's embattled union leaders. SPEA's 130 employees are not unionized, and it does not yet belong to an employer's association. It is thus not part of the centralized system of labor relations to which most of German industry belongs."[14]

Similarly, the tax laws force the chief executive officers of new companies to start paying out dividends from earnings almost as soon as they appear, pre-empting high re-investment policies. In addition, bankruptcy laws in Germany make it clear that to start a new business and to fail is socially unproductive. After two bankruptcies the entrepreneur is legally left only with the option of becoming an employee. He may not legally rely upon his experience from the bankruptcies to start a third enterprise.

Industrial policy towards science, or science policy also needs to be reformed in Europe. Hubert Markl, the President of the reorganized Berlin-Brandenburg Academy of Science, which is the successor the prestigious former Prussian Academy of Science, recently commented in *Science* magazine, "It comes to no

---

[11] "Where's the Venture Capital?" Newsweek, 31 October, 1994, p. 44.

[12] Similar sentiment was expressed by Joschka Fischer, parliamentary leader of the Green Party in Germany, who laments, "A company like Microsoft would never have a chance in Germany" ("Those German Banks and Their Industrial Treasures," The Economist, 21 January, 1995, pp. 63-64.

[13] "German Innovation: No Bubbling Brook," The Economist, 10 September, 1994, pp. 75-76.

[14] "Out of Service?" The Economist, 4 February, 1995, pp. 63-64.

surprise that Germany, half a decade after the breakdown of a precarious political stability and facing the challenges posed by reunification and global economic markets, is struggling to find its new position in the world. Perhaps spoilt by past success, Germans are learning the hard way that a successful future depends on making the best use of one's innovative talents...The best path for science to take is to encourage and support the highest quality and originality in all endeavors and to reform in ways that will realize the potential of the most talented."[15] Markl observes that, "It is alarming to note that unified Germany has fallen behind major competitors in terms of percentage of gross national product allocated to research and development. However, funds will increase only when the public believes that the autonomy enjoyed by the academic and research community is used to serve the whole society."[16] That is, the links between research and applications are sufficiently weak in Germany as to deter the approval of additional support for research. Markl concludes that the creation of an enabling environment is essential to making Germany more innovative: "The spirit of scientific innovation could then provide impetus for reform in all sectors of German society, from overly restrictive *Ladenschluss* (Shop closing hours) to excessive *Arbeitszeitverkuerzung* (reduction in working hours). Hard choices lie ahead for a Germany that has lived under the illusion that it had a subscription to economic miracles."

The university systems in European countries also need to be reformed in order to refocus on excellence in research and teaching on the one hand, and applicability and commercialization on the other. A recent article in *Science* magazine proclaimed "The Decline of German Universities".[17] While the investment in buildings and physical renovation in Berlin is breathtaking, the budget cuts in university education and research could prove to be devastating. Investments in physical capital may have bestowed the comparative advantage in earlier decades. But in the European context of the late 1990s, it is investments in creating and applying new knowledge that will bestow the comparative advantage. Perhaps investing in people rather than buildings would have a greater return.

Raimer Luest, former head of the European Space Agency has described that state of German universities as a "hopeless-looking dead end where bureaucrats set

---

[15] MARKL, H., "German Science in a Changing World," Science, Vol. 270, 27 October 1995.
[16] MARKL, H., "German Science in a Changing World," Science, Vol. 270, 27 October 1995.
[17] "The Decline of German Universities," Science, Vol. 273, 12 July 1996, pp. 172-174.

the direction."[18] The universities are underfunded and overcrowded, particularly in western Germany. Students typically must struggle through poorly organized curricula provided by only a minimal of guidance. Facilities and research labs have often become outdated. The incentive structure does not encourage scientific performance. Resources are typically divided equally among professors, regardless of their productivity. The *Wissenschaftsrat*, or Science Council, Germany's top scientific advisory body reports that there is a projected shortage of $1.1 billion in building and infrastructure funds. As *Science* magazine reports, "Perhaps the most contentious issue is funding: If Germany is to stay near the top of world science and technology, it cannot continue dropping the proportion of national income spent on universities, where it is now low on the list of major industrial nations."[19]

The institutional structure - or what some prefer to call the national systems of innovation - within the European Union seem to have been designed for industrial stability and the application of new technological knowledge only within the existing technological trajectories. And yet, as the comparative advantage of the nation increasingly becomes based on the earlier stages of the industry life cycle, the underlying knowledge conditions associated with tacit knowledge, such as greater uncertainty, asymmetries, and significant costs of transaction, dictate not stability, but rather mobility. Individuals and organizations embodying knowledge have to be as little impeded as possible to seek out ways of combing with complementary knowledge inputs in order to appropriate the value of their knowledge. And this means more movement, both of individual economic agents - that is workers - and firms. Europe held the comparative advantage in moderate-technology and traditional industries during the last three decades. This meant that to adapt existing technology along existing technological trajectories and make incremental improvements was sufficient to preserve the international competitiveness of firms and a rising standard of living for the domestic population. However, a shift in the comparative advantage of Europe away from such traditional industries has left a void. The economic challenge confronting Europe at the turn of the century will be to shift its industrial structure away from mature industries and products and towards newly emerging technologies and industries.

---

[18] "The Decline of German Universities," Science, Vol. 273, 12 July 1996, p. 172.
[19] "The Decline of German Universities," Science, Vol. 273, 12 July 1996, p. 174.

5.7 The EU's R&D Framework: Opportunities for New Initiatives

Through demand from the public sector, the government bodies on European, national and below-national levels offer a high demand potential, which in Europe has until now been only inadequately used for R&D policy. The dialogue referred to above should also therefore cover the further clarification of the question of how the public authorities can competently provide demand in order to successfully encourage innovations which result from the technology of the early twenty-first century. Innovative companies will attract incentives if a need for certain innovative products becomes clear to them at an early stage through the structure of the framework conditions and state demand, as long as the markets are still too small to give reliable signals. These aspects should also be further discussed in the proposed alliance of social players so that they can be formulated more clearly prior to a follow-up activity.

In view of the typical mature phases of science-related technological innovations, it can generally be assumed that everything that will dominate high-technology markets in ten years' time is already recognizable today. On the other hand, strategic planning is necessary for European R&D policy, aiming towards horizons even further in the future, because new technologies, especially those which will contribute to long sought after solutions to problems, must be weighed up at an early stage.

From the normative point of view, the direction to be taken in the future may be seen from the increasing demands made on technological development in terms of minimal use of resources, elimination of emissions, circular economy and sustainable development. These require the creation of the necessary framework conditions, especially those of a non-technical nature, for example legal regulations. Scarcely less important than the ecological problems is the socio-political dimension. From the point of view of technology policy, the requirement here is for a form of technological development which encourages wide-ranging participation by players from various sectors and of varying size and leads to an open market with no specific centralized structure.

This long-term view of technological development offers, in short, various starting points for European R&D policy, which overlap the individual subject areas, e. g. (compare GRUPP, 1994a):

- to encourage new physical, chemical and biological *basic effects* which can influence innovation in various technical areas;
- to *provide manufacturing technologies* which promote the rapid conversion of basic effects into innovative products;
- to take up technologies which may be *linked with the available know-how* and manufacturing structures so that new solutions may be produced on the basis of the available experience with restricted volumes of investment;
- to promote technologies which are expected to lead to short-term *multiplier effects* while under development (that is, during or immediately after the period in which they are promoted);
- to set up *framework conditions*, in particular legal regulations, which point technological development in the direction of sustainable development and the protection of scarce resources;
- to take account at an early stage of *non-technical factors* such as service areas, user guidance, questions of standardization, working organization and skill levels;
- to *promote opportunities for communication and co-operation* which bring the partners together from various fields of activity and in particular ensure that innovative companies (including small and medium-sized companies) can rely on an adequate knowledge base (oriented basic research) both at home and abroad;
- to set up *cross-disciplinary facilities at educational and research institutions*, which can develop new non-subject-related perspectives;
- to *encourage wide-ranging participation* by those involved in research and development and to produce and maintain an open market for innovations without special centralized structures.

It is in the nature of a long-term foresight that it is burdened with a high degree of uncertainty as to the probability of it coming about; it is not unusual for wishful thinking, arising from the most diverse motives, to be presented as a probable future event. On the other hand, modified technical, economic and social "cultures" have to be observed in periods of up to 50 years to understand their full significance and reality. In this way the technology of the early twenty-first century will be a pointer to the technical and social status of society in the middle of the next century.

Taking the long view, the motivating power of guiding visions is helpful in that it releases energies and the willingness to undertake concerted action. *Long-*

term lead projects in R&D policy can produce lasting motivation and unite powers which can work towards problem-solving requirements recognizable in the long term but also producing successes along the way (multiplier effects).

On the question of tangible ways of taking this subject further, since it is not a central theme of the study, it is suggested that the findings of the German, the British and the French Delphi survey on future science and technology be further analyzed in a follow-up study on long-term developments. The detailed evaluations produced on more than 1,000 individual subjects up to the year 2020 in the three countries should provide an adequate base to give more tangible form to the accessibility of various speculative lead projects in R&D policy in the above sense. This would also have to involve the elucidation of the inter-relationships between the projected scientific discoveries and technical achievements and the requirements of the technology at the beginning of the next century.

Lead projects in R&D policy which represent outline solutions to large, global, economic, social, societal and ecological problems, and above all the visionary view of technological development and the challenges now facing us throw up other, more radical questions of R&D policy than those set out above in respect of the short-term view. It was not the aim of this study to give those concrete form. It was however possible to indicate that the trends described in technology policy up to the start of the twenty-first century can themselves provide the key to further-reaching changes in future policy and the technology of the next decade can point the way to the lead projects of the twenty-first century. R&D policy for the day after tomorrow must be in place by tomorrow.

5.8 Labor Market Reforms for EU Competitiveness and Employment Growth

We here discuss labor market reforms in the narrow and more general senses. The narrow context encompasses the controversial question of employment protection legislation and other labor market regulations, while the broader context is education and training. Given the breadth of each area, we shall paint with a very broad brush, and be more interested in drawing out key issues rather than in deriving detailed recommendations per se. In each case the linking theme is enhanced flexibility.

The job protection issue is controversial precisely because the empirical evidence is mixed, and the econometric exercises often unsophisticated. Our understanding of the effects of employment protection mandates is rudimentary, and we are currently unable to identify with any precision the scale of disemployment and unemployment effects. The evidence is, then, only suggestive and even here we would also note that well-designed studies providing internally consistent results need not be generalizable to the policy issues at hand. Economic theory can support the case for a number of employment mandates, at least on a general level, based on a variety of market failure arguments. Equity concerns may often strengthen the case for state intervention in the workplace. At a more precise level, however, the predicted effects of mandates depend crucially on the assumptions being made and the setting in which regulations are implemented. Policy debate over mandates often accords all too little attention to the milieu of considerable firm and worker heterogeneity in which policies must be implemented as well as to the market adjustments that evolve in response to mandates. And it should not go unsaid that the actual policies adopted and implemented as a result of the political process need not mesh with the lines of action suggested by theory.

The analyses of employment protection, briefly reviewed in section 1.3, indicate that some mandates (the example cited was advance notice of redundancy) may have beneficial labor market outcomes even if the generality of such measures seem to be associated with reduced employment and possibly higher unemployment. But the negative outcomes that have been associated with employment regulation constitute at best a partial explanation of Europe's unfavorable labor market performance. Some countries do not appear to fit the mold. This diversity of experience is perhaps not unexpected in the sense that the web of rules governing the social protection of workers in a nation state are endogenous. But such rules are also a determinant of a country's competitive position and in an important sense are put up for adoption by the market. Ultimately they have to stand a market test. Those systems that survive (and adapt) are presumably competitive. If past experience is any guide, then it may be argued after PAQUÉ (1997) that "the cultural space of Europe provides enough leeway for a broad social search process which may lead to very different results depending on the mentality of the population and the particular local conditions." The notion of experimentation that is explicit in Paqué's treatment cannot be overemphasized.

Viewed from this perspective - though we would wish to underplay the results that no fault dismissals protection is associated with disemployment and that other regulations (and social security charges) have acted to the disadvantage of part-timers and unskilled workers - the real threat from employment protection regulation in the

European Union comes less from nation state intervention than it does from supranational regulation because this places a straightjacket on experimentation with different social systems and labor relations at the nation state level. This is perhaps the real issue confronting labor market reform in the Union. We think it critical that the move toward labor market harmonization within Europe - as evidenced by the social charter and social chapter experiments - be subjected to very careful scrutiny. In particular, to what extent can supranational regulation of the labor market improve on the actions arrived at by nation states and individuals? Frankly, although charged with the obligation to assess the economic consequences of its mandates, the Commission has not adequately conducted impact effect studies. Specifically, the following issues need to be addressed. What is the rationale for ional legislation? What are the likely effects? And could the objectives be better attained through other measures or levels? This would seem to require that the evaluative apparatus of DG5 be fundamentally upgraded. This assessment is not grounded in the presumption that efficiency considerations are the be-all-and-end-all of policy but rather to argue that economic analysis is a guide to policy. Arguably, a case could be made that the well-intentioned pursuit of social policy objectives by the European Union has proceeded in an economic vacuum.

It is perhaps appropriate at this stage to note that the US labor market is not to be viewed as an template any more than individual member states of the Community. Presumably both blocs have something to learn from one another. We think it interesting to note in this context that the US labor market has itself become both more regulated and more litigious in recent years, leading some observers to cite the benefits of low cost administrative rules found in at least some European countries (see ADDISON, 1997).

We feel it crucial to underscore the heterogeneity/complexity of labor markets. The US is rightly viewed as having a flexible and fluid labor market. Its job creation and destruction rates are indeed very large. For manufacturing industry, 1973-78, 10.3% of jobs were destroyed annually. Reflecting the shrinkage of the sector, annual job creation rates were 9.1%. Job reallocation thus averaged 19.4%. Equally important, the US is not an outlier in large-scale job reallocation. Table 14 indicates that European countries demonstrate a similar reshuffling of employment opportunities across locations.

Table 14: Net and Gross Job Flow Rates in Selected Countries
(Annual averages as percentages of employment)

Country	Interval	Sector	Job Creation	Job Destruction	Net Employment Groth	Job Reallocation
US	1973-78	Manufacturing	9.1	10.2	-1.1	19.4
France	1978-84	Private Nonfarm	11.4	12.0	-0.6	25.8
Germany	1978-88	Private	8.3	7.7	0.6	16.0
Sweden	1982-84	All employees	11.4	12.1	-0.8	23.5
Italy	1984-89	Social Security Emplyees	9.9	10.0	-0.1	19.9
Denmark	1983-89	Private	16.0	13.8	2.2	29.8
Finland	1986-91	Private	10.4	12.0	-1.6	22.4

Source: DAVIS, S.J., HALTIWANGER, J.C. and SCHUH, S. (1996b), Job Creation and Destruction, Cambridge, MA: MIT Press, Table 2.2.

Within-sector shifts in employment dominate between-sector shifts, irrespective of whether the sector is defined by industry, plant size, product specialization and so on. This is what we mean by heterogeneity. It is this heterogeneity that complicates the task of evaluating the effects of policies that place restrictions on job and worker reallocation. Existing analyses rely on aggregated data at the industry level - and often higher levels of aggregation - which obscure most of the underlying flows of workers and jobs. An important task for future research is to analyze the effect of regulations on the flows of workers and jobs as well as the creation and destruction of firms. But the extant analysis of gross job flow data, and in particular high rates of job destruction, patently underscores the need for a flexible workforce in terms of its skills. As DAVIS, HALTIWANGER, and SCHUH (1996b) point out, labor has to be equipped to respond to the large-scale job reallocation activity that seems to characterize both the US and European labor markets.

Before turning to consider policies that tend directly to increase flexibility, we pause to note that in the US more job creation and job destruction are accounted for by firms being born or dying than by the expansion or contraction of existing firms. In Europe the opposite is the case. This hints at greater entrepreneurialism in the US and this may assist in explaining its better performance in generating employment.

Arguably, the fundamental source of flexibility is the adaptability of the workforce and this has ultimately to do with formal schooling. Prior to addressing this issue, however, we note some more or less related reforms that might seem to commend themselves to the Community. Reform of the unemployment insurance (UI) system is perhaps the most obvious of these. UI in the Community is not experience rated so that employers do not bear the costs of laying off workers. There is scope for making contributions related to the firm's layoff experience. Moreover, UI should not be a vehicle of quasi-permanent income support and disincentive effects should be minimized. (The empirical evidence for the US not only confirms disincentive effects but also indicates that UI does not lead to significantly higher post-unemployment earnings and better and more stable job matches - see ADDISON and BLACKBURN, 1996.) Subject to the caveats entered below, the focus of UI systems should shift from passive reemployment assistance to active reemployment assistance, involving profiling of claimants and job search assistance. Innovations in UI such as reemployment bonuses paid to workers who terminate their search early (and/or to the employers who employ them), should be evaluated using demonstration initiatives and in all cases initiatives should be rigorously evaluated through random assignment of clients to experimental and control groups. We would note in passing that close attention has to be paid to the likely strategic responses of workers and firms to permanent programs (see MEYER, 1995).

Another flexibility issue resides in wage and labor costs. A number of observers have pointed to the need for the reform of European wage setting procedures to make settlements more closely accord with local realities at the enterprise level. This is a multifaceted issue that involves such diverse elements as worker representation, collective voice, the unsettled debate over corporatism, and insider/outsider considerations. We choose not to comment directly on the redesign of the European collective bargaining apparatus except to make three points. First, little support can be adduced for formal procedures that extend the terms and conditions of collective bargains to third parties, via so-called erga omnes agreements. Second, product market deregulation and trade liberalization would appear the most important means of improving flexibility in wage determination. Third, the Community must pay careful attention to the consequences of its facilitating European-wide collective bargaining.

We turn in conclusion to education, which we earlier identified as the most fundamental means of achieving labor market flexibility. As is well known, workers with more education earn significantly more than their less educated counterparts. It is also the case that empirically there is a strong complementarity between formal schooling and the return to post-schooling investments (MINCER, 1962). Accordingly, more educated workers receive more training. And as we have seen there have occurred dramatic shifts against low skill workers. In this light and given the positive association between labor force quality and economic growth it is not surprising that policy makers in all countries have increasingly turned their attention to education and training development.

In the US although the Federal government only provides 7% of the total funding for public elementary and secondary school training, it has authorized three substantive initiatives in the form of the Goals 2000: Educate America Act, the reauthorization of the Elementary and Secondary Education Act, and the School-to-Work Opportunities Act. (The Head Start program, dating from 1965, seeks to provide educational, nutritional, and health services up to the age of 5 for the children of poverty-level families. The program currently covers 0.75 million children and has a budget of $3.5 billion.) Goals 2000 provides grants to facilitate state and local school reform to raise standards of achievement. The Elementary and Secondary Education Act was reauthorized under the Improving America's Schools Act, and seeks to coordinate Federal aid with systemic reform at state level. Its keynote is improvement in allocating funds for the education of disadvantaged students. Another facet of the reauthorization is support for the creative use of technology in schools, including challenge grants to partnerships of schools, colleges, and the private sector for the development and demonstration of educational technology. The Schools-to-Work initiative provides Federal monies to states and communities to assist young people in transitioning to work. As is so often the case in the US, the hallmark of Federal action is the variety of initiatives that are spawned as a result. Dissemination of the results of the various services should provide a useful guide to future policy action.

The Federal role is much greater in higher and secondary education, where it accounts for one quarter of all revenues. Recent initiatives at this level have sought to address the widening gap in college enrollment rates by race and family income, which would appear to reflect the impact of tuition increases. Thus, the Federal government has attempted reform of student aid policy, to include more flexible options for repayment. As a matter of record, the proportion of college-age youth (aged 18 to 24 years) enrolled in college rose by more than one third (to 35%) between 1980 and 1994 and the numbers of associate, bachelor's, and doctoral degrees awarded grew by 28%, 25%, and 29%, respectively between 1980 and 1993, over which interval the population of college-age youth declined by 15%. We should also point out more generally that there are no signs of a decline in the educational skills of the workforce - the average educational attainment of the workforce has increased by two years since 1963 - and that test scores in math and science have risen for all groups since 1980, even if much of that improvement has been in lower level computational skills rather than higher level problem solving. And as was noted in section 1.3 there are now signs that the rise in the premium enjoyed by college educated manpower produced by demand outstripping supply has leveled off and actually begun to contract.

There is very broad agreement on the crucial role of schooling as a long-term solution to the problems of low skill - although here we have not addressed areas of disputation such as the widely perceived need to increase the degree of consumer choice in the educational system - but the position is altogether more difficult in respect of policy toward post-school training. Thus, for example, the percentage of those who go through a formal apprenticeship in the US is extremely low by European standards and the same appears true of formal company training. (That being said, it has also been shown that there is a substantial quantity of informal and thus hard to measure investment activity on the job, on which see MINCER, 1993.) This has led to the suggestion that the US should introduce a training tax and that the skills acquired should be certificated through some nationally recognized process (COMMISSION ON THE SKILLS OF THE AMERICAN WORKFORCE, 1990). The current administration is working in this direction through its National Skill Standards Board, even if it has eschewed for the present training taxes. As far as facilitating retraining is concerned, the administration is proposing replacing a very complex government-assisted system (encompassing no less than 70 training and related programs) with a single, choice-based system to enable displaced and low-income workers to take up "skill grants" of up to $2,620 per year for a two year period to undertake an associate degree. (Also under the so-called Middle Class Bill of Rights workers going back to school will be granted a $10,000 tax deduction per year for qualifying educational expenses.) A further approach is associated with the notion of the high-performance workplace encountered earlier in section 3.2.

These are interesting proposals that should stimulate interest in Europe. But at issue is their effectiveness. A trenchant criticism of the of "new consensus" on training has recently been offered by HECKMAN, ROSELIUS and SMITH (1994). The authors are critical of the market failure arguments, of certification, and in particular of the notion that American workers are provided with insufficient training investments. Policy makers in Europe would profit from the authors' critique. One of specific conclusions reached by Heckman et al. that will cause great disquiet is the suggestion that it may not be worthwhile to train low skill workers. Given their skepticism of market failure arguments and the fact that private sector training yields a higher payoff than public training, the typical exclusion of low skill workers from private sector training leads them ineluctably to this conclusion. On this view, training which has a low payoff should not be provided. It is a waste of resources pure and simple: an inefficient transfer policy as well as an inefficient investment policy. Since they recognize that there are societal advantages to inculcating the work ethic, the authors ultimately come down in favor of (inefficient) job subsidies rather than investment subsidies.

This is a very pessimistic evaluation and is in our view overdrawn in even a US context. But the low rate of return on public policies that target less-skilled and poorly educated workers is consistent with the shifting patterns of opportunity in the labor market noted in this section. Since the currently low-skilled, or more accurately a subset of them, confront real problems what is to be done?

US studies, which have the best experimental design, suggest that public programs can have positive and long-lasting effects for disadvantaged workers (see LALONDE, 1996). This is true for a variety of program services but is most clear cut for job search assistance. Yet the gains are only consistently observed for economically disadvantaged adult women. For adult males on the other hand the evaluations are mixed and marginal at best; for disadvantaged youth, the findings are rather pessimistic with the exception of Job Corps. The Job Corps program offers disadvantaged youth a very comprehensive array of services in a residential setting. It is an expensive program costing in the region of $16,000 per participant per year (down from $38,000 in 1966, in constant dollars.) By way of comparison, the average program cost under the main manpower instrument, the Job Training Partnership Act, is around $3,000 per participant. The Job Corps program has been credited with net social gains although the estimates hinge importantly on extrapolated earnings gains, estimates of the value of output produced during the training period, the value of reduced criminal behavior, and the value of savings in other transfer and training programs.

On net, this evidence can indeed be read in a pessimistic vein. Our interpretation is more positive by reason of the improved employment continuity of participants if not in their wages (as opposed to earnings). Also the improvement in the position of truly disadvantaged should not be expected to be other than incremental. This is why one should not necessarily be worried about the scale of typical program benefits being insufficient to take workers out of poverty. It is a start upon which more intensive and more expensive services can build, with carefully targeted subsequent measures. The problem here is one of resource availability.

If there are any lessons of the US experience, the chief among them are the need for flexibility in program design and for proper evaluation of programs. The presence of an underclass in the US is less likely to obtain in the Community, which limits points of comparison in the post-school training context. But European concerns about rising low skill unemployment are equally real and there continues to be real ambiguity concerning program efficacy.

Once one strays too far from the widely accepted recognition of the needs to improve the quality of initial and secondary education, to facilitate the school-to-work transition, and to raise access to higher education, one enters a minefield when it comes to second chance educational and training programs - that is, helping those currently most at risk. The European case is further distinguished by artificial barriers to employment that dissipate skills and prevent younger workers gain access to the first rungs of the job ladder. But growing wage polarization in the US and employment polarization in Europe are phenomena that demand immediate attention. There is alas no 0single method of dealing with the position of the currently least skilled. Experimentation with measures to deal with identified skill deficits is required though general, large-scale measures are not indicated precisely because these are least likely to redound to the advantage of the disadvantaged. The enhanced dissemination of the results of individual programs and support for new localized initiatives and demonstration projects favored by Community policy is to be warmly applauded, even if the notion that employers "undertrain" is unlikely to provide a sensible basis for policy.

5.9 Complementary Reform Options for Competitiveness and Full Employment

A main finding of this study is the fact that many newcomers from eastern Europe and Asia will conquer EU markets and that know-how will become more mobile due to the global information society. Therefore unskilled labor will suffer either wage reductions or unemployment (at given labor costs). Support for the creation of new firms and the expansion of the service industry is required in the EU. The process of job creation will be only successful if adequate policies are adopted - a perception which is similar to that of FREEMAN and SOETE (1994).

Long-term unemployment - especially among unskilled workers - is a serious problem in almost all EU countries. Retraining efforts have to be strengthened in member countries and higher investment in public and private universities is required.

Employees aged over 50 have particular problems in finding new jobs after being made redundant. If they have worked for many years in the same firm - as usually the case - they have acquired considerable firm specific human capital. In a future high technology society, which puts a premium on learning, redundancies of older workers tend to be permanent because hiring by new firms implies lower wages which will hardly be accepted by the worker in the presence of unemployment insurance benefits. At the same time firms will be reluctant to hire older workers because training on the job will have a short pay-off period compared to hiring younger workers. To avoid such effects older workers which are laid off and accept a new job within a short-term period could get a temporary tax benefit.

6. Summary and Conclusions

Basic Conclusions

Comparing the EU as a group of 15 countries with the US and Japan is somewhat misleading, since R&D policies at the EU-level is largely insignificant in terms of expenditure. Thus, R&D and innovation policies are determined at the national level and varies substantially between different EU member states. International competitiveness of EU firms can often be strengthened by increasing product variety and a broader research portfolio. Nevertheless, some concentration of R&D efforts of EU industry could be useful in the future, namely to the extent that this reflects economies of scale, specialization gains and the impulses of integrated EU capital markets.

To the extent that monetary integration creates bigger and efficient EU capital markets (WELFENS, 1997c and 1997d), one may expect rising intra-EU merger activities, which already were reinforced by the single market dynamics. Efficient capital markets could indirectly encourage firms to specialize in certain research fields. It should not be overlooked that coordinating and harmonizing national R&D policies of EU member countries can only be achieved at considerable political and economic transaction costs.

The analysis has shown that the US job miracle offers (mutatis mutandis) some valuable lessons for the EU. Deregulation of labor markets could help to stimulate job creation; a reduction of gross wage costs could contribute to higher employment. This basically points to the need for social security reforms and lower costs in the health industry. Technological change has intensified but is not necessarily reducing the number of jobs in Europe. A major problem in the EU is insufficient net investment in core EU countries and this in turn is partly due to insufficient profitability of real capital formation but also to administrative impediments by new firms. Finally, strong EU outward FDI in combination with low FDI inflows in continental EU countries (except for the Netherlands and the UK) point to problems in overall capital formation, namely that investors from the US and Asia do not find conditions appropriate for high investments.

Facing economic opening up of eastern Europe and intensified international competition in innovation EU countries will have to stimulate R&D and target the education system more directly towards crucial market requirements. When considering various alternatives for liberalizing the telecommunication sector, EU countries should be encouraged to pursue rather vigorous reforms that lead to full competition and hence price reductions. Such price reductions are a prerequisite for the expansion of value-added services as well as for a better use of telecoms networks and the creation of virtual research networks and virtual multinational companies.

R&D typically is financed by the national government, which hands out subsidies to companies located within the respective country. With the increasing importance of multinational companies which organize both R&D activities and production on an international - sometimes even a global scale - the link between national R&D subsidies and positive national employment and tax revenue effects is weakening. In the open EU economies therefore the question arises which role supranational R&D financing could play in the future. There is also the question which type of national R&D policy is still promising. Technology intensive and innovative firms are often launched from university campuses and the entrepreneurial potential of universities certainly is not fully exhausted in OECD countries. In the coming information age the question arises whether universities - traditionally enjoying cheap access to powerful networks - are not becoming increasingly important for starting new business. Compared to the US continental Europe has a poor venture capital system so that one should look carefully into the sometimes underestimated future role of small and medium businesses.

The EU is underspecialized in innovation compared to the US and Japan. This clearly points to the benefit from the coordination of some national R&D programs, but also from R&D competition within the Community - such competition will force firms to specialize more strongly. One may warn against generally supporting mainly large firms, since small and medium firms are particularly flexible and adjust to changing global innovation patterns more easily. While the traditional universal banking system of continental Europe has worked rather well in the past, the new century with its stronger focus on R&D is likely to require a stronger role of capital markets and venture capital markets in particular. As regards venture capital financing, continental EU countries are rather underdeveloped relative to the UK or the US The EU could stimulate the creation of venture capital in the whole EU through an initial seed financing pool. Tax laws could be refined in a way which makes long-term investment in stocks more attractive; special benefits could encourage workers to save for investment funds.

A reform of the unemployment insurance system in EU countries is urgently needed. Incentive compatible contribution schemes should be introduced - possibly only after regaining full employment - namely lower (higher) contribution rates for regions and sectors with below (above) national average unemployment rates.

Older employees laid off during recession and structural change could be brought back to work by special temporary tax concessions which make this group of workers willing to accept a new less well-paid job in a new firm. Administrative and tax impediments against labor mobility should be removed by comprehensive reforms. Taxes levied on the acquisition of land - as in Germany (increased in 1996/97) - are absolutely counterproductive in this respect. Regional policies could be modernized in the EU, namely in a way which would encourage timely adjustment in poor regions. 10 % of the EU structural funds could be set aside as a premium pool to support regions which in the past made the fastest progress in economic catching-up and job creation.

Several research avenues are worth exploring in the future:
- To which extent could higher economic growth reduce unemployment in the medium term (over five years)?
- Which effects will the globalization process have on R&D in the EU and on employment growth in western Europe?
- Which supranational and national R&D policies are most suitable for the new setting of globalization?
- What is the effect of EU foreign direct investment (inward and outward) on employment in Europe?
- Which role will eastern Europe play in a new intra-European division of labor and know-how?

The EU could regain full employment within a decade, but one might face the problems of the 1980s soon again if there are no serious attempts at policy reforms. Such reforms could include persistent scientific monitoring of labor markets, evaluation of the dynamics of new firms and analysis of public R&D policies; in particular whether national and supranational R&D policies are consistent on the one hand, and, on the other hand, are encouraging stronger EU specialization in innovations.

Appendix I: Tables and Figures

Table A1: Labor Force Participation Rates[a] (Percentages)

	1973	1979	1983	1993	1994	1995[b]
France	67,8	68,4	66,4	66,7	67,3	67,3
Germany	69,4	68,3	67,5	71,7	71,5	71,0
Italy	58,7	60,2	60,1	58,9	59,3	59,6
Spain	62,7	57,7	56,7	58,9	59,1	59,3
United Kingdom	73,0	74,3	72,4	74,7	74,2	73,8
Australia	69,8	69,2	69,3	73,7	74,2	75,4
Austria	65,1	64,9	65,6	69,2	71,6	71,3
Belgium	62,2	62,8	62,8	63,7	64,6	65,0
Canada	66,7	73,4	75,3	75,1	75,2	74,8
Czech Republic	..	..	..	75,3	75,5	75,0
Denmark	75,9	79,8	80,9	82,6	79,1	78,7
Finland	71,7	75,5	77,4	73,9	73,5	73,9
Greece	57,1	55,4	59,9	58,9	59,6	60,0
Iceland	71,3	73,1	77,3	85,1	85,1	85,8
Ireland	63,5	62,4	62,7	62,4	62,9	63,3
Luxembourg	64,8	64,4	63,3	62,5	62,5	60,4
Mexico	..	..	..	64,2	65,2	65,4
Netherlands	57,6	56,5	59,0	67,5	68,4	68,8
New Zealand	64,5	66,3	65,3	73,2	74,4	74,9
Norway	68,7	75,6	76,5	76,5	76,9	77,8
Portugal	64,0	73,6	71,4	71,2	71,4	70,8
Sweden	75,5	80,5	81,3	77,6	76,3	77,0
Switzerland	77,7	73,8	74,5	83,4	82,6	81,9
Turkey	74,0	71,2	64,7	57,7	57,8	58,4
Japan	71,7	71,8	73,0	76,1	76,4	76,5
United States	68,4	72,1	73,2	76,8	77,9	77,8
North America[c]	68,2	72,2	73,4	74,0	74,9	74,9
European Union	66,2	66,3	65,7	67,4	67,5	67,5
OECD Europe[c]	67,1	67,0	65,8	66,7	66,8	66,8
Total OECD[c]	68,2	69,5	69,5	70,9	71,3	71,4

a) Defined as the total labour force divided by the working-age population (15-64)
b) Secretariat estimates based on OECD Economic Outlook, No.59, June 1996
c) Above countries only

Source: OECD (1996a), Employment Outlook, July 1996, p. 2.

Table A2: Indicators for Internationalization of Production and R&D in Industrial Companies in Selected Countries, 1993 (Percentages)

Indicators	Germany	USA	Japan	France	United Kingdom	Canada
activities abroad						
Share of exports in gross value added of production (export dependence)	29,9	12,3	11,6	30,2	29,7	44,8
Number of foreign employees relative to domestic employees	23,5	22,4	8,1	32,5	..	..
Direct investment[a] abroad relative to exports	26,2	51,7	32,6	30,9[b]	59,0	34,1
R&D expenditures of companies relative to domestic R&D expenditures	15,0	10,0	2,0	..	..	..
Share of patents of domestic companies where the invention took place abroad	14,9	7,8	1,0	14,3	42,1	33,0
domestic activities						
Share of imports in domestic demand[c]	25,4	15,9	5,7	28,8	33,7	46,2
Number of employees in foreign owned companies relative to total domestic employees	15,9	11,6	1,1	23,9	16,2[d]	48,0
Foreign direct investment[a] relative to imports	19,5	32,2	10,3	20,9	31,7	48,4
Share of R&D expenditures by foreign owned companies in total domestic R&D expenditures	15,8	14,9	8,2	15,2	25,8	40,8
Share of patents of foreign companies where the invention took place at home	17,0	..	..	18,0	41,0	..

a) stock at the end of the year
b) direct investment stock in 1992
c) imports as a share of gross value added in production minus exports plus imports (in percent)
d) 1990

Source: DIW (1996), DIW Wochenbericht 16/96, p. 263.

Table A3:   **Technology Intensity[a] and Employment Development in OECD Countries, 1970-1991, (Average annual growth rate in percent)**

Country	High-Techno-logy Sector	Medium-Techno-logy Sector	Low-Techno-logy Sector	Manufacturing Industry
Denmark	0.6	0.7	-1.3	-0.6
Germany[b]	0.4	0.5	-1.5	-0.5
France	0.1	-0.8	-1.7	-1.1
UK	-1.4	-2.1	-2.6	-2.2
Italy	0.0	-0.1	-0.4	-0.3
Netherlands	-0.5	-0.4	-1.7	-1.2
USA	0.7	0.2	-0.6	-0.1
Japan	1.9	0.8	-0.3	0.4
OECD-13[c]	0.6	0.0	-0.9	-0.4
	(19.1)	(29.0)	(51.9)	(100)

[a] Classification of the OECD in 1986.

[b] West Germany.

[c] Including Australia, Canada, Finland, Sweden und Norway; in ( ) share of employment in whole industry employment in 1991 in percent.

Source: OCHEL, W. and PENZKOFER, W. (1995), Internationale Wettbewerbsfähigkeit und ihre Implikationen für die Europäische FuE-Politik, Ifo-Institut, Munich, p. 32.

Table A4: European Applications Filed and Euro-PCT Applications Entering the Regional Phase in 1995

Country of origin	Applications	
	number	per cent
Austria	546	0,91%
Belgium	737	1,23%
Switzerland	2084	3,47%
Germany	11789	19,62%
Denmark	414	0,69%
Spain	295	0,49%
France	4667	7,77%
United Kingdom	3212	5,35%
Greece	28	0,05%
Ireland	89	0,15%
Italy	2071	3,45%
Liechtenstein	99	0,16%
Luxembourg	62	0,10%
Monaco	13	0,02%
Netherlands	2293	3,82%
Portugal	18	0,03%
Sweden	1025	1,71%
Sub-total	29442	49,01%
Japan	10190	16,96%
United States of America	17579	29,26%
Others	2867	4,77%
Sub-total	30636	50,99%
Total[a]	60078	100,00%

a)   Rounding differences may lead to totals not being 100%

Source: EUROPEAN PATENT OFFICE, Annual Report 1995, p.72.

Appendix

187

Table A5: Stock Market Capitalization in Selected OECD Countries (End of November 1996)

Country	Stock Circulation (Bill. DM)[1]	Stock Market Capitalization Coefficient[2]
USA[3]	13,354	122
Japan[4]	4,881	63
Great Britain	2,544	152
Germany	1,002	27
France	892	38
Canada[5]	756	88
Switzerland	624	135
The Netherlands	555	93
Italy	386	23
Sweden	357	103
Spain[6]	332	39
Belgium	180	44
Denmark	105	40
Finland	90	47
Norway	85	38
Austria	48	14

Notes: 1 - prices of domestic stocks listed on the stock exchange; 2 - stock circulation in percent of the 1995 nominal GNP; 3 - New York Stock Exchange and NASDAQ; 4 - Tokio Stock Exchange; 5 - Toronto Stock Exchange; 6 - Madrid Stock Exchange

Source: DEUTSCHE BUNDESBANK (1997), Monthly Report, January 1997.

Figure A1:Employment Growth in the European Community and Elsewhere, 1960-1995
(Index 1960=100)

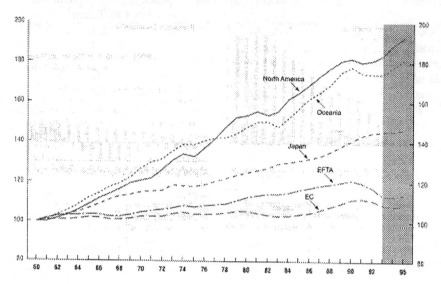

Note: OECD projections in shaded area.

Source: OECD (1994a), OECD Jobs Study, Part I, Chart 2.1.

Figure A2: Unemployment Rates in the European Community and Elsewhere, 1970-1995

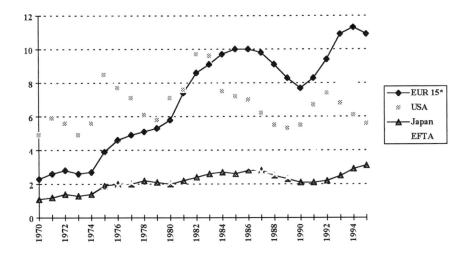

* *Since 1991 including East Germany.*
Source: Eurostat/European Commission.

Figure A3: Unemployment Rates in OECD Regions, 1950-95
(As a percentage of the labor force)

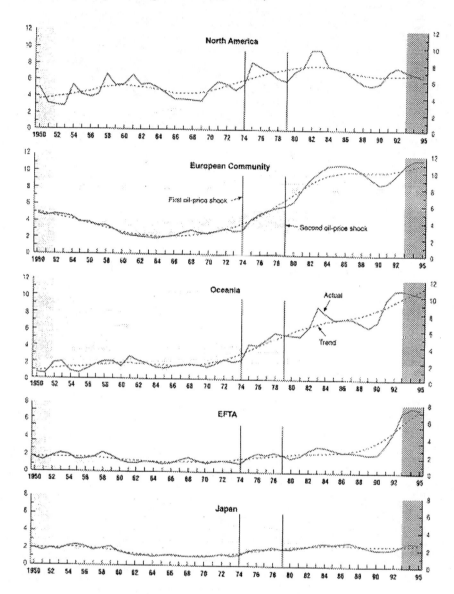

Note: OECD projections in shaded area.

Source: OECD (1994a), OECD Jobs Study, Part I, Chart 1.12.

Figure A4: Growth in Various Measures of Real Pay in the US, 1963-91

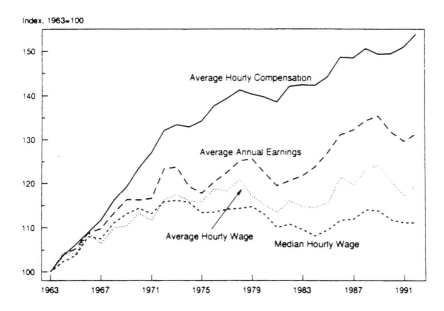

Index, 1963=100

Note: CPI-U-X1 is used as the deflator.

Source: Economic Report of the President (1995), Chart 5-2.

Figure A5: Real Wages and Employment in the European Community and the US,
      1970-92 (Index 1970=100)

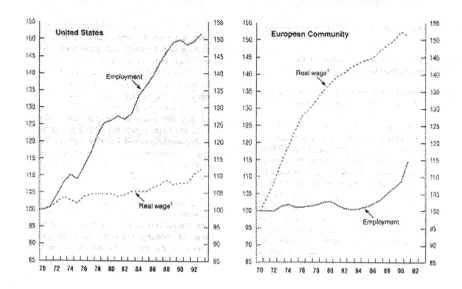

Source: OECD (1994a), OECD Jobs Study, Part I, Chart 2.3.

Figure A6: Expenditure on R&D Relative to GDP

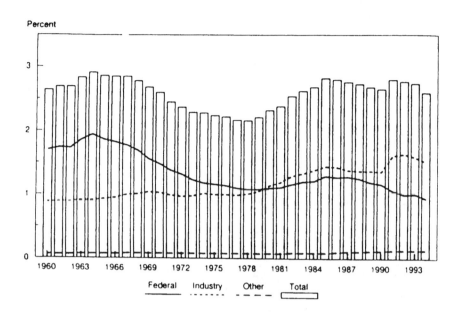

Notes: *"Other" includes R&D funded by universities and the non-profit organizations. Observations after 1980 not strictly comparable with earlier years.*

Source: *Economic Report of the President (1995), Chart 3-6.*

Figure A7: Educational Expenditure as a Percentage of GDP by Type of Institution
(1992)

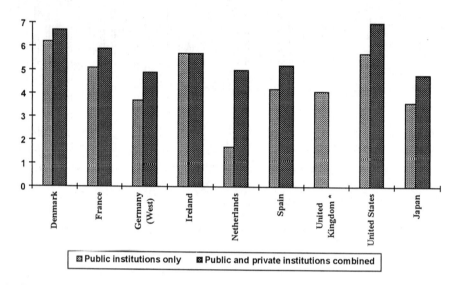

* *For the United Kingdom only Data for public institutions were available.*

Source: OECD (1995c), Education at a glance, OECD Indicators, Paris, p. 73..

Appendix II: R&D Policy in Korea

During the 1980s South Korea had to face a number of structural problems (CHUNG, 1996, p. 215). Up to then Korea had specialized in labor-intensive products. This was due to the low wage level which offered the possibility to export goods like cars, machinery, ships, textiles, shoes, and electronics at low prices. The firms primarily focused on the reduction of actual cost issues instead of long-term competitiveness through an altered product assortment or rising product quality. With the emergence of further new competitors such as China, India or Taiwan and rising wage claims at home Korea's comparative advantage in labor-intensive products - i.e. the low labor costs - was eroded. Hence, the weakness of the Korean economy became obvious: it had failed to undertake technological innovation, especially in the field of process technologies.

Though Korean firms acknowledged this challenge, they had difficulties in developing and applying new production technologies. There are mainly two reasons for this. First, in the late 1980s and early 1990s the Korean economy was in a recession so that managers, especially those of potentially innovative SMEs, often abstained from investment in R&D. Second, the Korean R&D capacities were underdeveloped. Up to the early 1980s the share of R&D expenditures in GNP was less than 1%, of which the government bore more than 50% (CHUNG, 1996, p. 109). The R&D personnel in Korea amounted to only 35,000 in 1981, compared to a figure 10 times higher in Germany that year. Research was predominantly pursued in state R&D institutes and in 1981 only 32.7% of R&D expenditures were spent in the private business sector (compared to 68.9% in Germany). Thus no implementable technologies were yet developed in order to raise productivity and overcome the structural crisis.

During the 1980s and early 1990s the share of R&D expenditures in Korean GDP increased from 0.8% in 1981 to 2.0% in 1991. The respective figure for Germany was 2.8% in 1991. Above all private R&D activities expanded greatly, while public R&D relatively lost in importance. Thus the share of privatly-sponsored R&D rose up to 80.4%, whereas the state share fell from 53.5% in 1981 to the internationally low level of 19.4% in 1991.[1] 71.3% of R&D activities were pursued in private institutes and firm departments. The rapid development of private R&D can be explained by the effective support through state R&D policy and the rising recognition in firms that R&D contributes to economic success (CHUNG, 1996, p. 116). Besides this the Korean state R&D policy focused on big projects in the frame of the National R&D Programme that was initiated in 1982. Within this program some key industries were selected and supported in their R&D activities. In the forefront of R&D activities stood applied R&D that was directly relevant for industries. Technologies from abroad were imitated, adapted and further developed.

---

[1] Most developed countries finance more than 30% of the whole national R&D expenditures such as Germany with 35% in 1989, the US with 46% in 1990, France with about 50% in 1989 and the UK with 37% in 1988. Just Japan recorded a state share of only 17% in R&D expenditures in 1989 (CHUNG, 1996, p. 126).

In the 1990s the focus of R&D policy shifted from applied and close-to-industry R&D, that is now mainly undertaken by private, firms to more sophisticated and new high and top technology. The aim is to widen the technological basis of the Korean economy in order to catch up with the highly developed western economies. Korea, therefore, has to concentrate on high technology products which can be exported and on high technology production methods which secure a high product quality. Thus improvement is strived for in the fields of sensorical techniques, precision manufacturing, semiconductor technology and Computer Integrated Manufacturing and Flexible Manufacturing Systems. The government sees its role in establishing the basis for and stimulating further private R&D. Furthermore the university system has to be developed. Besides the education and qualification of R&D personnel which is required in industry and administration, a strengthening of basic research and the cooperation of industry and sciences is needed. Altogether the Korean government plans to raise the share of R&D expenditures in GDP to 5% by 2001 in order to reach the stated aim of catching-up.

Appendix III: Statement of Professor Welfens for the Hearing of the European Parliament, Committee on Research, Technological Development and Energy in Brussels, October 1, 1996

On the eve of the 21st century, which will be characterized by technological and ecological changes as well as by global shifts in the economic power of different regions, the EU faces nine main challenges in the area of R&D:

(1) Neighboring Eastern Europe is opening up and several transforming economies - as future EU member countries - will have to be integrated in the EU wide division of labor in the field of R&D. With ex-CMEA countries, especially those attracting high foreign direct investment inflows, moving up the technology ladder (like Asian and Latin American NICs), western European firms will have to focus more on advanced and high technology and EU innovation policy will have to shift its main focus accordingly.

(2) Since the end of the Cold War the US has been redirecting R&D resources strongly towards civilian projects so that the EU is likely to face a reinforced technological challenge from the US. Only in France and the UK a reduction in military R&D expenditures will allow an 'easy' increase in civilian R&D activities. Germany's traditionally dominant focus on civilian R&D - an exclusive position shared with Japan among large OECD economies - will be undermined as R&D resources at a global level increasingly focus on civilian projects. The innovation race will intensify and the EU will have to raise R&D expenditures relative to GDP. Moreover, efficiency of R&D policies will have to be raised. Since intra-EU merger activities have accelerated there is a risk that Europe compared to the US will lack aggressive innovative newcomers.

(3) R&D in the service sector - notoriously underestimated - will become ever more important in OECD countries moving towards knowledge-based societies. Sustained EU economic growth and full employment cannot be achieved without a much stronger promotion of the service industry in general and R&D in the service sector in particular. Developments in the US during the last quarter of the 20th century have shown that a service boom can create millions of additional jobs. With a rising global supply of unskilled labor and a globally intensified high technology race skilled personnel is and will be available at a premium in the labor market. EU countries and the Community itself - with a new policy area - should increasingly support education, retraining and teleteaching for adults projects in cooperation with the private sector.

(4) The Community of the 21st century will be comprised of many more member countries than at the time of foundation in 1957, so that policy cooperation will become both more important and more difficult. Evaluation of innovation policies at the regional, national and supranational level will have to be reinforced in order to maintain efficieny.

(5) As innovation becomes more important in the 21st century efficient and new modes of financing R&D and innovation need to be developed. Besides improved seed-financing (early stage of venture capital financing) for technology-oriented start-up companies the EU is in need of stronger stock market activities which could be nurtured both by tax

incentives for households, special forms of mass privatization and a switch away from pay-as-you-go pension schemes. If old-age pension programs in continental EU countries (except for the Netherlands which already implemented serious reforms) were to rely more on accumulated savings, capital markets could play a much greater role as a source of risk capital than has been the case in the 1980s and early 1990s. The intrinsic asymmetry of information between the innovator and the bank as a potential creditor creates serious problems for efficient R&D financing in an increasingly knowledge-based society. If an R&D project is financed by a bank, the project is evaluated only when or immediately before the credit is extended. By contrast, equity markets provide continuous monitoring and provide firms with the incentive to build up a reputation in innovation. This reinforces growth.

(6) Since due to globalization and intensified technology races unskilled labor is likely to experience a fall in its relative income position, new special savings incentives and new forms of employee ownership of capital will become important as a means to avoid social conflicts. High unemployment and social conflicts could create in the EU a climate hostile to innovation. This in turn would endanger prosperity in the EU and undermine the Community's stability.

(7) Globally, intellectual property rights will become more important in the firms from the knowledge-based OECD economies. At the EU level, the regional and the global level (e.g. OECD, WTO) serious attempts to improve the system of property rights should be undertaken. A special emphasis should also be on how to facilitate international investment as a substitute to trade because higher international investment flows mean increasingly mobile technology. To the extent that trade growth is thereby reduced - without impairing prosperity - international traffic and hence emissions will fall.

(8) As life expectancy in Europe and health expenditure-GDP shares rise medical R&D and innovations in health cost management will become increasingly important. New programs at both the national and the EU level are appropriate in this field.

(9) The new information technologies in combination with liberalized telecommunications will offer novel opportunities to organize international R&D joint ventures and to accelerate the diffusion of innovations. Telecommunications will be highly important for structural adjustment and economic growth in both the EU and Eastern Europe (WELFENS and GRAACK, 1996; WELFENS and YARROW, 1996), where empirical analysis for Germany shows a signifant contribution of telecommunications to economic growth (JUNGMITTAG and WELFENS, 1996). New communication technologies could stimulate not only economic growth in Europe but also facilitate European support for transition and development in Eastern Europe, Latin America, Africa and Asia. Teleconsulting and teleteaching as well as international virtual companies could provide new ways to promote prosperous market economies worldwide.

R&D programs in the EU should be strengthened, with due attention to be paid to the principles of subsidiarity, cooperation and efficiency. Given serious regional and global ecological challenges environmental R&D projects should receive increased funding which could be diverted from the present agricultural budget. Special programs could also encourage R&D projects in the triade EU-US-Asia. Finally, there is the risk that the rising number of cooperative R&D projects - exempt from antitrust restrictions - will encourage cooperation at the production stage, too, thereby reducing competition. This in turn would undermine long term innovativeness in Europe.

Appendix IV: Coping with Environmental Problems: Positive Employment Effects?[2]

Usually the discussion about environmental protection starts from the thesis of a trade-off between a clean environment and a competitive economy. According to this a strengthening of environmental policy results in additional costs for the production sector and hence less competitiveness. These costs derive from a rise in the factor costs of the environment. The environment is used in the production sphere either as an input factor - such as water in the fishing industry or soil in agriculture - or as a receptacle of waste - such as the atmosphere for the CO_2 emissions of the energy sector. In addition the environment functions as a consumption good: individuals need clean air to breathe or a beautiful landscape to recreate.[3] Economic growth (as observed in the last decades) and the increasing world population have caused a rise in the demand for the environment. At the same time the supply of a clean environment with a certain quality has remained constant or even decreased due to the environment's limited capacity to absorb pollution and to recreate itself.

In a market economy such a demand/supply constellation with competing uses for one scarce good usually leads to rising market prices. Higher market prices would encourage an adjustment process in which excess demand would be reduced through factor substitution, i.e. substitution between the environmental input factor and other inputs (labor and capital). The consumers of environmental goods would shift their purchasing power to other relatively cheaper goods. This substitution process would continue until a new market equilibrium is reached. However, in the case of environmental goods such a market process does not take place due to a lack of adequately defined and exclusive property rights for the use of the environment (SIEBERT, 1995, p. 97). Thus, the costs of using the environment are not internal to the market and reflected in prices but external in the form of environmental pollution.

This is the point at which environmental policy intervenes. With the help of environmental instruments the existing excess demand for the environment is managed. In the context of competitiveness of industries the discussion primarily focuses on the policy method for handling the demand for the environment as a receptacle of waste. If a company is forced to pay a pollution tax or to fulfill product or production standards the costs of using the environment can no longer be externalized to the economy as a whole. Instead entrepreneurial decisions have to take into account that costs concerning the joint „bads" of environmental pollution are influencing profits. These costs emerge directly in the form of a tax which has to be paid or a transferable discharge permit which has to be acquired, and indirectly in the form of the costs following from the fulfillment of these standards. Thus, in the case of the first two market instruments - tax or permit - firms can either keep their

---

[2] This appendix is based on WELFENS, P.J.J. and HILLEBRAND, R. (1997), Growth, Innovation and Full Employment: Challenges for a New Environmental Policy, EIIW Discussion Paper, University of Potsdam, forthcoming.
[3] Besides this individuals also need the environment as a receptacle of waste for their rubbish or the air pollution caused by the car emissions on a spare time trip. This use of the environment could be handled similarly to the commercial demand for a receptacle of waste.

production processes unchanged and pay for the subsequent pollution or they can reduce pollution by changing the production processes. The latter could be achieved by installing so-called end-of-pipe technology, such as filters, or by reorganizing the production process, such as investing in less pollutive production methods in the frame of an integrated pollution control approach. In the case of standards the firms do not have to pay for the emissions which are permitted by the standard, but have to avoid excess emissions through a reduction in production or pollution.

It then can be argued that the rising costs connected with environmental policy erode the competitiveness of environmentally intensive branches and the economy as a whole (SPRENGER, 1996, p. 6). In principle there are two strategies that firms can adopt in response to the cost increases. On the one hand firms could pass on the costs in the form of higher prices for the good, thereby causing a reduction in demand. In this case production capacities and employment would diminish. Falling demand and the resulting downsizing would also affect other branches and enterprises via the underlying input-output relations. If the price elasticity of demand is very low so that rising prices cause little change in demand, adverse crowding out effects on other markets facing high income elasticities of demand will occur. On the other hand - if firms do not pass on costs and hold prices constant - profits and hence the financial basis for investment will decrease (LINTZ, 1992, p. 17). Hence, future economic growth will ceteris paribus, be lower with negative effects on employment. This second strategy is especially pursued in global markets where the producers of tradable goods compete with foreign suppliers facing lower environmental standards and ,therefore, lower costs. In conclusion, one would expect environmental policy to lead to higher costs of production and hence a loss in competitiveness. The economy, thus, would have to downsize and reduce employment in order to adjust to the globally determined cost and price level.

Though these adverse effects of environmental policy on competitiveness and employment cannot be denied, empirical estimations suggest that the cost burden for the economy as a whole is still relatively low in the OECD countries (BLAZEJCZAK and LÖBBE, 1993, p. 37). This is indicated by the share of pollution abatement and control expenditures of the business and the public sector in GDP (see Table A6).

Table A6: Pollution Abatement and Control Expenditures in Percent of GDP, 1990

	Public Sector[a]	Business Sector	Total
Denmark	1.0	..	..
Spain	0.6	..	..
Switzerland[b]	0.8	..	..
France	0.6	0.3	1.0
Canada[b]	0.8	0.3	1.1
Norway	..	..	1.2
USA	0.6	0.8	1.4
Netherlands[b]	0.9	0.6	1.4
Portugal	0.4	0.2	0.6[a]
UK	0.4	1.1	1.5
Japan	..	..	1.6
Germany	0.8	0.8	1.6
Austria[c]	1.0	0.7	1.7
Italy[b]	0.5	0.4	0.9

a) *The public expenditures are mostly financed by general tax revenues of which the business sector bears asignificant share.*
b) *1989.*
c) *1988.*

Source: OECD (1994b), OECD Environmental Indicators, Paris, p.137.

But these figures have to be interpreted very cautiously. Though they remained relatively unchanged during the late 1980s, the rising significance of environmental problems and the following strengthening of environmental policy requirements is likely to result in a perceptibly higher level of pollution abatement and control expenditure shares in the future. Thus, the discussions on CO_2 emission taxes and stricter standards in the field of waste management are still going on and will - once they are passed into law - encumber the economy further (LÖBBE and WENKE, 1995, p. 16). Moreover, no information on the structural distribution of the cost burden is included. Certain branches such as the chemical industry or the electricity sector, suffer more from the additional costs through environmental policy than others. A true quantification of the cost effects on employment is difficult to make due to such methodological problems (HORBACH and KOMAR, 1996, p. 6). Thus, the labor intensity, the price and income elasticity of demand of the affected branches would have to be taken into consideration.

Furthermore some theoretical arguments against the cost thesis have to be adduced: First of all every policy of environmental protection in the first line has to aim at an amelioration of the environmental performance. It cannot be its target to focus primarily on competitiveness issues or employment problems which have to be dealt within other policy fields. From an economic point of view environmental policy corrects the distorted factor costs structure in which the use of the environment - especially as a receptacle for waste - is not charged and therefore assumed to be free. By internalizing the external costs up to the optimal level of the externality[4] and thereby abolishing the shadow subsidies of free environmental use a higher welfare level can be reached. Nevertheless employment and competitiveness issues are of importance in a macroeconomic view of an environmental policy approach: accordingly a cost-benefit analysis has to reveal the net welfare effect of every policy. Hence the effects on economic growth, competitiveness and employment have to be taken into account as potential costs when evaluating environmental policy. Besides the benefit of an improved environmental quality there are further economic benefits that have to be considered.

Second, the improving performance of the environment entails a fall in other cost categories. Those branches that require a clean environment as an input factor like forestry, fishing or especially tourism gain a cost advantage from reduced input prices. Hence they expand and according to the labor intensity of the branch new employment is created. Furthermore the depreciations on buildings, material infrastructure and other real capital stock can be lowered because the environmental damage due to emissions is lower and the amortization horizon longer. The costs of maintenance and repair also decrease. Though there will be some job losses in the maintenance branch, resources formerly spent on the restoring of the real capital stock are now free to be spent in new benefit-creating activities. From this a positive employment effect is likely to occur. Furthermore, if the health of employees improves due to cleaner air, soil and water and less noise, social security costs may fall and factor prices decrease, resulting in higher employment. In addition, environmental performance is increasingly seen as a soft factor of location. The demand for a clean environment is positively correlated to income and education. Hence high qualified and high income employees may only be attracted to enterprise locations - at a relatively lower wage - if the surroundings are in adequate condition. Finally, a sustainable environment is the precondition of any long-term and stable economic growth.

Third, environmental policy - as well as the increasing environmental consciousness of consumers - encourages the development of a market for environmental goods. Following the implementation of emission standards enterprises are forced to acquire additional process techniques like filters, new pollution abating machinery or special waste management services in order to fulfill the standard requirements. This demand only arises due to political decisions and leads to a better use of capacities in those sectors that offer environmental protection technology or services.[5] In addition to the direct positive employment effects in the mentioned industries further demand for goods and labor results from upstream intermediate industries. The development of high technology markets for environmental protection goods offers the opportunity to realize first mover advantages in international trade with these goods: as foreign countries also tighten their environmental standards, domestic enterprises

---

[4] A maximal internalisation is not rational because of the costs connected with the internalisation. In the case of environmental pollution these costs are the ones of abatement.

[5] But one has to admit that crowding out effects are likely to occur. Starting from a given level of financial equipment other investments have to be reduced in order to finance the environmentally determined expenditures.

can at once supply well-proven products to foreign enterprises. By exploiting this export potential further jobs could be created. In the case that firms already operate at full capacity additional investment becomes necessary which again causes multiplier effects. Further positive employment effects derive from government or state institutions which are involved in the process of planning, executing and monitoring environmental policy.

A recent study by four leading German economic research institutes[6] attempts to estimate these employment effects caused by the demand in the environmental goods market (BUNDESMINISTERIUM FÜR UMWELT, NATURSCHUTZ UND REAKTORSICHERHEIT, 1996). What makes every empirical estimation in this field difficult is the fact that the environmental goods sector is not explicitly delineated in official statistics. The lack of integrated environmental and economic accounting makes an exact quantification of the demand-based employment effects of environmental policy impossible. Thus, any quantitative study on this topic has to be interpreted very carefully. Environmental goods are mainly produced in the following traditionally measured sectors: construction industry, mechanical engineering, electric/electronics, optical and precision instruments industry, chemical industry and steel and metal industry. So, researchers cannot draw any conclusions from the supply-side information collected in statistics but have either to collect the information themselves or to rely on demand-side approaches. The above-mentioned study follows such a demand-side-based approach.

The study reveals that in Germany in 1994 nearly 1 million jobs resulted from environmental protection spendings.[7] Thus, the share of employment of an aggregated environmental protection sector in the whole employment adds up to 2.7% in Germany (SPRENGER, 1996, p. 9). This figure is nearly equal to the share of the important motor vehicles sector. 47% of the created jobs are induced by environmentally motivated spending in investment and material inputs while about 53% of the jobs are created due to spending in personnel, mainly in the fields of waste management services, environmental bureaucracy and other environment-related institutions. Concerning the structural split of the environmentally induced employment, the study shows that about 420,000 jobs in the manufacturing sector - especially in the sectors mentioned above - depend on environment protection spendings. But the majority of jobs - more than 530,000 - has been created in the services sector. Besides the rising importance of direct environmental services such as in governmental administration or in the waste management sector the trend towards jobs in services also relies on the increasing importance of production-related services. Especially engineering, planning, consulting and financial management services gain more weight in environmental protection induced markets as the technological level of the goods rises quickly. Thus, the economy-wide shift towards the services sector can also be recognized in the course of ecological modernization. For comparison, some other estimations may be

---

[6] The four institutes are the DIW in Berlin, the RWI in Essen, the Ifo-institute in Munich and the IWH in Halle.

[7] To clearify: not included in the figure of 1 million jobs are the adverse employment effects caused by the cost push effect of the environmental protection. Moreover, possible crowding out effects in other branches are also neglected.

mentioned: the OECD calculates that the number of jobs associated with environmental expenditures in the US were roughly 4 million in 1992 (OECD, 1996d, p. 136), whereas Italy recorded about 300.000 jobs directly or indirectly linked to the environment (OECD, 1994c, p. 92), .

Fourth - and eventually the main objection to the cost-push argument: the trade-off between a clean environment and a competitive economy is analyzed merely from a static point of view (PORTER and VAN DER LINDE, 1995). It is assumed that economic parameters such as technology, products, production processes and consumer needs remain constant with only the degree of regulation rising. Accordingly, environmental policy implies additional costs, less competitiveness and adverse employment effects. But, from a dynamic perspective the economic parameters are not fixed but alterable.

- On the demand side, an increase in consumers' environmental consciousness leads to a shift in the structure of product demand towards less environmentally intensive goods. *Ergo* a change on the supply side will have to follow and the utilization of the environment for economic purposes will *ceteris paribus* decrease.
- On the supply side, even with constant consumers' preferences, enterprises have an incentive to use environmentally friendly production methods: since the implementation of adequate policy instruments internalizes and thereby raises the costs of the environmental use, firms will have to raise the productivity of the environment in order to maximize profits. This holds due to the neoclassical condition for profit maximization which requires that the cost of a factor is in line with its marginal productivity. A rise in the productivity of the entrepreneurial use of the environment as a receptacle of waste can be realized by a decrease in the emission intensity of the output. From a dynamic perspective the opportunity of redesigning and modernizing the production process offers the possibility to reduce emission intensity. Incomplete material utilization and insufficient controls of production processes can be eliminated or less-pollution-intensive new production technologies introduced. Thus, less material input is needed to produce the same amount of output. Consequently, cost reductions can be achieved in the field of input costs - e.g. less energy input (LINTZ, 1992, p. 15) - and the field of otherwise necessary abatement costs caused by end-of-pipe technologies. In conclusion, therefore, environmental pollution constitutes an act of wasting resources and a status of sub-optimal production structures, even from a microeconomic point of view. Firms, thus, have the incentive to produce in a less environment-intensive way.

If a modernization of the production process and the range of products takes place the following effects on the employment situation are likely to occur:

- Progress in the field of natural resource productivity due to integrated technologies lessens the pressure on labor rationalization measures in the face of international cost races. Therefore, the goal of higher living standards determined by high employment and productivity can be reached more easily (EUROPEAN COMMISSION, 1996, p. 4). At the same time the aim of sustainable development becomes achievable and, thereby, raises welfare further.

- Though a satisfactory empirical study on the macroeconomic employment effects of integrated environmental technologies is impossible due to methodological problems and lack of data, the net effect is expected to be positive (BLAZEJCZAK, EDLER and GORNIG, 1994, p. 35-36). On the one hand the eco-industry producing end-of-pipe-technologies will contract as will those downstream branches like the energy sector whose inputs will be diminished. On the other hand, the negative growth and employment effects are likely to be overcompensated in the long run by rising productivity due to an integrated pollution control approach. These innovation and productivity effects are not limited to the environment sector but will spread through the whole economy.

   To sum up: the trade-off between sustainable development and high competitiveness and, thus, high employment could be overcome if the focus of environmental policy shifts from the end-of-pipe approach to the integrated pollution control approach. Only from a static short-term view does environmental regulation necessarily lead to additional costs. Given a constant production process the entrepreneur has to implement end-of-pipe technology which requires additional capital and labor inputs and results in lower productivity. If environmental improvement is considered as an incentive to raise input productivity, sustainable development goes hand in hand with higher competitiveness and employment. In order to manage the shift to an integrated approach to pollution prevention two major preconditions have to be satisfied:

1. Environmental policy has to incorporate a framework which is innovation-friendly. PORTER and VAN DER LINDE (1995) suggest such an „innovation-friendly regulation" in the field of environmental policy.
   - First of all environmental policy has to shift from an abatement technology based view to an outcome-based view. By fixing one technology as the „best available technology", such as in the case of catalysts or scrubbers for air pollution, innovation is discouraged. Innovations do not only lead to lower costs in achieving the politically-set standard but in the medium-term result in an adjustment of the term „best available technology" (BROCKHOFF, 1995, p. 34). This interdependence lowers the incentive for enterprises to innovate. A superior approach would be to focus on a reduction target that depends on ecological requests but not on technological availability. The private actors can then find out the most efficient way to achieve the proclaimed aim. This provides firms with an incentive to innovate in order to maximize the profit.
   - The environmental instruments should as far as possible include market incentives instead of command and control approaches. Regulation by standards forces enterprises to adjust only to the level of permitted pollutions because the marginal costs of further use of the environment are zero. *Ergo* further emission reductions are useless in the eye of the entrepreneur. In contrast, market instruments like transferable discharge permits or taxes give the incentive to reduce emissions to the optimum level in the interest of profit maximization due to the positive marginal costs that are associated with the use of the environment as a receptacle of waste. Up to now and despite the announcements in the 5th Environmental Action Program of the EC

Commission current EC environmental policy still predominantly relies on command and control approaches (EUROPEAN ENVIRONMENT AGENCY, 1995, p. 17). Only slow progress towards the use of market instruments is made in some EU member states.[8]

- Furthermore it is important to make the regulation process predictable and stable in order to reduce insecurity and thereby make investment decisions more profitable. The reorganization of the product design and the production process is an investment with a long horizon. Well-defined phase-in periods of new reduction targets will give enterprises time to adjust by innovating and investing rather than implementing the long-run expensive end-of-pipe technologies. It is important that the regulation is strict enough for innovation to appear profitable. Lax standards and a week regulation authority invite enterprise behavior directed at fighting these standards through lobbyism instead of encouraging a strategy of higher resource productivity Industries should be involved in the regulation process in order to gain necessary insider information and to erect realistic and bearable regulation schemes. The regulation process should be transparent and run through at a minimum time. This makes it more difficult for lobbyism to adversely influence the results.

2. In addition to these institutional prerequisites for an innovation process, R&D are necessary to enable a shift towards an integration pollution approach.
- Firstly, it is necessary to define the emission limits that guarantee sustainable development. Hence, basic and applied research activities on the carrying capacity of the environment and the pollution effects of emissions have to be strengthened. Though it appears to be impossible to fix bearable emission limits, progress in the field of environmental cause-effect-issues has to be made. The concrete reduction or emission target that is likely to guarantee sustainable development then has to be deduced politically (BONUS, 1996, p. 22) and has to be adjusted to the respective present state of science. Further research is necessary on the evolution of an adequate legal and institutional framework that allows the realization of the innovation-friendly and competitiveness-promoting environmental regulation.
- Second, research and development is needed to create and apply new knowledge on environmental-friendly products and production processes.

---

[8] For instance, in Germany and Italy an environmentally motivated tax differentiation between unleaded and leaded petrol has been introduced, while in Austria several taxes are environmentally relevant but only bear a share of 8% of all tax revenues (OECD, 1993b, p. 91-92).

Figure A8: Environmental R&D and International Competitiveness

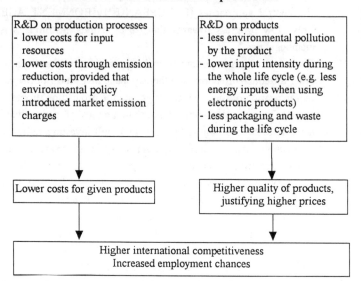

R&D has to focus on production processes as well as on products. By this either the same products can be produced with lower costs or the quality of the products can be improved so that higher prices can be charged. Hence, the international competitiveness of products rises which may result in higher employment. As far as the outcome of the R&D activities is codifiable in patents and accordingly the higher competitiveness of the goods offered can be limited to the firm, an incentive to pursue environmentally motivated R&D exists. This is because the competitive advantages following R&D expenditures can be gained exclusively. First-mover-advantages and long-run advantages have to be taken into account, too.[9]

Finally, one can conclude that negative employment effects will occur in the context with a strong environmental policy. But they are likely to be overcompensated by positive effects on the job markets in those branches that require the environment as an input factor and those ones that are suppliers in the market for environmental goods. Moreover, a rise in competitiveness and thereby in employment is very likely to occur when firms adopt integrated pollution control approaches in order to fulfill the environmental policy goals. Therefore R&D both in the field of environmentally friendly products and production processes is indispensable.

---

[9] For instance, although the adjustment of the American car manufacturers to standards in favor of cleaner cars in California in the 1970s caused costs for technological innovations the overall competitiveness has been risen: nowadays the cars can compete with „clean" cars from other countries that also have implemented high environmental standards (OECD, 1996d, p. 136).

Appendix V: Wages and Technology

An important question related to technological progress and wages concernes the dynamic evolution of industry. There is new empirical evidence that wage premia are due to technology leadership of firms. Plants that employ less technology pay lower than average wages when worker and establishment characteristics are controlled for. This shows that technology has a positive effect on wages. However, high unemployment can increase workers' resistance to new technology. With high unemployment rates in EU countries workers dismissed face a low probability of finding a new job. This will stimulate resistance against new technology and investment and could lead to resource absorbing conflicts over jobs and employment. To the extent that this reduces prospects for higher investment-output ratios and higher growth, there is a tendency for sustained unemployment.

US studies showed that shifts among plants favoring skilled workers are related to exports. Rising exports tend to raise required skill levels. Dynamic high growth plants are important in determining industry performance. Such plants significantly contribute to well paid and relatively secure jobs (ALEXANDER, 1996). As regards the development of earnings it is often argued that real earnings per employee have fallen after 1973. However, switching from a narrow wage concept to the broader definition of wages and salaries per employee real wages have been stable; including non-wage benefits employees have enjoyed a real income gain of 10% in the two decades after 1973. Taking into account higher government transfers net of taxes and profits accruing to households real household income per head has grown by amost 40% since 1973, roughly the same rate as per capita GDP (BIS 1996, p. 22,).

References:

AGEGAZ, B., DILLON, P., FELDMAN, D.H. and WHITELEY, P.F., eds. (1994), The Challenge of European Integration: Boulder: Westview Press.

ACS, Z.J. and AUDRETSCH, D.B. (1988), Innovation in Large and Small Firms: An Empirical Analysis, American Economic Review, 78(4), September, 678-690.

ACS, Z.J. and AUDRETSCH, D.B. (1990), Innovation and Small Firms, Cambridge: MIT Press.

ADDISON, J.T. (1997), Sectoral Change and the State of the Labor Market in the United States, in: SOLTWEDEL, R. ed., The Market and the State, Kiel: Institut für Weltwirtschaft.

ADDISON, J.T. and BLACKBURN, M.L. (1996), Unemployment Insurance and Postunemployment Wages, Unpublished Paper, University of South Carolina (May).

ADDISON, J.T. and GROSSO, J.-L. (1996), Job Security Provisions and Employment: Revised Estimates, Industrial Relations 35 (October), pp. 585-603.

ADDISON, J.T. and TEIXEIRA, P. (1996), Dismissals Protection and Employment: Does the Lazear Model Work for Portugal?, Unpublished Paper, Department of Economics, University of South Carolina.

AIZENMAN, J. (1997), Entwicklungsländer: Wachstumsursachen - Wachstumshindernisse, in: VON HAGEN, J., WELFENS, P.J.J. and BOERSCH-SUPAN, A., eds., Springers Handbuch der Volkswirtschaftslehre, Vol. 2, Heidelberg: Springer, pp. 407-442.

ALEXANDER, L.S. (1996), Technology, Economic Growth and Employment: New Research from the US Department of Commerce, in: OECD, Employment and Growth in the Knowledge-based Economy, Paris, pp. 307-325.

ALLEN, S. G. and FREEMAN, R. B. (1995), Quantitative Flexibility in the US Labor Market, Unpublished Paper, Harvard University.

AMENDOLA, G., DOSI, G. and PAPAGNI, E. (1993), The Dynamics of International Competitiveness, Weltwirtschaftliches Archiv 129 (3), pp. 451 - 471.

ARROW, K. (1962), Economic Welfare and the Allocation of Resources for Invention, in: NELSON, R.R. (ed.), The Rate and Direction of Inventive Activity, Princeton: Princeton University Press, pp. 609-626.

ATKINSON, A.B. and MICKLEWRIGHT, J. (1991), Unemployment Compensation and Labor Market Transitions: A Critical Review, Journal of Economic Literature, Vol. 29 (December), pp. 1679-1727.

AUDRETSCH, D.B. (1989), The Market and the State: The Role of Government Towards Business in Europe, Japan and the United States, New York: New York University Press.

AUDRETSCH, D.B. (1995), Innovation and Industry Evolution, Cambridge: MIT Press.

AUDRETSCH D.B. (1997), Industrieökonomik, in: VON HAGEN, J., WELFENS, P.J.J. and BOERSCH-SUPAN, A., eds., Springers Handbuch der Volkswirtschaftslehre, Vol. 1, Heidelberg: Springer, pp. 177-227.

AUDRETSCH, D.B. and FELDMAN, M.P. (1996), R&D Spillovers and the Geography of Innovation and Production, American Economic Review, 86(3), June, pp. 630-640.

AUDRETSCH, D.B. and FRITSCH, M. (1995), Creative Destruction: Turbulence and Economic Growth in Europe, in: HELMSTÄDTER, E. and PERLMAN, M., eds., Behavioral Norms, Technological Progress, and Economic Dynamics: Studies in Schumpeterian Economics, Ann Arbor: University of Michigan Press.

AUDRETSCH, D.B. and STEPHAN, P.E. (1996), Company-Scientist Locational Links: The Case of Biotechnology, American Economic Review, 86(3), June, pp. 641-652.

AUDRETSCH, D.B., VAN LEEUWEN, G., MENKVELD, B.J. and THURIK, R. (1995), Sub-Optimal Scale Firms and Compensating Factor Differentials in Dutch Manufacturing, Centre for Economic Policy Research (CEPR) Discussion Paper No. 1162.

BALDWIN, J.R. and PICOT, G. (1995), Employment Generation by Small Producers in the Canadian Manufacturing Sector, Small Business Economics, 7(4), pp. 317-331.

BALDWIN, J.R. and RAFIQUIZZAMAN, C. (1995), Learning and Survival, International Journal of Industrial Organization, 12 (4), pp. 346-352.

BALDWIN, R.E. (1989), The Growth Effects of 1992, Economic Policy, No. 9., pp. 247-281.

BALDWIN, R.E. (1994), Towards an Integrated Europe, London: CEPR.

BALDWIN, W.L. and SCOTT, J.T. (1987), Market Structure and Technological Change, New York: Harwood Academic Publishers.

BARTELS, A.P. and LICHTENBERG, F.R. (1987), The Comparative Advantage of Educated Workers in Implementing New Technology, Review of Economics and Statistics, Vol. 69, pp. 1-11.

BEAN, C.R. (1994), European Unemployment: A Survey, Journal of Economic Literature, Vol. 32 (June), pp. 573-619.

BIRCH, D.L. (1981), Who Creates Jobs?, The Public Interest, 65, Fall, pp. 3-14.

BIS (1996), 66th Annual Report, Basle: Bank for International Settlement.

BLACKBURN, M.L., BLOOM, D. and FREEMAN, R.B. (1990), The Declining Position of Less Skilled American Men, in: BURTLESS, G., ed., A Future of Lousy Jobs - The

Changing Structure of US Wages. Washington, D.C.: The Brookings Institution, pp. 31-67.

BLAZEJCZAK, J. and LÖBBE, K. (1993), The protection of the environment and business conditions for Industry, Report for the Federal Environmental Agency, Berichte 1/93 des Umweltbundesamtes, Berlin.

BLAZEJCZAK, J., EDLER, D. and GORNIG, M. (1994), Grüne Arbeitsplätze, in: Aus Politik und Zeitgeschichte, Beilage zur Wochenzeitung Das Parlament, B37/94, 16. September 1994, pp. 29-36.

BONUS, H. (1996), Institutionen und Institutionelle Ökonomik: Anwendungen für die Umweltpolitik, Discussion Paper No. 231, Economic Faculty, University of Münster.

BORJAS, G.J., FREEMAN, R.B. and KATZ, L.F. (1992), On the Labor Market Effects of Immigration and Trade, in: BORJAS, G.J. and FREEMAN, R.B. eds., Immigration and the Work Force. Chicago, IL: University of Chicago Press, pp. 213- 44.

BOYER, R. (1996), Training and Employment in the New Production Models, in: STI Science Technology Industy, Review No. 15, pp. 105-131.

BRANDER, J.A. and SPENCER, B. (1981), Tariffs and the Extraction of Monopoly Rents under Potential Entry, Canadian Journal of Economics, Vol. 14, pp. 371-389.

BRANDER, J.A. and SPENCER, B. (1985), Export Subsidies and International Market Share Rivalry, Journal of International Economics, Vol. 18, pp. 83-100.

BROCKHOFF, K. (1994), Forschung und Entwicklung, Planung und Kontrolle, 3rd edition, München: Oldenbourg, 1992, and 4th edition.

BROCKHOFF, K. (1995), F&E und Umwelt, in: JUNKERNHEINRICH, M., KLEMMER, P. and WAGNER, G.R., eds., Handbuch zur Umweltökonomie, Berlin: Analytica, pp. 30-37.

BROERSMA, O. and GAUTIER, P. (forthcoming), Job Creation and Job Destruction by Small Firms: An Empirical Investigation for the Dutch Manufacturing Sector, Small Business Economics.

BROWN, C., CONNOR, J., HEERINGA, S. and JACKSON, J. (1990), Studying Small Business with the Michigan Employment Security Commission Longitudinal Data Base, Small Business Economics, 2(4), pp. 261-278.

BROWN, C., HAMILTON, J. and MEDOFF, J., (1990), Employers Large and Small, Cambridge: Harvard University Press.

BROWN, W.H. and HIRBAYASHI, M.J. (1996), Patents with Multiple Inventors Residing in Different Countries, in: OECD, Innovation, Patents and Technological Strategies, Paris.

BUNDESMINISTER FÜR FORSCHUNG UND TECHNOLOGIE (1993), Bundesbericht Forschung 1993, Bonn: BMFT.

BUNDESMINISTERIUM FÜR UMWELTSCHUTZ, NATURSCHUTZ UND REAKTORSICHERHEIT (1996), Umweltpolitik: Aktualisierte Berechnung der umweltschutzinduzierten Beschäftigung in Deutschland, Study jointly produced by DIW, ifo, IWH and RWI, Bonn.

BURGESS, S.M. (1994), The Reallocation of Employment and the Role of Employment Protection Legislation, Discussion Paper No. 193, Centre for Economic Performance, London School of Economics (April).

BURTLESS, G. (1987), Jobless Pay and High European Unemployment, in: LAWRENCE, R.Z. and SCHULTZE, C.L., eds., Barriers to European Growth - A Transatlantic View. Washington, D.C.: The Brookings Institution, pp. 105-74.

BURTLESS, G. (1990), Introduction and Summary, in: BURTLESS, G., ed., A Future of Lousy Jobs? The Changing Structure of US Wages. Washington, D.C.: The Brookings Institution, pp. 1-30.

BURTLESS, G. (1995), International Trade and the Rise in Earnings Inequality, Journal of Economic Literature, Vol. 33 (June), pp. 800-16.

CARLSSON, B. and STANKIEWICZ, R. (1991), On the nature, function and composition of technical systems, Journal of Evolutionary Economics 1(2), pp. 93 - 118.

CHUNG, S. (1996), Technologiepolitik für neue Produktionstechnologien in Korea und Deutschland, Heidelberg: Physica.

COHEN, W. and LEVIN, R.C. (1989), Empirical Studies of Innovation and Market Structure," in: SCHMALENSEE, R. and WILLIG, R., eds., Handbook of Industrial Organization, Vol. 2, Amsterdam: North-Holland, pp. 1059-1107.

COHEN, W. and LEVINTHAL, D., (1990), Absorptive Capacity: A New Perspective on Learning and Innovation, Administrative Science Quarterly, 35(1), pp. 128-152.

COMMISSION ON THE SKILLS OF THE AMERICAN WORKFORCE (1990), America's Choice: High Skills or Low Wages. Rochester, N.Y.: National Center on Education and the Economy.

CUHLS, K. and KUWAHARA, T. (1994), Outlook for Japanese and German Future Technology, Heidelberg: Springer-Physica.

DASGUPTA, P.S. and DAVID, P.A. (1987), Information Disclosure and the Economics of Science and Technology, in: FEIWEL, G., ed., Kenneth Arrow and the Ascent of Economic Theory, New York: Mac Millan.

DAVIS, S.J., HALTIWANGER, J. and SCHUH, S. (1996a), Small Business and Job Creation: Dissecting the Myth and Reassessing the Facts, Small Business Economics, 8(5), October 1996.

DAVIS, S.J., HALTIWANGER, J. and SCHUH, S. (1996b), Job Creation and Destruction in US Manufacturing, Cambridge, MA: MIT Press.

DE GRAUWE, P. (1992), The Economics of Monetary Integration, London: Macmillan.

DEPARTMENT OF COMMERCE (1996), Direct Investment on a Historical-Cost Basis, Survey of Current Business, July, Washington D.C., pp. 45-55.

DEUTSCHE BUNDESBANK (1994), Reale Wechselkurse als Indikatoren der internationalen Wettbewerbsfähigkeit, Monatsbericht, May, pp. 47 - 60.

DEUTSCHE BUNDESBANK (1996), Long Term Comparison of Technological Services in the Balance of Payments, Monthly Report, May, pp. 61-71.

DEUTSCHE BUNDESBANK (1997), Monthly Report, January.

DIW (1996), Internationalisierung von Forschung und Entwicklung in multinationalen Unternehmen, DIW Wochenbericht, 16/96, pp. 258-265.

DOSI, G. (1988), Sources, Procedures and Microeconomic Effects of Innovation, Journal of Economic Literature, Vol. 26, pp. 1120 - 1171.

DOSI, G., PAVITT, K. and SOETE, L. (1990), The Economics of Technical Change and International Trade, New York: Harvester Wheatsheaf.

ECONOMIC POLICY INSTITUTE (1996), The State of Working America, Washington D.C.

ECONOMIC REPORT OF THE PRESIDENT (1994), Washington, D.C.: United States Government Printing Office.

ECONOMIC REPORT OF THE PRESIDENT (1995), Washington, D.C.: United States Government Printing Office.

EMPLOYMENT POLICY FOUNDATION (1996), The American Workplace. 1996 Labor Day Report. Washington, D.C.: Employment Policy Foundation.

ERGAS, H. (1987), Does Technology Policy Matter?, in: GUILE, B.R. and BROOKS, H., eds., Technology and Global Industry: Companies and Nations in the World Economy, Washington, D.C.: National Academy Press.

ETHIER, W. (1982), Decreasing Costs in International Trade and Frank Graham's Argument for Protection, Econometrica, Vol. 50, pp. 1243-1268.

ETHIER, W. (1986), The Multinational Firm, Quarterly Journal of Economics, Vol. 101, pp. 805-834.

EU INFORMATIONEN (1995), February 1995, No. 2.

EUROPEAN COMMISSION (1993), Weißbuch 'Wachstum, Wettbewerbsfähigkeit und Beschäftigung', Bulletin der Europäischen Gemeinschaft, Beilage 6/93, Luxembourg.

EUROPEAN COMMISSION (1995a), Green Paper on Innovation, Vol. I, COM(95) 688 final, Brussels.

EUROPEAN COMMISSION (1995b), Green Paper on Innovation, Vol. II, COM(95) 688 final, Brussels.

EUROPEAN COMMISSION (1996), Benchmarking the Competitiveness of European Industry, Brussels: COM(96) 463 final.

EUROPEAN ENVIRONMENT AGENCY (1995), Environment in the European Union 1995, Copenhagen.

EUROPEAN PATENT OFFICE (1995), Annual Report 1995, Munich.

FAGERBERG, J.(1988), International competitiveness, Economic Journal 98, pp. 355 - 374.

FRANZ, W. (1997), Arbeitsmärkte, in: VON HAGEN, J., WELFENS, P.J.J. and BOERSCH-SUPAN, A., eds., Springers Handbuch der Volkswirtschaftslehre, Vol. 1, Heidelberg: Springer, pp. 135-175.

FREEMAN, C. and SOETE, L. (1994), Work for all or mass unemployment?,. London: Pinter.

FREEMAN, R.B. (1993), How Much Has Deunionization Contributed to the Rise in Male Inequality?, in: DANZIGER, S. and GOTTSCHALK, P. eds., Uneven Tides - Rising Inequality in America, New York: Russell Sage Foundation, pp. 133-63.

FROOT, K.A. and STEIN, J.C. (1991), Exchange Rates and Foreign Direct Investment: An Imperfect Capital Markets Approach, Quarterly Journal of Economics, November, pp. 1191-1217.

GALLAGHER, C.C., DALY, M.J. and THOMASON, J.C. (1991), The Growth of U.K. Companies and Their Contribution to Job Generation, 1985-1987, Small Business Economics, 3(4), pp. 269-286.

GARDNER, J.M. (1995), Worker Displacement: A Decade of Change, Monthly Labor Review 118 (April), pp. 45-57.

GIERSCH, H., PAQUE, K.-H. and SCHMIEDING, H. (1992), The Fading Miracle, Cambridge: Cambridge University Press.

GILDER, G. (1989), Microcosm, New York: Touchstone.

GLAESER, E.L., KALLAL, H.D., SCHEINKMAN, J.A. and SCHLEIFER, A. (1992), Growth of Cities, Journal of Political Economy, 100(4), pp. 1126-1152.

GORDON, R. (1996), Problems in the Measurement and Performance of Service-Sector Productivity in the United States, NBER Working Paper No. 5519. Cambridge, MA: National Bureau of Economic Research.

GORT, M. and KLEPPER, S. (1982), Time Paths in the Diffusion of Production Innovations, Economic Journal, 92(3), pp. 630-653.

GRAACK, C. (1996), Structure of the Telecoms Sector and Degree of Internationalization in Europe and Russia, Discussion Paper No. 17, Europäisches Institut für internationale Wirtschaftsbeziehungen (EIIW), Potsdam.

GRAAF, J. de V. (1957), Theoretical Welfare Economics, Cambridge: Cambridge University Press.

GRILICHES, Z. (1979), Issues in Assessing the Contribution of R&D to Productivity Growth, Bell Journal of Economics, 10, Spring, pp. 92-116.

GRILICHES, Z. (1990), Patent Statistics as Economic Indicators: A Survey, Journal of Economic Literature, Vol. 28, pp. 1661 - 1707.

GRILICHES, Z. (1992), The Search for R&D Spill-Overs, Scandinavian Journal of Economics, 94(S), pp. 29-47.

GROSSMAN, G.M. and HELPMAN, E. (1991), Innovation and Growth in the Global Economy, Cambridge, MA: MIT Press.

GRUBB, D. and WELLS, W. (1993), Employment Regulation and Patterns of Work in EC Countries, OECD Economic Studies, No. 21 (Winter), pp. 7-58.

GRUPP, H. (1994a), Technology at the Beginning of the 21st Century, Technology Analysis & Strategic Management 6(4), pp. 379 - 397.

GRUPP, H. (1994b), The measurement of technical performance of innovations by technometrics and its impact on established technology indicators, Research Policy 23, pp. 175 - 193.

GRUPP, H. (1995), Science, High Technology and the Competitiveness of EC Nations, Cambridge Journal of Economics 19, pp. 209 - 223.

GRUPP, H. (1997), Appropriation of Innovation Rents in a Science-Driven Market, forthcoming.

GRUPP, H. and HOHMEYER, O. (1986), A Technometric Model for the Assessment of Technological Standards and their Application to Selected Technology-Intensive Products, Tech. Forecast. Soc. Change 30, pp. 123 - 137.

GRUPP, H. and HOHMEYER, O. (1988), Technological Standards for Research-Intensive Product Groups and International Competitiveness, in: VAN RAAN, ed., Handbook of Quantitative Studies of Science and Technology, Amsterdam: North-Holland, pp. 611 - 673.

GRUPP, H. and MÜNT, G. (1996), Trade on High-Technology Markets and Patent Statistics - Leading-Edge Versus High-Level Technology, in: ARCHIBUGI, D. and MICHIE, J., eds., Trade, Growth and Technical Change, Cambridge, Cambridge University Press, (in print).

GRUPP, H., MÜNT, G. and SCHMOCH, U. (1994), Trade in High-Technology Products and Patent Statistics - Leading Edge Versus High Level Technology, paper presented for the 1994 Münster Conference of the International Joseph A. Schumpeter Society, August 17-20, „Economic Dynamism: Analysis and Policy".

GRUPP, H., MÜNT, G., GEHRKE, B. and LEGLER, H. (1996), Knowledge-intensive and resource-concerned structures: strength and weakness of high technology in Germany, in: KRULL and MEYER-KRAHMER, F., eds., Science and Technology in Germany, Harlow: Cartermill, pp. 46 - 62.

HAMEL, G. and PRAHLAD, C.K. (1994), Competing for the Future, Boston: Harvard Business School Press.

HANNAN, M.T. and FREEMAN, J. (1989), Organizational Ecology, Cambridge: Harvard University Press.

HÄRTEL, H.-H. (1988), Wachstums- und Struktureffekte des Umweltschutzes, Wirtschaftsdienst, Vol. 68, no. 5, pp. 245-252.

HECKMAN, J.J., ROSELIUS, R.L. and SMITH, J.A. (1994), US Education and Training Policy: A Re-evaluation of the Underlying Assumptions Behind the 'New Consensus', in: SOLMON, L.C. and LEVENSON, A.R., eds., Labor Markets, Employment Policy, and Job Creation, Boulder, CO: The Westview Press, pp. 83-121.

HELPMAN, E. and KRUGMAN, P.R. (1985), Market Structure and Foreign Trade, Cambridge, MA: MIT Press.

HIRSCHMAN, A.O. (1970), Exit, Voice, and Loyalty, Cambridge, MA: Harvard University Press.

HOLMSTROM, B. (1989), Agency Costs and Innovation, Journal of Economic Behavior and Organization, 12, pp. 305-327.

HORBACH, J. and KOMAR, W., (1996), Beschäftigung durch Umweltschutz in Deutschland, Institut für Wirtschaftsforschung Halle: Wirtschaft im Wandel, 15/1996, pp. 6-9.

HUFBAUER, G.C., ed (1990), Europe 1992. An American Perspective, Washington DC: Brookings.

INVERNIZZI, B. and REVELLI, R. (1993), Small Firms and the Italian Economy: Structural Changes and Evidence of Turbulence, in: ACS, Z.J. and AUDRETSCH, D.B., eds., Small Firms and Entrepreneurship: An East-West Comparison, Cambridge: Cambridge University Press, pp. 123-154.

IRVINE, J. and MARTIN, B. R. (1984), Foresight in Science. Picking the Winners, London: Dover.

JACKMANN, R., PISSARIDES, C. and AVOURI, S. (1990), Unemployment Policies, Economic Policy, October.

JACOBS, J. (1969), The Economy of Cities, New York: Random House.

JAFFE, A.B., TRAJTENBERG, M. and HENDERSON, R., (1993), Geographic Localization of Knowledge Spillovers as Evidenced by Patent Citations, Quarterly Journal of Economics, 63(3), August, pp. 577-598.

JENSEN, M.C. (1993), The Modern Industrial Revolution, Exit, and the Failure of Internal Control Systems, Journal of Finance, 68(3), July, pp. 831-880.

JOVANOVIC, B. (1982), Selection and Evolution of Industry, Econometrica, 50(2), pp. 649-670.

JOVANOVIC, M.N. (1992), International Economic Integration, London: Routledge.

JUHN, C.. and MURPHY, K.M. (1994), Relative Wages and Skill Demand, 1940-1990, in: SOLMON, L.C. and LEVENSON, A.R., eds., Labor Markets, Employment Policy, and Job Creation, Boulder, CO: The Westview Press, pp. 343-59.

JUNGMITTAG, A. and WELFENS, P.J.J. (1996), Telekommunikation, Innovation und die langfristige Produktionsfunktion: Theoretische Aspekte und eine Kointegrationsanalyse für die Bundesrepublik Deutschland, Discussion Paper No. 20, Europäisches Institut für internationale Wirtschaftsbeziehungen (EIIW), Potsdam.

KINDLEBERGER, C.P. and AUDRETSCH, D.B. (1983), The Multinational Corporation in the 1980s, Cambridge, MA: MIT Press.

KLEINKNECHT, A. (1989), Firm Size and Innovation: Observations in Dutch Manufacturing Industry, Small Business Economics, 1(3), pp. 214-222.

KLODT, H. (1992), Technology-Based Trade and Multinationals' Investment in Europe: Structural Change and Competition in Schumpeterian Goods, in: KLEIN, M. and WELFENS, P.J.J, eds., Multinationals in the New Europe and Global Trade, Heidelberg and New York: Springer, pp. 107-121.

KNIGHT, F.H. (1921), Risk, Uncertainty and Profit, New York: Houghton Mifflin.

KONINGS, J. (1995), Gross Job Flows and the Evolution of Size in U.K. Establishments, Small Business Economics, 7(3), pp. 213-220.

KREPS, D. (1991), Corporate Culture and Economic Theory, in: ALT, J. and SHEPSLE, K., eds., Positive Perspectives on Political Economy, Cambridge: Cambridge University Press.

KRUGMAN, P. A. (1981), Trade, accumulation and uneven development, Journal of Development Economics 8, pp. 149 - 161.

KRUGMAN, P.A. (1991), Geography and Trade, Cambridge: MIT Press.

KRUPP, H. (1984), Basic Research in German Research Institutions Excluding Universities and the Max-Planck Society, in: JAPAN SOCIETY FOR THE PROMOTION OF SCIENCE (ed.), Proceedings of the Japan-Germany Science Seminar, Tokyo, pp. 73 - 109.

KUHLMANN, S. and MEYER-KRAHMER, F. (1995), Practice of Technology Policy Evaluation in Germany: Introduction and Overview, in: BECHER, G. and KUHLMANN, S., eds., Evaluation of Technology Programmes in Germany, Dordrecht: Kluwer Academic Publishers.

LALONDE, R.J. (1996), The Promise of Public Sector-Sponsored Training Programs, Journal of Economic Perspectives 9 (Spring), pp. 149-68.

LANCASTER, K. J. (1991), Modern Consumer Theory, Aldershot: Edward Elgar.

LAZEAR, E.P. (1990), Job Security Provisions and Job Security, Quarterly Journal of Economics 105 (August), pp. 699-726.

LEGLER, H., GRUPP, H., GEHRKE, B. and SCHASSE, U. (1992), Innovationspotential und Hochtechnologie, Heidelberg: Physica-Verlag.

LENK, H. (1979), Pragmatische Vernunft. Philosophie zwischen Wissenschaft and Praxis, Stuttgart: Philipp Reclam.

LEONARD, J.S. (1986), On the Size Distribution of Employment and Establishments, Nation Bureau of Economic Research (NBER), Discussion Paper No. 1951.

LINDBECK, A. and SNOWER, D. (1990), Demand and Supply-side Policies and Unemployment: Policy Implications of the Insider-outsider Approach, Scandinavian Journal of Economics, Vol. 92, pp. 279-305.

LINTZ, G. (1992), Umweltpolitik und Beschäftigung, Beitrag zur Arbeitsmarkt- und Berufsforschung Nr. 159, Institut für Arbeitsmarkt- und Berufsforschung der Bundesanstalt für Arbeit, Nürnberg.

LÖBBE, K. and WENKE, M. (1995), Beschäftigung und Umweltschutz, in: JUNKERNHEINRICH, M., KLEMMER, P. and WAGNER, G.R., eds., Handbuch zur Umweltökonomie, Berlin: Analytica, pp. 16-21.

LOESCH, A. (1954), The Economics of Location, New Haven: Yale University Press.

LOVEMAN, G. and SENGENBERGER, W. (1991), The Re-Emergence of Small-Scale Production: An International Comparison, Small Business Ecnomics, 3(1), pp. 1-37.

LUCAS, R.E., Jr. (1993), Making a Miracle, Econometrica, 61(2), pp. 1002-1937.

LUHMANN, N. (1988), Die Wirtschaft der Gesellschaft, Frankfurt: Suhrkamp.

MACHLUP, F. (1962), The Production and Distribution of Knowledge in the United States, Princeton, N. J.

MATA, J. (1994), Firm Growth During Infancy, Small Business Economics, 6(1), pp. 27-40.

McKENZIE, G. and VENABLES, A.J. (1991), The Economics of the Single European Act, London: Macmillan.

McKINSEY (1996), Capital Productivity, Washington, D.C.

MEYER, B.D. (1995), Lessons from the US Unemployment Insurance Experiments, Journal of Economic Literature, Vol. 33 (March), pp. 91-131.

MILGROM, P. (1988), Employment Contracts, Influence Activities and Organization Design, Journal of Political Economy, 96(1), pp. 42-60.

MILGROM, P. and ROBERTS, J. (1987), Information Asymmetries, Strategic Behavior, and Industrial Organization, American Economic Review, 77(2), pp. 184-193.

MINCER, J. (1962), On the Job Training: Costs, Returns, and Some Implications, Journal of Political Economy 70 (Supplement), pp. 50-79.

MINCER, J. (1993), Investment in US Education and Training, Discussion Paper No. 671, Columbia University.

MONTHLY LABOR REVIEW (1993), The American Workforce, 1992-2005, Monthly Labor Review 116 (November).

MOSLEY, H., and KRUPPE, T. (1993), Employment Protection and Labor Force Adjustment - A Comparative Evaluation, Discussion Paper, Wissenschaftszentrum Berlin/WZB (April).

MUELLER, D.C. (1976), Information, Mobility, and Profit, Kyklos, 29(3), pp. 419-448.

MÜNT, G. (1996), Dynamik von Innovation und Aussenhandel, Entwicklung technischer und wirtschaftlicher Spezialisierungsmuster, Heidelberg: Physica-Verlag.

MURPHY, K.M. and WELCH, F. (1993), Industrial Change and the Rising Importance of Skill, in: DANZIGER, S. and GOTTSCHALK, P., eds., Uneven Tides - Rising Inequality in America. New York: Russell Sage Foundation, pp. 101-32.

NEFIODOW, L.N. (1991), Der fünfte Kondratieff: Strategien zum Strukturwandel in Wirtschaft und Gesellschaft, 2nd ed., Frankfurt/Wiesbaden: FAZ, Gabler.

NELSON, R.R. and WINTER, S.G. (1982), An Evolutionary Theory of Economic Change, Cambridge, MA: Cambridge University Press.

NEVEN, E. (1990), EEC Integration Towards 1992: Some Distributional Aspects, Economic Policy, pp. 14-46.

NIW/DIW/FHI/ZEW (1996), Zur technologischen Leistungsfähigkeit Deutschlands, Bericht an das Bundesministerium für Bildung, Wissenschaft, Forschung und Technologie, Hannover 1995, mimeo.

NOAM, E.M. (1993), Assessing the Impacts of Divestiture and Deregulation in Telecommunications, Southern Economic Journal, January 1993.

OCHEL, W. and PENZKOFER, W. (1995), Internationale Wettbewerbsfähigkeit und ihre Implikationen für die Europäische FuE-Politik, Ifo-Institut, Munich.

OECD (1993a), Frascati Manual 1992, Proposed Standard Practice for Surveys of Research and Experimental Development, Fifth Revision, Paris.

OECD (1993b), OECD-Umweltprüfberichte Österreich, Paris.

OECD (1994a), The OECD Jobs Study, Part I and II. Paris.

OECD (1994b), OECD Environmental Indicators, Paris.

OECD (1994c), OECD Environmental Performance Reviews: Italy, Paris.

OECD (1995a), Telecommunication Infrastructure. The Benefits of Competiton, Paris.

OECD (1995b), Science and Technology Indicators, Paris.

OECD (1995c), Education at a glance, OECD Indicators, Paris.

OECD (1996a), OECD Employment Outlook, July 1996, Paris.

OECD (1996b), Technology, Productivity and Job Creation, Vol. 1 Highlights, Paris.

OECD (1996c), Technology, Productivity and Job Creation, Vol. 2 Analytical Report, Paris.

OECD (1996d), OECD Environmental Performance Reviews: United States, Paris.

OOSTERBEEK, H. and VAN PRAAG, M. (1995), Firm-Size Wage Differentials in the Netherlands, Small Business Economics, 7(3), pp. 173-182.

PALINKAS, P. (1994), Forschungs- und Technologiepolitik, in: MICKEL, W.W., ed., Handlexikon der Europäischen Union, Cologne: Omnia.

PAPACONSTANTINOV, G. (1996), Globalisation, Technology and Employment: Characteristics and Trends, in: OECD, STI Review No. 15, pp. 177-235.

PAQUE, K.-H. (1997), Does Europe's Common Market Need a Social Dimension? Some Academic Thoughts on a Popular Theme, in: ADDISON, J.T. and SIEBERT, W.S. eds., Labour Markets in Europe: Issues of Harmonization and Regulation, London: The Dryden Press.

PAVITT, K. (1984), Sectoral patterns of technical change: Towards a taxonomy and a theory, Research Policy 13, pp. 343-373.

PAVITT, K. and SOETE, L. (1980), Innovative activities and export shares: some comparisons between industries and countries, in: PAVITT, K., ed., Technical Innovation and British Economic Performance, London: Macmillan.

PETERS, T. (1992), Rethinking Scale, California Management Review, 35, Fall, pp. 7-29.

PETIT, P. (1995), Technology and Employment: Key Questions in a Context of High Unemployment, in: OECD, STI Review, No. 15, pp. 13-47.

PIORE, M.J. and SABEL, C. (1984), The Second Industrial Divide, New York: Basic Books.

POLANYI, M. (1966), The Tacit Dimension, London: Routledge & Kegan,.

POLLAK, M. (1991), Research and Development in the Service Sector, The Service Economy (July).

PORTER, M. (1990), The Competitive Advantage of Nations, New York: Free Press.

PORTER, M.E. and VAN DER LINDE, C. (1995), Green and Competitive, in: Harvard Business Review, September-October 1995, pp. 120-134.

REGNIER, P. (1993), The Dynamics of Small and Medium-Sized Enterprises in Korea and Other Asian NIEs, Small Business Economics, 5(1), March, pp. 23-36.

REPORT (1995), Germany's Technological Performance, NIW, DIW, ISI, ZEW.

ROMER, P. (1986), Increasing Returns and Long-Run Growth, Journal of Political Economy, 94(5), pp. 1002-1037.

ROMER, P. (1990), Endogenous Technological Change, Journal of Political Economy, 98(1), pp. 71-102.

ROTHWELL, R. (1989), Small Firms, Innovation and Industrial Change, Small Business Economics, 1(1), pp. 51-64.

SANTERELLI, E. and STERLACCHINI, A. (1990), Innovation, Formal vs. Informal

R&D, and Firm Size: Some Evidence from Italian Manufacturing Firms, Small Business Economics, 2(2), pp. 223-228.

SAXENIAN, A. (1994), Regional Advantage, Cambridge: Harvard University Press.

SCHÄFER, T. and HYLAND, P. (1994), Technology Policy in the Post-Cold War World, Journal of Economic Issues, 28 (June), No. 2, pp. 597-608.

SCHERER, F.M. (1984), Innovation and Growth: Schumpeterian Perspectives, Cambridge, MA: MIT Press.

SCHERER, F.M. (1992), Schumpeter and Plausible Capitalism, Journal of Economic Literature, Vol. 30(3), pp. 1416-1433.

SCHERER, F.M. (1996), Industry Structure, Strategy, and Public Policy, New York: Harper Collins.

SCHMOCH, U., GRUPP, H., MANNSBART, W. and SCHWITALLA, B. (1988) Technikprognosen mit Patentindikatoren, Köln: Verlag TÜV Rheinland.

SERVAN-SCHREIBER, J.J. (1968), The American Challenge, London: Hamish Hamilton.

SEUFERT, W. (1996), Job Creation in the European Inforamtion Society, forthcoming in ADDISON, J. and WELFENS, P.J.J., eds., European Labor Markets and Social Security, Heidelberg and New York: Springer.

SIEBERT, H. (1991), Capital Flows in the World Economy, Symposium 1990, Tübingen: Mohr.

SIEBERT, H. (1995), Economics of the Environment, 4th ed., Heidelberg: Springer.

SKOLIMOWSKI, H. (1966), The Structure of Thinking in Technology, Technology and Culture 7, pp. 371 - 383.

SOETE, L. G. (1981), A general test of technological gap trade theory, Weltwirtschaftliches Archiv 117, pp. 638 - 660.

SOETE, L. G. (1987), The Impact of Technological Innovation on International Trade Patterns: The Evidence Reconsidered, Research Policy 16, pp. 101 - 130.

SONG, B.-N. (1990), The Rise of the Korean Economy, Oxford: Oxford University Press.

SORRENTINO, C. (1995), International Unemployment Indicators, 1983-93, Monthly Labor Review 118 (August), pp. 31-50.

SPRENGER, R.-U. (1996), Umweltschutz und Beschäftigung in Deutschland, in: ifo Schnelldienst, Vol. 49, no. 28, pp. 6-15.

STANKIEWICZ, R. (1992), Technology as an autonomous, socio-cognitive system, in: GRUPP, H., ed., Dynamics of Science-Based Innovation, Berlin: Springer, pp. 19 - 44.

STIFTERVERBAND (1995), Forschung und Entwicklung in der Wirtschaft, FuE-Info, Dezember 1995, Essen.

STRAUBHAAR, T. (1988), International Labor Migration within a Common Market: Some Aspects of EC Experience, Journal of Common Market Studies, pp. 45-62.

TEECE, D., RUMULT, R., DOSI, G. and WINTER, S. (1994), Understanding Corporate Coherence: Theory and Evidence, Journal of Economic Behavior and Organization, 23(1), pp. 1-30.

TICHY, G. (1992), Theoretical and Empirical Considerations on the Dimension of an Optimum Integration Area in Europe, Aussenwirtschaft, Vol. 47, pp. 107-137.

TILLY, R. and WELFENS, P.J.J., eds. (1996), European Economic Integration as a Challenge to Industry and Government, Heidelberg, New York: Springer.

TIRONI, E. (1982), Customs Union Theory in the Presence of Foreign Firms, Oxford Economic Papers, pp. 150-171.

TOPEL, R.H. (1993), What Have We Learned from Empirical Studies of Unemployment and Turnover?, American Economic Review 83 (May), pp. 110-15.

UNCTAD (1996), World Investment Report 1996, New York and Geneva.

US BUREAU OF THE CENSUS (1995), Statistical Abstract of the United States 1995, 115th edition, Washington, D.C.: United States Government Printing Office.

UTTERBACK, J. M. and ABERNATHY, W. J. (1975), A Dynamic Model of Process and Product Innovation, Omega 3, pp. 639 - 656.

UTTERBACK, J. M. and SUÁREZ, F. F. (1993), Innovation Competition and Industry Structure, Research Policy 22, pp. 1 - 21.

VAN DIJK, M.P. (1995), Flexible Specialization, the New Competition and Industrial Districts, Small Business Economics, 7(1), February, pp. 15-28.

VAN PARIDON, C.W.A.M. (1992), Technology Policy in a Small and Open Economy: the Case of the Netherlands, in: SCHERER, F.M. and PERLMAN, M., eds., Entrepreneurship, Technological Innovation and Economic Growth, Ann Arbor: University of Michigan Press.

VERNON, R. (1966), The Product Cycle Hypothesis in a new International Environment, Oxford Bulletin of Economics and Statistics, 41(4), pp. 255-267.

VON HIPPLE, E. (1994), Sticky Information and the Locus of Problem Solving: Implications for Innovation, Management Science, 40(4), pp. 429-439.

WAGNER, J. (1994), Small-Firm Entry in Manufacturing Industries, Small Business Economics, 5(3), pp. 211-214.

WAGNER, J. (1995), Firm Size and Job Creation in Germany, Small Business Economics, 7(6), pp. 469-474.

WAGNER, J. (forthcoming), Firm Size and Job Quality: A Survey of the Evidence from Germany, Small Business Economics.

WELFENS, P.J.J. (1992a), Privatization, M&As, and Inter-Firm Cooperation in the EC: Improved Prospects for Innovation?, in: SCHERER, F.M and PERLMAN, M., eds.,

Entrepreneurship, Technological Innovation, and Economic Growth. Studies in Schumpeterian Tradition, Ann Arbor: University of Michigan Press, pr. 119-140.

WELFENS, P.J.J. (1992b), The Economic Challenges of Privatization and Foreign Direct Investment in Eastern Europe, Managment International Review, Vol. 32, No. 3, pp. 199-218.

WELFENS, P.J.J. (1996a), European Monetary Integration, 3rd revised and enlarged edition, Heidelberg and New York: Springer.

WELFENS, P.J.J. (1996b), Economic Aspects of German Unification, 2nd revised and enlarged edition, Heidelberg and New York: Springer.

WELFENS, P.J.J. (1996c), The EU Facing Economic Opening-Up in Eastern Europe: Problems, Issues and Policy Options, in: TILLY, R. and WELFENS, P.J.J., eds, European Economic Integration as a Challenge to Industry and Government, Heidelberg, New York: Springer, pp. 103-172.

WELFENS, P.J.J. (1997a), Growth and Full Employment in the EU?, forthcoming in ADDISON, J. and WELFENS, P.J.J., eds., European Labor Markets and Social Security, Heidelberg and New York: Springer.

WELFENS, P.J.J. (1997b), Product-Market Integration in the Presence of MNCs and Unemployment: Towards a New Theory of Economic Integration, EIIW working paper, Potsdam University, forthcoming.

WELFENS, P.J.J., ed. (1997c), Banking, International Capital Flows and Growth in Europe, Heidelberg and York: Springer.

WELFENS, P.J.J., ed. (1997d), European Monetary Union: Transition, International Impact and Policy Options, Heidelberg and New York: Springer .

WELFENS, P.J.J. (1997e), The Single Market and the Eastern Enlargement of the EU, Heidelberg and New York: Springer, forthcoming.

WELFENS, P.J.J. and GRAACK, C. (1996), Telekommunikationswirtschaft: Deregulierung, Privatisierung und Internationalisierung, Heidelberg: Springer.

WELFENS, P.J.J. and HILLEBRAND, R. (1997), Growth, Innovation and Full Employment: Challenges for a New Environmental Policy, EIIW Discussion Paper No, University of Potsdam, forthcoming.

WELFENS, P.J.J. and YARROW, G., eds. (1996), Telecommunications and Energy in Transforming Economies, Heidelberg and New York: Springer.

WIELAND, B. (1995), Telekommunikation und vertikale Integration am Beispiel des Bankensektors, Heidelberg: Physica.

WILLIAMSON, O.E. (1975), Markets and Hierarchies: Antitrust Analysis and Implications, New York: Free Press.

WINTER, S.G. (1984), Schumpeterian Competition in Alternative Technological Regimes, Journal of Economic Behavior and Organization, 5, Sept.-Dec., pp. 287-320.

WOLFF, E.N. (1996), Technology and the Demand for Skills, in: OECD, Special Issue on Technology, Productivity and Employment, STI Review No. 18, pp. 95-123.

WONG, P.-K. (1993), Small, Newly Industrializing Economies Facing Technology Globalization: A Singaporian Perspective, paper presented at the fourth international symposium on the management of technology, Montreal, Canada, 13-14 October.

WYCKOFF, A. (1996), The Growing Strength of Services, OECD Observer, June, No.200, pp.11-15.

ZENIT (1996), Evalutation of the impacts of the structural policies on the economic and social cohesion of the Union: Germany, Final Report: Mülheim.

List of Figures

List of Tables

Innovation Data on OECD Countries

Table A7: Research and Development Intensities
(Gross Expenditures per Gross Domestic Product in Percentages)

	1975	1980	1985	1990	1991	1995
Germany*	2.24	2.4	2.72	2.76	2.61	2.28
France	1.8	1.84	2.25	2.41	2.41	2.34
United Kingdom	2.03	2.3	2.27	2.18	2.11	2.05
Italy	0.93	0.86	1.13	1.3	1.32	1.14
Belgium	1.3	1.5	1.68	---	1.65	---
Netherlands	2.02	1.89	2.09	2.15	2.05	---
Denmark	1.08	1.04	1.25	1.63	1.7	1.82
Ireland	0.86	0.7	0.82	0.86	0.96	1.4
Greece	0.2	0.2	0.34	---	0.37	---
Spain	0.35	0.4	0.55	0.85	0.87	0.8
Portugal	0.3	0.33	0.4	0.54	0.6	0.61
Austria	0.92	1.1	1.27	1.42	1.5	1.53
Sweden	1.8	2.0	2.89	2.9	2.89	3.02
Finland	0.91	1.1	1.57	1.91	2.07	2.32
EU			1.91	1.99	1.96	1.84
Switzerland	2.4	2.3	2.7	2.9	2.8	---
Norway	1.34	1.27	1.62	1.8	1.65	1.59
Iceland	0.94	0.7	0.75	0.99	1.16	1.46
Turkey	0.2	0.6	0.7	0.32	0.53	0.38
Canada	1.15	1.17	1.43	1.47	1.52	1.61
USA	2.38	2.46	2.89	2.81	2.84	2.58
Japan	2.01	2.22	2.77	3.04	3.0	3.0
Australia	1.0	1.0	1.2	1.38	---	---
New Zealand	0.87	1.0	0.88	1.0	0.99	---

*   until 1990 West Germany

Source: OECD: Main Science and Technology Indicators.
Calculation by Fraunhofer (ISI).

Table A8:   Patent Applications at the European Patent Office in R&D-intensive aeras (per million employees)

	1989	1990	1991	1992	1993	1994	1995*
USA	86	90	90	90	90	92	100
Japan	149	147	128	114	113	106	122
Germany**	245	224	172	173	173	185	199
United Kingdom	85	78	72	74	74	74	77
France	123	120	118	111	114	117	117
Switzerland	316	294	258	254	261	279	275
Canada	26	24	28	28	29	32	34
Sweden	115	124	128	143	154	196	213
Italy	56	56	56	52	59	60	63
Netherlands	154	146	138	136	132	136	147

*   1995 estimated

** up to 1990 West Germany

Source: Data base EPAT; classification and calculation Fraunhofer (ISI)

Further Publications by *Paul J. J. Welfens*

P. J. J. Welfens
European Monetary Union
Transition, International Impact and Policy Options
1997. X, 467 pp. 50 figs., 31 tabs. Hardcover
ISBN 3-540-63305-7

P. J. J. Welfens, D. Audretsch, J. T. Addison, H. Grupp
Technological Competition, Employment and Innovation
Policies in OECD Countries
1997. VI, 236 pp. Hardcover ISBN 3-540-63439-8

P. J. J. Welfens, H. C. Wolf
Banking, International Capital Flows and Growth in Europe
Financial Markets, Savings and Monetary Integration in
a World with Uncertain Convergence
1997. XIV, 458 pp. 22 figs., 63 tabs. Hardcover
ISBN 3-540-63192-5

P. J. J. Welfens, G. Yarrow
Telecommunications and Energy in Systemic Transformation
International Dynamics, Deregulation and Adjustment in
Network Industries
1997. XII, 501 pp. 39 figs., Hardcover
ISBN 3-540-61586-5

R. Tilly, P. J. J. Welfens
**European Economic Integration as a Challenge to
Industry and Government**
Contemporary and Historical Perspectives on
International Economic Dynamics
1996. X, 558 pp. 43 figs., Hardcover ISBN 3-540-60431-6

P. J. J. Welfens
Economic Aspects of German Unification
Expectations, Transition Dynamics and International Perspectives
2nd rev. and enlarged ed. 1996. XV, 527 pp. 34 figs., 110 tabs.
Hardcover ISBN 3-540-60261-5

P. J. J. Welfens
Market-oriented Systemic Transformations in Eastern Europe
Problems, Theoretical Issues, and Policy Options
1992. XII, 261 pp. 20 figs., 29 tabs. Hardcover
ISBN 3-540-55793-8

M. W. Klein, P. J. J. Welfens
Multinationals in the New Europe and Global Trade
1992. XV, 281 pp. 24 figs., 75 tabs. Hardcover
ISBN 3-540-54634-0

Druck: Strauss Offsetdruck, Mörlenbach
Verarbeitung: Schäffer, Grünstadt